076876
428DOR
Cuc

WJEC Eduqas GCSE English Language specification overview

The exam papers

The grade you receive at the end of your WJEC Eduqas GCSE English Language course is entirely based on your performance in two exam papers. The following provides a summary of these two exam papers:

Exam paper	Reading and Writing questions and marks	Assessment Objectives	Timing	Marks (and % of GCSE)
Component 1: 20th Century Literature **Reading and Creative Prose Writing**	**Section A: Reading** Exam text: • Extract from one unseen 20th-century literature prose text (about 60–100 lines) Exam questions and marks: • Five reading questions (40 marks in total)	Reading: • AO1 • AO2 • AO4	1 hour 45 minutes	Reading: 40 marks (20% of GCSE) Writing: 40 marks (20% of GCSE) Component 1 total: 80 marks (40% of GCSE)
	Section B: Writing Creative prose writing Exam questions and marks: • Choice of four titles – students respond to one task (24 marks for communication and organization; 16 marks for technical accuracy)	Writing: • AO5 • AO6		
Component 2: 19th and 21st Century Non-Fiction **Reading and Transactional/ Persuasive Writing**	**Section A: Reading** Exam texts: • Two unseen non-fiction texts (about 900–1200 words in total), one from the 19th century and the other from the 21st century Exam questions and marks: • Six reading questions (40 marks in total)	Reading: • AO1 • AO2 • AO3 • AO4	2 hours	Reading: 40 marks (30% of GCSE) Writing: 40 marks (30% of GCSE) Component 2 total: 80 marks (60% of GCSE)
	Section B: Writing Transactional/persuasive writing Exam question and marks: • Two compulsory tasks (20 marks for each task – 12 for communication and organization and 8 for technical accuracy)	Writing: • AO5 • AO6		

What will you be studying and learning?

Reading

Across the two GCSE English Language components, you will be studying the following:

- Critical reading and comprehension
- Summary and synthesis
- Evaluation of a writer's choice of vocabulary, form, grammatical and structural features
- Comparing texts

Writing

Across the two GCSE English Language components, you will be studying the following:

- Producing clear and coherent texts
- Writing for impact

Component 1 gives you opportunities for writing to describe and narrate, and imaginative and creative use of language. Your response should be narrative or recount.

Component 2, across the two tasks, gives you the opportunity to write for a range of audiences and purposes, adapting style to form and to real-life contexts in, for example, letters, articles, reviews, speeches, etc.

Spoken Language

As well as preparing for the two GCSE English Language exams, your course also includes Spoken Language assessment. This is **not** an exam. Instead you will be completing one formal presentation or speech where you will be:

- Presenting information and ideas
- Responding to spoken language
- Expressing ideas using Standard English

Spoken Language assesses AO7, AO8 and AO9. Your achievement in Spoken Language will be reported, but it will not form part of your final GCSE English Language qualification mark and grade.

> **A note on spelling**
> Certain words, for example 'synthesize' and 'organize', have been spelt with 'ize' throughout this book. It is equally acceptable to spell these words with 'ise'.

The Assessment Objectives

AO1	• Identify and interpret explicit and implicit information and ideas. • Select and synthesize evidence from different texts.
AO2	Explain, comment on and analyse how writers use language and structure to achieve effects and influence readers, using relevant subject terminology to support their views.
AO3	Compare writers' ideas and perspectives, as well as how these are conveyed, across two or more texts.
AO4	Evaluate texts critically and support this with appropriate textual references.
AO5	• Communicate clearly, effectively and imaginatively, selecting and adapting tone, style and register for different forms, purposes and audiences. • Organize information and ideas, using structural and grammatical features to support coherence and cohesion of texts.
AO6	Use a range of vocabulary and sentence structures for clarity, purpose and effect, with accurate spelling and punctuation.
AO7	Demonstrate presentation skills in a formal setting.
AO8	Listen and respond appropriately to spoken language, including to questions and feedback on presentations.
AO9	Use spoken Standard English effectively in speeches and presentations.

Introduction to this book

How this book will help you

Develop your reading and writing skills

The primary aim of this book is to develop and improve your reading and writing skills. Crucially, however, in this book you will be doing this in the context of what the exam papers will be asking of you at the end of your course. So, the skills you will be practising throughout this book are ideal preparation for your two GCSE English Language exam papers.

Explore the types of texts that you will face in the exams

In your English Language exams you will have to respond to a number of unseen texts. In order to prepare you fully for the range and types of texts that you might face in the exam, this book is structured thematically so you can explore the connections between texts. This is ideal preparation for your exams as the unseen texts in your exam papers will be of different types (fiction and non-fiction), from the 19th, 20th and 21st centuries and will, in some instances, be connected.

Become familiar with the Assessment Objectives and the exam paper requirements

Assessment Objectives are the skills that underpin all qualifications. Your GCSE English Language exam papers are testing six Assessment Objectives (see pages 4–5). Chapters 1 to 5 of this book develop your reading and writing skills in the context of these Assessment Objectives. Chapter 6 pulls all the skills together that you have been practising in order to help prepare you for 'mock' exam papers at the end of the book.

Practise the types of tasks you will face in the exams

Chapters 1 to 5 in this book include end-of-chapter assessments that enable you to demonstrate what you have learned and help your teacher assess your progress. Each of these assessments includes tasks that prepare you for the types of tasks that you will be facing in your GCSE English Language exams. The sample papers in Chapter 6 give you the opportunity to bring together all that you have been learning and practising in a 'mock' exam situation.

How is the book structured?

Chapters 1 to 5

Chapters 1 to 5 develop your reading and writing skills within different themes. Each chapter opens with an introductory page that introduces the theme, explains the skills you will be developing and links the learning to the exam requirements.

The chapters then include a range of fiction and non-fiction texts, from the 19th, 20th and 21st centuries, to help you develop your reading skills. Across the chapters you will be developing responses in the context of all of the reading Assessment Objectives and you will encounter all of the text types from the 19th, 20th and 21st centuries that your exam paper texts will be taken from.

Your writing skills are also developed throughout every chapter, including a focus on improving your technical accuracy (also known as SPAG – Spelling, Punctuation and Grammar).

Chapter 6

Chapter 6 pulls all of the skills together that you have learned throughout the course, revisiting key points and providing you with revision practice. The chapter and book concludes with sample exam papers to enable you and your teacher to see how much progress you have made.

What are the main features within this book?

Activities, Stretch and Support

To develop your reading responses to the wide range of texts included in this book, as well as developing your writing skills, you will find many varied activities. The 'Support' feature provides additional help with some activities, while the 'Stretch' feature introduces further challenge to help develop a more advanced response.

Tips, Key terms and glossed words

These features help support your understanding of key terms, concepts and more difficult words within a source text. These therefore enable you to concentrate fully on developing your reading and writing skills.

Exam link and Progress check

The 'Exam link' box explains how the skills you are developing relate to the exam papers. In addition to the summative end-of-chapter assessments, you will also find regular formative assessments in the form of 'Progress checks'. Through peer and self-assessment, these enable you to assess your learning and establish next steps and targets.

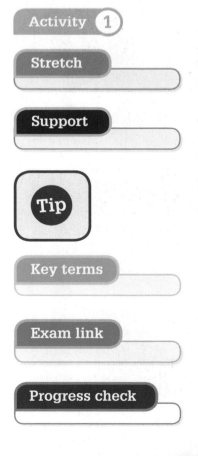

Further GCSE English Language and GCSE English Literature resources

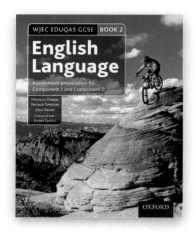

WJEC Eduqas GCSE English Language Student Book 2: Assessment Preparation for Component 1 and Component 2

Student Book 2 provides you with all the exam preparation and practice that you need to succeed. The book is divided into Reading and Writing sections (like in the exams) and further divided into chapters which guide you through the Assessment Objective and exam paper question requirements. The book features:

- a range of texts and tasks similar to those you will encounter in the exam
- activities to practise and reinforce the key skills, with advice on how to improve your responses
- marked sample student responses at different levels
- opportunities for self-assessment and peer-assessment
- sample exam papers.

WJEC Eduqas GCSE English Literature Student Book

This Student Book provides in-depth skills development for the English Literature specification, including:

- comprehensive coverage and practice of the poetry anthology and unseen poetry requirements
- advice and activities to support Shakespeare, the 19th-century novel and modern prose and drama
- sample student responses at different levels and sample exam-style tasks to help prepare you for the exam paper questions
- 'Stretch' and 'Support' features to ensure all students make progress.

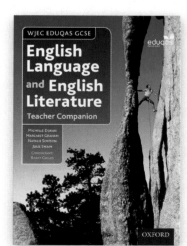

WJEC Eduqas GCSE English Language and English Literature Teacher Companion

The Teacher Companion provides holistic support for teachers to help them plan and deliver their GCSE programme, including:

- specification insight and planning guidance to aid planning and delivery of the specifications
- teaching tips and guidance for effective lesson delivery to all students of the material in Student Book 1, with additional support for differentiation and personalization
- extensive exam preparation guidance and planning, with links to English Language Student Book 2 and English Literature Student Book
- guidance and support for delivering Spoken Language assessments
- links to, and guidance on, the additional resources on Kerboodle.

WJEC Eduqas GCSE English Language and English Literature Kerboodle: Resources and Assessment

What is Kerboodle?

Kerboodle is a brand new online subscription-based platform provided by Oxford University Press.

Kerboodle: Resources and Assessment

This WJEC Eduqas GCSE English Language and English Literature Kerboodle: Resources and Assessment provides comprehensive support and resources to enable English departments and individual teachers to plan their GCSE courses and deliver effective, personalized lessons that prepare students for the requirements of the exams. Resources include:

- Teaching and learning materials, linked to the corresponding Student Books and Teacher Companion, including:
  - differentiation, personalization and peer/self-assessment worksheets and teaching resources
  - a bank of assignable spelling, punctuation and grammar interactive activities to improve technical accuracy

- Assessment resources, including:
  - marked sample answers to the Student Book 1 and Student Book 2 assessments, with mark schemes
  - editable versions of the end-of-chapter Student Book assessments and sample exam papers

- Professional development materials, including:
  - six specially-commissioned film-based CPD units, written by Geoff Barton, with classroom lesson footage, additional interviews (with Phil Jarrett and Michelle Doran) and supporting written resources – ideal for departmental meetings
  - a SPAG guide for GCSE teaching

- Planning resources, including:
  - editable sample schemes of work and medium-term plans, with guidance on what to consider when planning your GCSE course
  - CPD units supporting discussion around departmental GCSE planning

- Digital books including:
  - all three Student Books in digital format*
  - a bank of tools enabling personalization

*Also available individually for student access

1 EXTREMES

In this chapter you will develop your ability to read and write non-fiction texts. You will encounter a range of activities that will build on what you already know to help you become a more effective reader and writer in this style. The activities will also give you the chance to plan and produce some writing of your own.

The focus of this chapter is 'Extremes'. You will examine how extremes can be presented in non-fiction. You will also have the opportunity to reflect on what makes an event extreme and how they make you, as a reader, feel and react. The chapter is divided into three units and each one will focus on different types of extreme – sports, weather and travel in a range of different environments. While you are working through the chapter, try to consider the impact of these extremes both on the people experiencing them and the world around them.

'Tell the truth, or someone will tell it for you.'
Stephanie Klein

'I enjoy doing the research of non-fiction; that gives me some pleasure, being a detective again.'
Joseph Wambaugh

'In non-fiction, you have that limitation, that constraint, of telling the truth.'
Peter Matthiessen

What is non-fiction?

For our purposes, non-fiction can be defined as:
- writing that deals with facts and events rather than imaginative narration

or

- a class of literature that includes books in all subjects other than fiction.

Almost everything that you see in the media is non-fiction. Most of the conversations you have with friends and family will be based on true or non-fiction events.

Non-fiction writing covers a huge range of texts. Any writing that is based on facts, real-life stories, real people and real events can be classed as non-fiction. Writing that is imagined or written in a creative or exaggerated manner is fictional.

Reading non-fiction

Throughout each day you will encounter many pieces of non-fiction writing. From the texts found on cereal packets, newspapers or online news reports to the textbooks you use at school, all of these are non-fiction. We read non-fiction accounts to acquire information, to learn about a new topic or if we want to research a real-life event. Non-fiction reading can be a factual exercise, but it can also be an emotional activity as we may read about glorious achievements, harrowing real-life stories or global issues that may affect our lives.

Writing non-fiction

You will have produced many non-fiction or transactional pieces of writing during your years at school. Transactional writing is writing that has a clear purpose and audience. It will aim to argue, persuade, inform or advise a reader or audience. Examples include letters, articles, reviews, reports and leaflets. Producing a non-fiction text requires a writer to carefully consider a number of factors such as the audience for the writing, the reasons behind it (also known as the purpose of the writing) and the ideas a writer wishes to explore.

Exam link

Exam relevance

The study of non-fiction is very important for GCSE English Language. One of the exams you will take at the end of your course is largely based on this type of reading and writing. In the first section of the exam you will be asked to read two non-fiction texts and answer questions. In the second section you will be asked to write two non-fiction or transactional pieces of writing.

In this chapter you will:

- read and explore a range of different non-fiction texts
- start to plan and prepare for the Writing section of the exam
- develop some of the skills that will help you in the exam.

Exploring extremes

Learning objectives

- To explore the theme of extremes
- To consider your own experience of extremes

Introduction

The title of this chapter is 'Extremes'. The word 'extreme' can be used in many different **contexts**, from describing people and their personal actions and achievements, to the natural environment and world we live in. You will begin by thinking about the overreaching theme of extremes and what part extremes may have played in your own lives.

For our purposes, 'extreme' can be defined in two ways.

As an **adjective** it can mean:

- very great or intense
- furthest away, outermost: *the extreme edge*
- going to great lengths in actions or opinions, not moderate.

As a **noun** it can mean:

- either end of something
- something extreme, either of two concepts or opinions that are as different from each other as they can be.

Activity 1

Consider what the word 'extreme' means to you:
- Think about your own experiences of extremes. Write down any words or phrases that you associate with this idea.
- Discuss with a friend the ways you think this word can be used. Share your ideas and write down any new ones.
- Using the ideas you have discussed, write your own definition for this term.

Activity 2

Look at the images on this page. What can you see? Why do you think these pictures could be described as extreme? Write down any words or phrases you would use to describe the extremes pictured in them.

Activity **3**

Choose one of the images from Activity 2. Imagine you are the photographer who took the photograph and answer the following questions.

1. Why did you take the photograph?
2. Where were you when you took the photograph?
3. Describe the weather conditions in your location.
4. Write down five words to describe how you feel when you look through your camera lens.

Key terms

Context: the words that come before and after a particular word or phrase and help to clarify its meaning; the circumstances or background against which something happens

Adjectives: words like *big*, *exciting* and *unexpected*. They describe what is named by nouns, noun phrases or pronouns

Nouns: words like *girl*, *book*, *Mary*, *school*, *year*, *money*, *happiness*, *Brighton*. One of their main jobs is to identify a person, place or thing

The language or words you chose may have helped to convey the extreme nature of the location. Choosing language carefully is essential when writing, as it allows your reader to picture what you are describing. If you are describing an extreme environment or location, you should think about choosing words and phrases that express intensity.

Activity **4**

Think about the TV programmes you have watched, the news reports you have read or listened to, or any books you have read. All of these will have, at some time, included information about extremes. During the last week you may have come across some extreme events or people. Even the weather can be described as extreme if it is unusually severe. Can you think of any other situations where you may have encountered extremes?

Design and complete a table to show your recent experiences of extremes in non-fiction.
For example:

Source of extremes	What happened
BBC News	Deadly heatwaves and devastating floods have sparked popular interest in understanding the role of global warming in driving extreme weather.

Think carefully about the words and phrases you choose to convey the intensity of the situation.

Extreme sports

① Reading techniques

Learning objectives

- To develop reading skills
- To understand different ways of gathering information when you read
- To explore how to read a text for different purposes or to achieve different results

Key terms

Perspective: a particular way of thinking about something

Purpose: something you intend to do or achieve; an intention or aim

Fact: something that is known to have happened and/or to be true

Introduction

In recent years, extreme sports have become increasingly popular. Although many people think they are dangerous, for participants they produce high levels of adrenaline, excitement and challenge. In this unit you will learn new skills and improve on your existing reading skills, using texts on extreme sports to inspire you.

Because we learn to read when we are young, reading becomes a skill that we rarely think about. Being able to read and understand a text is a crucial skill for life, school and exams. When reading a text, there are a number of different techniques that you can use:

Close reading

This will enable you to understand a text in detail. It will help you to understand the writer's overall meaning and **perspective**, and the **purpose** of the text. When you read closely you need to try to understand each sentence and what the writer is trying to convey.

Skimming

This is much quicker than close reading. When you skim a text, you do not read every word but try to take in the overall meaning and organizational structure of the text by moving your eyes throughout the passage. Headings and topic sentences are really useful for this technique – these features help you to locate main ideas, topics or information quickly.

Scanning

You use this technique if you are looking for a particular piece of information or a key word. If you were asked to find out why an event was dangerous, you could begin by scanning the text for the word *danger*. This technique is useful if you are asked to locate a **fact** or phrase.

Activity ①

Read the extract on page 15 closely ('Base jumpers: the men who fall to earth'). It includes some difficult words and phrases that you may not understand. Your teacher may ask you to write these down and try to work out what they mean. Even though a text may have some complicated sections, if you read it closely you can usually work out the *overall* meaning.

Base jumpers: the men who fall to earth

What would drive someone to risk life, limb and liberty by breaking into the world's tallest building and jumping off the top of it with just one small parachute? Ed Caesar infiltrates[1] the secret society of the death-defying base jumpers.

In the early hours of April 9, 2008, a 44-year-old Englishman and a 48-year-old Frenchman sat silently on the edge of the windowless 155th floor of the Burj tower – the tallest building in the world – watching dawn bleed over Dubai. From their eyrie[2] half a mile up, they saw the desert turn from blue to pink and heard the muezzins[3] call the faithful to prayer. In that moment, remembers the Frenchman, 'everything below seemed to belong to us. We felt like kings, and this was our kingdom'.

Their reign was short. At 5.30am, the men could see truckloads of workers arriving at the site, ready to start construction for the day. It was time to go. They rose to their feet. The Englishman looked at his friend, counted to three, and launched himself from the building. The Frenchman followed a moment later.

The Englishman fell like a shot pheasant for ten long seconds. He then drew his small pilot chute, which caught, filled with air, and released the blossom of his main canopy. The Frenchman took more time. He was wearing a wingsuit – a webbed overall that allows a parachutist to travel forward as well as down. As he fell, he spread his arms wide, raised his chest to the dawn, and glided away from the building. When he had flown as close as he dared to a nearby skyscraper, he deployed[4] his parachute and descended[5] to safety. The pair had done it – they had pulled off one of the greatest coups[6] in the history of base jumping. Why? Why would someone be so stupid as to jump from a building with only a small parachute on their back? An answer (perhaps not the answer, but an answer) is that people have been doing this kind of thing, if not for ever, then at least for 150 years. Ever since Charles Blondin strutted across Niagara Falls on a tightrope in 1859, ever since Houdini first broke from his shackles, ever since the most famous wirewalker of all, the Man on Wire, Philippe Petit, danced between the twin towers in 1974, men – and it is almost always men – have needed to touch the void.

[1]infiltrate – to enter a place or organization gradually and without being noticed
[2]eyrie – the nest of an eagle or other bird of prey
[3]muezzin – a Muslim crier who proclaims the hours of prayer from a minaret
[4]deploy – to bring something into effective action
[5]descend – to move down
[6]coup – a sudden and unexpected successful action

Activity 2

Once you have read the extract, think about what you have learned about base jumping and what the writer thinks about it. Now discuss the following with a partner.

• What do you learn about base jumping from this article?

• Why do you think Ed Caesar wrote this text?

• If you had to tell someone about this text in 50 words, what would you say?

Activity

Now you need to use skimming and scanning reading skills to locate the following information from the extract on page 15. Some tips have been provided to help focus your search. See how quickly you can find the information.

1. What is base jumping?
2. When did the event take place?
3. How did the Frenchman feel?
4. What was the Frenchman wearing?
5. Write down any words that show how Ed Caesar feels about the jump.

Tip

1. A definition of base jumping is crucial to understanding the extract, so start at the beginning and skim the text. Don't forget to look at the title.
2. Looking at the **topic sentence** for each paragraph is a good place to start.
3. Scan the text and look for the word *feel* or *felt*.
4. Scan the text looking for the word *wearing*.
5. Skim back through the whole passage looking for any words that might suggest his opinion about the jump.

The language or words and phrases used by a writer help a reader to understand exactly what is being said. Writers are often deliberate in the language they choose. Carefully selected language can paint a clear image for a reader so they can visualize what the writer is describing. Language can also make a reader feel a range of emotions such as anger, sympathy and surprise.

> **Key term**
>
> **Topic sentence:** often the first sentence in a paragraph, it tells the reader what the paragraph is about, and is followed by other sentences which give more detail

Activity 4

Look at the following phrases about base jumpers and see if you can work out why the writer has chosen specific words.

> 'watching dawn bleed over Dubai'

What does the word 'bleed' suggest about the colour of the morning sun? What does it suggest about how the colour is merging with the rest of the sky?

> 'fell like a shot pheasant'

What is your image of the pheasant? How do you think it is falling, given the fact that it has been shot?

> 'the blossom of his main canopy'

Why has the writer used the word 'blossom' to describe the parachute? What image do you get of the shape of the parachute?

2 Recognizing different text types

Learning objectives

- To understand what different text types look like
- To explore some of the features different text types might have

In English, you will be asked to read and produce a range of text types. Writers often have to produce text of a particular type, which is linked to its purpose. For example, a journalist will produce articles for a newspaper or magazine, while a school will often use a letter or email format to send information home.

Activity 1

Look at the extracts on pages 19–21. These are some of the kinds of popular texts you encounter in everyday life. Look at the features of each extract carefully. Can you match the definitions below to the extracts on pages 19–21?

A Article – a short, self-contained piece of writing often found in a newspaper or magazine.

B Blog – a website where someone writes about their own opinions, activities and experiences. Blogs are usually structured so that other people can comment or begin discussions about the topics included in the blog.

C Webpage – a page within a given website that can be found on the Internet.

D Letter – a written message to a specific audience. Letters can be **formal** or **informal**, depending on the audience. The level of formality will determine the style and content of the letter.

E Book extract – a passage or section from a book. An extract may cover an entire event, or it may simply give a character outline or a snapshot of a larger main event.

F Leaflet – a printed sheet of paper giving information, especially one given out for free. Most leaflets are produced to encourage or persuade a reader to do something (for example, to visit an attraction or donate money), or to give out information (for example, a leaflet found at a doctors' surgery about a medical condition like meningitis).

Extract 1

Dear Editor,

I was appalled to read that last weekend's weather not only played havoc with my hydrangeas but that it also sparked what can only be described as a sport for lunatics. For those of you not yet acquainted with this latest craze, let me explain. Tombstoning is the 'art' of diving off rocks, cliffs and bridges into the, often shallow and rocky but almost always dangerous, waters below. This fad has claimed more than twenty lives in the last five years but is growing in popularity…

Extract 2

Extract 3

◄ ► C ✖ +

JAN 20

Expert Interview with Nina Nordling of High Heaven

Extreme News and Views

Hi Nina, thanks for talking to us. We hear you're embarking on a pretty exciting venture this year and we can't wait to hear more about it. Please start by telling us a little about yourself, and how you got into the extreme sports industry:

I started riding motocross a couple of years back, and I discovered I just loved everything to do with adrenaline [...] I founded a motocross team for women and got really interested in the action sports industry, being active in skate, surf and a ton of motorsports, as well as the TV host of the Swedish MX Championships. As a first-time entrepreneur I realized I needed a kickass team and today we are three super-ambitious team members working with the startup High Heaven.

Extract 4

Free runners hit the streets as urban craze sweeps Britain

It's seen on TV and the web, and free running is now soaring in popularity in UK cities. But as schools embrace it and the world championships come to London, critics say it's highly dangerous.

It is one of the hottest days of the summer and outside London's South Bank Centre Jake Penny, 15, and his friend, Joe Scandrett, 13, are hurling themselves around a warren of concrete pedestrian underpasses.

Using ledges, metal handrails and anything else within reach, the two teenagers cause passers-by to gape by executing back-flips and somersaults high into the air, each time landing gracefully and silently on the pavement.

Extract 5

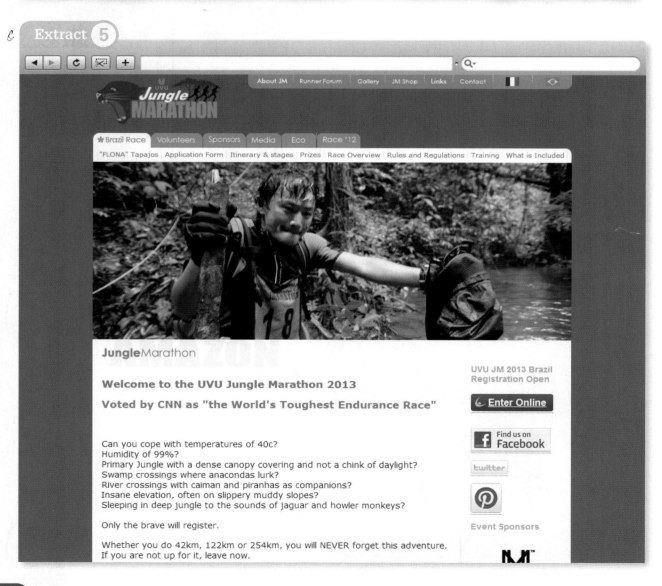

About JM | Runner Forum | Gallery | JM Shop | Links | Contact

★ Brazil Race | Volunteers | Sponsors | Media | Eco | Race '12

"FLONA" Tapajos | Application Form | Itinerary & stages | Prizes | Race Overview | Rules and Regulations | Training | What is Included

JungleMarathon

Welcome to the UVU Jungle Marathon 2013

Voted by CNN as "the World's Toughest Endurance Race"

Can you cope with temperatures of 40c?
Humidity of 99%?
Primary Jungle with a dense canopy covering and not a chink of daylight?
Swamp crossings where anacondas lurk?
River crossings with caiman and piranhas as companions?
Insane elevation, often on slippery muddy slopes?
Sleeping in deep jungle to the sounds of jaguar and howler monkeys?

Only the brave will register.

Whether you do 42km, 122km or 254km, you will NEVER forget this adventure.
If you are not up for it, leave now.

UVU JM 2013 Brazil Registration Open

⟲ Enter Online

Find us on Facebook

twitter

Event Sponsors

Extract ⑥

Across the world seemingly ordinary people are undertaking extraordinary challenges that will push their limits to achieve the improbable – by sea, bike, foot or sled. From the Badwater Ultramarathon in the unforgiving heat of Death Valley in California to the freezing wilderness of Alaska, these once-in-a-lifetime experiences are increasingly popular, and strangely addictive. For a certain breed of competitor, there is an unbreakable drive to see exactly how much the body and will can endure.

Activity ②

1. Can you think of any other text types? Discuss with a partner and write them down.

2. Write down any features you can think of that these text types might have in common.

3. Look closely at the letter. It is a formal letter; can you see anything that is missing?

Stretch

Select one of the text types and read it closely. Who is the intended audience? What features has the writer used to make it appealing to the target audience?

3 Analysing the writer's perspective

Learning objectives

- To understand what is meant by a writer's perspective
- To explore a writer's perspective

Understanding why a person has written an article and what they think about the topic can often help you to explore the text fully.

Activity 1

Read the extract below closely and think about the writer and what they might have thought about when writing this article. Some of this text has been annotated with the techniques the writer has used to get their message across.

SPAG

Imperative verbs command the reader to become engaged with the text.

This is a superlative adjective, used here to suggest that compared to any other race this is the <u>most</u> difficult.

Questions are asked for dramatic effect, 'pain' and 'danger' show that the writer can't comprehend the big attraction of the ice mile and will explain why in the rest of the article.

Similes give vivid comparisons using things we are familiar with so we can clearly imagine what the writer is trying to explain. They use the words 'as' and 'like' to make the comparison.

Lists can be used to show there are multiple reasons.

Meet the ice mile: the toughest swimming test on the planet

There's a new favourite pastime for swimming masochists: doing a mile without stopping in water colder than 5°C. With pain a certainty and the danger very real, what's the big attraction?

A few years ago I travelled to Finland to compete in the Winter Swimming Championships. It was one of their mildest winters for years but, even so, the water was still –0.7°C. Adrenaline got me through the very short race – but afterwards I felt like my hands had been slammed in a car door and that my feet had been pounded by mallets. It was brutal.

For the past 10 years I've been swimming outdoors throughout the winter. I've swum regularly, sometimes gloriously and sometimes painfully, in water gradually dropping to around 1°C or 2°C. [...] People ask me why I do it. I think it's a kind of invigorating, tingling, mad high – and a serious adrenaline rush. I love it. [...]

However there is one thing I have not contemplated, and have absolutely no wish to take part in. It's something that is gaining popularity among outdoor swimmers and endurance athletes around the world. It's a cold-water challenge called the 'ice mile'.

The basic rules for swimming an ice mile are pretty straightforward. Find a body of water that is below 5°C, and swim one mile under supervision wearing only your swimming costume, a pair of goggles and one silicone swimming hat. [...] It's a serious, serious endeavour that should not be taken lightly.

I have no desire whatsoever to swim an ice mile. Swimming a few hundred metres in water much below 10°C is enough of a challenge to me, and hurts like hell. It does to most regular cold-water swimmers. For every degree below 10°C, your feet and hands hurt more, your muscles contract so much it's hard to make your arms and shoulders stretch out to pull your stroke. Your hands splay as you lose motor function. You can have massive ice-cream headaches. And once you stop generating heat while swimming and are out of the water, the recovery is appalling and you can be cold all day. [...]

An ice mile to me seems punishing in the extreme. [...]

I have to admit to thinking that there is something macho about ice milers. It's a level of punishment and pain that I can't fathom and don't want to experience.

Repetition is used to reinforce or stress a point of view.

Use of the personal pronoun 'I' reinforces the personal nature of the experience.

Sometimes a writer will explicitly state their view about something, for example, 'It was brutal.' Sometimes you need to work like a detective and look for clues or unpick words and phrases to help you understand the implicit point the writer is trying to get across.

Activity 2

Titles are carefully worded so you become instantly attracted to the text and continue to read. Look at the words highlighted below. Why do you think the writer may have selected these specific words?

Meet the ice mile: the toughest swimming test on the planet

In an exam situation there isn't time to analyse every single word. The following questions will help you focus on how to pick out explicit and implicit meaning.

Activity 3

Read the article again, recording words or phrases that give a positive or negative **impression** of cold-water swimming.

Positive language	Negative language
gloriously	painfully

Stretch

Choose one or two examples from each column and explain what the words suggest about cold-water swimming.

Key terms

Impression: effect produced on the mind, ideas

Simile: a figure of speech in which one thing is compared to another using the words *like* or *as*, as in *He's as fit as a fiddle*

Exam link

In an exam, you will be asked to explain the effect of words and phrases and you may choose to pick out some words from the text to help you. You must make sure that your explanation of their effect is clear and concise.

Activity 4

The text has been annotated with some techniques we use when explaining how a writer might achieve an effect. For example, the writer may use the question 'With pain a certainty and the danger very real, what's the big attraction?' to emphasize the fact that she can't understand why anyone would willingly experience pain and danger for fun and that she questions the motives for swimming.

For each of the annotations around the extract:

• copy the relevant word or phrase

• copy the technique and explanation

• discuss why you think the writer has chosen to use this phrase and technique

• write down an explanation to show why you think each phrase is effective.

'I felt like my hands had been slammed in a car door'. **Similes** give vivid comparisons using familiar things so we can clearly imagine what the writer is trying to explain. They use the words 'as' and 'like' to make the comparison.

The simile is effective because we can imagine the intense pain that would be felt from slamming your hand in a car door and can imagine just how painful the swim must have been.

4 Changing perspective

Learning objective

● To understand a writer's perspective and how this can change

A writer's perspective is made up of the views and opinions they have about a topic. These views may change depending on when they write about an event. When deducing a writer's perspective, you need to understand exactly what that person thinks and feels about their topic.

Bungee jumping involves jumping from a tall structure while tied to an elastic cord. Buildings, bridges and cranes are commonly used, but extreme jumpers have been known to throw themselves from moving objects, such as hot-air balloons or helicopters. The thrill comes from free-falling and then being thrust back into the air as the cord recoils.

Activity 1

1. Imagine you have decided to take part in a bungee jump for charity. Use a table to record how you felt before, during and after your jump.

2. Discuss with a partner why your feelings might change.

Read the newspaper extract on page 25, which documents the writer's feelings before and after a bungee jump.

Activity 2

1. Look at the first section of the extract ('The fearful adventurer…'). Write down words or phrases that tell you how the writer is feeling.

2. Next to each word or phrase, write down one word that you think sums up how he feels.

3. What effect do these words and phrases have on you?

How the writer feels	One-word summary	Effect on reader
'apprehension is beginning to creep in'	uneasy	His nervousness is escalating so we sympathize with him.

Activity 3

Having completed the bungee jump, the writer explains his fear in the second section of the extract ('Fight the fear'). With a partner, make a list of the reasons he gives to explain why he found bungee jumping so difficult.

Stretch

Look back at the two sections of the text. Make a list of any similarities and any differences that you can see. Do you think the writer has changed his writing style and opinion after the bungee jump has taken place?

The fearful adventurer: confronting my demons at the world's highest bungee jump

I'm standing a few feet from the edge of the Bloukrans River Bridge. [...] It's famous for being home to the world's highest commercial bungee bridge jump.

My feet have been tied together, and two men are helping me hop to the edge. For the past hour while waiting my turn I've been trying to remain calm, but apprehension is beginning to creep in. I cautiously look down to where the Bloukrans River, several hundred metres below us, snakes its way to the nearby Indian Ocean. I quickly look up. 'Bloody hell', I think to myself. I decide not to look down again, but rather focus on the panoramic view in front of me.

I'm advised to jump outwards as much as possible, so I'll get a better bounce at the end. Is a better bounce a good thing? I'm not sure.

I take a deep breath and try to block out the voice in my head that's screaming, 'It's not too late to change your mind!' But I'm not going to chicken out – after all, I'm only doing this 216m-high escapade for one reason: to rebel against the fear that's begun to grip me as I get older.

The words 'Three, two, one, go!' ring out. I throw caution to the wind and jump.

Fight the fear

There was, of course, absolutely no reason for me to be afraid. Face Adrenalin have seen an average of 110 jumps every day for the past 16 years – with a 100pc safety record. That's 642,400 people who've managed to conquer their fears and, more to the point, survive to tell the tale. [...]

Nonetheless, it was a big deal for me. [...] I've run hundreds of kilometres across deserts in the searing heat, plunged off ferries at dawn into ice-cold black water, skidded along mountain ridges on a bike, and ploughed through heavy jungle foliage – none of which has fazed me too much. I have no problem with the thought of being uncomfortably cold, hot, wet or sleep deprived.

But ask me to jump off a bridge? In an act where I have no control? Well, that requires tapping into an entirely different set of resources and switch off my natural life-protecting instinct. It's something I find increasingly difficult.

A writer's perspective before an event is often based on their opinions and knowledge about the topic. When a writer has formed an opinion without having experienced something for themselves, they are speculating. We use clues in a text to **speculate** about what might happen.

When a writer has a first-hand experience and then gives their views, this can be classed as factual, since their views are based on something that has happened. The writer in this text **reflects** on what happened and how he feels about it. Good readers can spot the difference between fact and speculation and use this to help them explain the effect of a text.

> ### Key terms
>
> **Speculate:** to form an opinion about something without knowing the facts
> **Reflect:** to think deeply or carefully about something

5 Understanding sentence types

Learning objectives

- To understand different sentence types
- To experiment with a range of sentence types for effect

Key term

Verb: a word like *eat*, *think* or *walk*. Some verbs identify an action; others identify thoughts and feelings

---

Writers use different types of sentences to add variety to their work. If a writer used the same type of sentence throughout a piece of work it would sound very repetitive. In this section you will look at the different types of sentences and learn how to use them for effect.

Simple sentence – a sentence made up of a simple clause with one main **verb**, for example, 'The bike flew down the hill.'

Compound sentence – a sentence made up of two clauses which are coordinated using conjunctions such as *and* or *but*. These clauses will be about the same subject and the conjunction will join the ideas together. Each clause can make sense on its own, for example, 'The bike flew down the hill *and* it was a blur of red and silver.'

Complex sentence – a sentence made up of a main clause and at least one subordinate (dependent) clause. The subordinate clause usually adds extra information to the sentence, but doesn't make sense on its own, for example, 'The bike, like a magnificent soaring bird, flew down the hill.' The clause 'like a magnificent soaring bird' is a subordinate clause as it does not make sense on its own.

Activity 1

Read the paragraph below. While you are reading you need to think about the following:

- What type of sentences have been used?
- Does the passage sound interesting?
- Does the writing sound fluent?

White water rafting

The instructor held the dinghy[1] in the water. I climbed into the dinghy. It was yellow rubber. There were six of us in the boat. We were told exactly where to sit. Each person was given an oar. We were instructed to use the oars to paddle. Oars can also be used to push away from rocks.

The instructor pushed us away from the side. We were immediately sucked into the middle of the rapids[2]. The water thrashed against the rubber craft. Waves crashed into the boat. Water swirled around my feet. The water current was violent. We raced towards a waterfall.

I took a deep breath. Our boat surged over the top.

[1]dinghy – a small inflatable rubber boat
[2]rapids – a fast-flowing part of a river

Activity 2

1. Write down two or three sentences to explain what you think about the way the paragraph has been written. **SPAG**

2. With a partner, write a list of additional words that you would use to describe the rapids and the dinghy. Think about words to describe the movement, the sound and their appearance.

3. Rewrite the paragraph using compound and complex sentences to add extra detail. Try to include a range of simple, compound and complex sentences. You can change the order of words, phrases and sentences to make your work sound more interesting.

Exam link

Try consciously to use different sentence types in your written work, as by adding more detail they will make your writing more interesting. In the exam you should try to include a range of different sentence types, but make sure you punctuate them correctly.

Progress check

Now you have completed the first unit of work in this chapter, think about how confident you feel about reading and analysing non-fiction texts. Read each skill listed below under 'Where am I now?' and complete the box that reflects how you feel about it. Give a reason or example to support your choice, for example, an occasion when you have struggled or an activity you felt very confident about.

Where am I now?	Very pleased – I think I am good at this skill	OK – I do need more practice	One of my weaker areas so I need more practice
Using different reading skills to locate information			
Understanding the features of different texts			
Understanding a writer's perspective and how this can change			
Using different sentence types in my work			

Extreme weather

6 Exploring text structure

Learning objectives

- To understand text structure
- To consider the different ways that a text can be structured

Tip Always track through a text chronologically (from beginning to end), so you can fully appreciate how the writer's argument develops.

Introduction

Extreme weather is often difficult to predict and can cause havoc both to people and environments. In this unit you will develop your descriptive writing skills as you analyse and respond to how weather is presented in non-fiction writing.

Understanding text structure is important. When reading, think about how the writer has put together their ideas. When writing, think carefully about how to bring together information to maximize the effect of your writing on a reader, teacher or examiner. Planning the structure and content of your writing is essential. It will help you to avoid running out of ideas and losing track of your argument.

Features of structure

Within a text, a writer may use one or more of these structural features:

Chronological — this will be arranged in the order in which things happened

Descriptive — this will give plenty of detail and will describe events without making any judgements. Descriptive details help readers visualize information, often giving the 'who, what, where, when, why and how' of a topic/subject

Problem and solution — this describes a problem and presents one or more solutions

Features of structure

Compare and contrast — this will look at differences and similarities

Cause and effect — this describes events and identifies reasons (causes) why the event happened

Sequence and order — the writer may sequence or order the text in a specific way for impact. A charity letter, for example, may start with facts and information before concluding with a direct appeal

Read the following extract closely. Think about the different structural features discussed on page 28.

UK must adapt for weather extremes says Environment Agency

We cannot escape the fact that we have witnessed and experienced some extreme weather in the UK over the past decade. From Hurricane Hercules which attacked much of Cornwall and Wales over the Christmas period in 2013 to the subsequent severe floods which were catastrophic for areas like Sheffield, Salisbury and Dorset, to name but a few. Often the UK seems ill equipped to deal with these weather extremes, but given their frequency and the untold damage they cause, the Environment Agency suggests that urgent action is required.

Almost half the days in 2012 were during either periods of drought or flooding during one of the most extreme years of weather on record, according to Government figures. [...]

The flipside of climate change was also in evidence as dry weather in the later months of 2011 led to widespread drought in the summer of 2012. The Government ordered a hosepipe ban affecting 20 million people and the Environment Agency said 95 days had been in drought, more than a quarter of the year.

More extreme weather is inevitable and will exacerbate many of the problems that we already deal with, including flooding and water scarcity. Taking action today to prepare and adapt homes, businesses, agricultural practices and infrastructure for the future is vital.

Activity

Look at the four sections which have been highlighted in the extract above. Match the structural features to the correct section of the text.

A Cause and effect

B Compare and contrast

C Problem and solution

D Descriptive

Stretch

The argument in this text has been carefully structured. Look at each of the examples above and think about what they add to the text and the writer's argument and how they are effective.

Activity

1. Look at the question below and write a list of points that you think would help you to answer the question.

   How does the writer of the article above try to persuade us that the UK needs to adapt for extreme weather?

2. Look at the following section of a sample answer. Consider how you could improve it, and then write it out with your amendments.

   > The writer persuades us that we need to adapt to extreme weather because we have seen for ourselves the damage caused, 'we have witnessed and experienced some extreme weather in the UK over the past decade'. The lengthy timescale (ten years) suggests that the problem has been continual and that we need to find a solution.

Tip Work through the extract from the title to the end and think about both the content and structure of the writer's argument. Remember that content includes what the writer has to say and any techniques they use to help them convey their message.

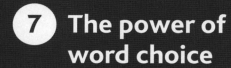

7 The power of word choice

Learning objectives

- To understand how words and phrases are used in a text
- To consider the effect of specific words and phrases in a text

Writers select words and phrases carefully to influence their readers. When you are looking at a text, identify words and phrases that are significant or relevant, and then think about what the writer is trying to achieve by using them. The language (words) a writer uses can be very effective. Language that is used to manipulate or evoke the reader's feelings is known as emotive language.

Activity 1

Read the extract below. Jot down brief notes or words to describe how the article makes you feel.

Experience: I was swept away by a flood

'Shocked, tossed and buffeted, I gasped for breath and tried to keep my head above water'

It was after midnight last December and we were driving home from a party. The weather in Devon had been awful. [...] We were in our Ford Ranger pick-up truck, which always felt safe. Paul, my husband, was driving and my seven-year-old son, Silas, was in the back.

[...] One minute we were halfway home and driving up to a familiar bridge, the next there was water rising over the bonnet. Deep floodwater was coursing across from a nearby railway line and surrounding fields, and we were caught in the middle of it. [...]

Water was instantly around my ankles. I reached my hand back and felt it around Silas's, too. Paul climbed out through a window, at which point Silas woke up, confused and disoriented. I managed to pass him through the window to Paul, who was now on the truck's roof. [...]

He grabbed my hood to help, but he was at a precarious angle and I could hear Silas crying, so I told him to let go – Silas needed him. [...] As I saw his empty, outstretched hand, the water took me away. I'm a strong swimmer, but had no option but to shoot down the rapids. Shocked, tossed and buffeted, I gasped for breath and tried to keep my head above water. There was a horrendously loud noise, like a huge wall of bubbles swirling in my ears. Bewildered, I remember saying, 'Oh God, oh God, oh God!' I never expected to die of drowning.

Washed over a garden wall, I joined the River Taw. [...] It was extremely dark but I could just make out trees. As I passed, I reached out and grabbed two branches no bigger than my index finger with a perfect tight grip. Somehow my feet wedged in a firm foothold and I hugged the tree with my knees. One minute longer and I'd have

been sucked beneath a railway bridge. [...]

After nearly 40 minutes, I saw a small spotlight. I started to shout for help. Someone glimpsed my movement and a firefighter tried to talk to me, but I couldn't hear her above the roar of the water.

The light of a helicopter made me out in the tree. [...] My husband, who had been rescued with my son was nearby with a policewoman. She reassured him that so long as they could hear me, there was hope.

Guided to me by the helicopter, the rescue team managed to steer the boat to my shoulder. Four strong arms lifted me into the boat and I felt sheer relief and utter safety. [...]

My rescuers were volunteers who have since received medals [...]. In the isolation of that tree, I found a strength of character I didn't know I possessed – but I'm still flabbergasted I survived at all.

Activity 2

In this article, Vanessa Glover has described her experience of being swept away by a flood. Remind yourself what a verb is (page 26).

1. Complete the table below by listing ten verbs from the extract.

2. Write down the effect of each verb. To do this, think about the meaning of the verb and why it has been used. Think about how the verb contributes to describing Vanessa's overall experience.

Verb	Effect
'tossed'	This makes it sound like she is being thrown around effortlessly in an uncontrolled manner and this emphasizes the intense power of the flood.

Activity 3

At the beginning of the text Vanessa Glover tries to convey the fact that she did not know whether she would survive. Write down any phrases that suggest she felt terrified and afraid during her ordeal.

Activity 4

The passage is written in the **first person**. Do you think the first person or the **third person** is more effective for this type of writing? Why do you think this?

Stretch

Remind yourself of the work on structure on pages 28–29. Think about the order of the events. How does the writer use the structure of the text to build tension?

Key terms

First person (*I/we*): using first-person narrative allows you to tell a story from the perspective of a character in the text. In non-fiction texts it can be seen as a biased view because it only tells one side of the story

Third person (*he/she/it/they*): using third-person narrative means the story is told from an independent point of view so you can see what all the characters think and feel. In non-fiction texts it is regarded as an unbiased voice

8 Fact or fiction?

Learning objective

- To understand and explore the differences between factual and fictional accounts

A writer's style may be influenced by their audience. If they are reporting information for a newspaper article, it is likely that the information will be factual and based on actual events. If a writer is reporting information to entertain or persuade, they may use exaggeration to have an emotional impact on the reader.

A typhoon is a tropical cyclone. You are going to read two texts that describe typhoons. The first text is a news report of Typhoon Haiyan's approach to the Philippines. The second is an extract from a novel called *Typhoon*. The narrator describes the effects of the terrible storm on a ship.

Extract 1

Philippines: thousands evacuated as Typhoon Haiyan strikes

Enormous storm predicted to be largest ever recorded, topping hurricane Camille in 1969, hits north Pacific

Typhoon Haiyan has hit the Philippines with winds of 195mph, with experts saying 'catastrophic damage' will result from what is predicted to be the strongest tropical cyclone to make landfall in recorded history.

Thousands of people have been evacuated and thousands more have fled their homes as the category five storm sent waves as high as 5m ashore [...] overturning powerlines and leaving streets knee-deep in water.

Haiyan – the Philippines' 25th typhoon so far this year – is expected to barrel through the archipelago close to Cebu, the nation's second-largest city and home to around 2.5 million people.

Extract 2

Extract from *Typhoon* by Joseph Conrad

The seas in the dark seemed to rush from all sides to keep her back where she might perish[1]. There was hate in the way she was handled, and a ferocity[2] in the blows that fell. She was like a living creature thrown to the rage of the mob; hustled terribly, struck at, borne up[3], flung down, leaped upon. Captain MacWhirr and Jukes kept hold of each other, deafened by the noise, gagged by the wind; and the great physical tumult[4] beating about their bodies, brought, like an unbridled[5] display of passion, a profound[6] trouble to their souls. One of those wild and appalling shrieks that are heard at times passing mysteriously overhead in the steady roar of a hurricane, swooped, as if borne on wings, upon the ship, and Jukes tried to outscream it.

[1] perish – to die or be destroyed
[2] ferocity – savagery, viciousness, wildness
[3] borne up – from the verb 'to bear', to raise aloft, to support

[4] tumult – a loud noise usually made by a crowd of people
[5] unbridled – not controlled or restrained
[6] profound – very deep or intense

Activity 1

1. Now you have read the extracts, look at the adjectives below and match each one to the correct extract.

descriptive	factual	fictional	informative

persuasive	exaggerated	emotional	entertaining

2. What do you think the **purpose** of each text is?

3. The extracts describe the typhoons very differently. List five words or phrases used to describe each typhoon. For example, Conrad: 'like a living creature thrown to the rage of the mob'; the report: 'largest ever recorded'.

Stretch

You began to consider how the writers described typhoons differently in question 3 above. Which do you think is the most effective description, and why?

You should think about:

- the words used to describe the typhoons
- which writer makes the typhoon sound most powerful and how they do this
- which you prefer and the reasons for your choice.

When a writer uses **personification** they represent an idea or an object in human form or give it human characteristics. For example, they may describe a tree as a withered old person with gnarled hands and a stooped posture.

Tip Remember, a text can have more than one purpose. Use the adjectives from question 1 to help you.

Key terms

Purpose: the purpose of a text is what the writer deliberately sets out to achieve. They may wish to persuade, encourage, advise or even anger their reader.

Personification: the attribution of a personal nature or human characteristics to something non-human

Activity 2

1. Conrad refers to 'she' in the passage. Who or what is he referring to?

2. What is the effect of personifying the typhoon?

Extreme travel

9 How a writer influences the reader

Learning objective

- To explore the question 'how does a writer...?'

Introduction

Some people choose to visit and explore extreme environments. From hostile, uninhabited islands to jungles, deserts, mountains and vast areas of ice and snow, there are many extreme areas on our planet. These are often dangerous and conditions can be life-threatening.

Students are often asked to think about a writer's techniques and how a writer may try to manipulate feelings. From holiday brochures to charity adverts, writers try to appeal to us and change the way we feel. When we are asked to consider, 'how does the writer...?' we need to think carefully about:

- what the writer actually says
- how the contents might affect the reader
- the writer's method.

Activity 1

Read the extract opposite. The article suggests that this is Sir Ranulph Fiennes' 'greatest challenge to date'.

1. Look at the subheading and write down anything that the writer says here to suggest this is a great challenge.

2. Now look at the rest of the article. How does the writer present the trek as a challenge? Use these questions to help you.

> Do any of the words suggest it is a challenge?

> Does the writer use any numbers or statistics to make the trek sound more challenging?

> What have other people said about the area?

> What will make this adventure difficult?

Activity 2

Now think about each piece of information you have chosen. Can you explain why each of these suggests that the trek will be a challenge?

Support

The writer mentions Captain Robert Falcon Scott and Apsley Cherry-Garrard in the text. Who do you think these people are? Why do you think the writer mentions them?

Stretch

Some of the language is extreme and paints a bleak picture of the expedition. Given the adversity he faces, why do you think Sir Ranulph Fiennes wants to embark on this 'appalling challenge'?

You should look for both explicit and implicit reasons. Remember to support your answer with textual references.

Sir Ranulph Fiennes to attempt record winter Antarctica trek

Veteran explorer describes planned 2,000-mile trek in temperatures as low as –90°C as his greatest challenge to date

The appalling challenge of a six-month 2,000-mile walk across the south pole, in the perpetual darkness of the Antarctic winter when temperatures can plummet to –90°C, proved, perhaps inevitably, irresistible to the veteran explorer Sir Ranulph Fiennes. [...]

Fiennes' hero, Captain Robert Falcon Scott, wrote 'great God, this is an awful place' when he finally reached the south pole a century ago, before freezing and starving to death with his team on the return journey. Apsley Cherry-Garrard called his own trek 'the worst journey in the world'. [...]

Those journeys were made in summer. Nobody before has attempted [...] crossing the pole in winter. In a prepared statement, Fiennes said: 'This will be my greatest challenge to date. We will stretch the limits of human endurance.' [...]

However, in person, at the launch at the Royal Society of The Coldest Journey, Fiennes could not really explain why anyone should contemplate such a venture, still less a man aged 68 who has survived cancer, major heart surgery, and the loss of most of the frozen finger tips on one hand – which he cut off himself with a saw bought specially for the purpose. 'It's what I do,' he said, looking slightly puzzled at the question.

Activity 3

Using all the skills you've looked at in Activities 1 and 2, write two paragraphs to answer the following question:

How does the writer persuade us that this will be a great challenge?

Exam link

The following steps can help you answer 'How...' questions in the exam:

1. When analysing what a writer says, work out who the writer is – in this case it is journalist Maev Kennedy, not Sir Ranulph Fiennes.

2. Look carefully at what the question asks you to do. Are you being asked how the writer persuades you to do something or why you are persuaded that this is a difficult task?

3. Once you understand what you are being asked to look at, start focusing on what the writer says and how they put their ideas together.

4. Pick out words, phrases, techniques or methods and explain how these work in relation to the question.

   Picking out words and phrases or stating a technique or method can be meaningless unless you are able to explain how they work in the context of the question. For example:

   Where is the emotive language?

   The writer uses a wealth of emotive language in the passage.

   Why does the writer use emotive language? Why does it suggest the trek is challenging?

10 Effective content

Learning objective

● To explore how the content of a text can influence a reader

The content of a text will often have an impact on a reader. Carefully written content can make a reader feel a range of different emotions including guilt, embarrassment, pity or elation. Writers will often construct their content very carefully to manipulate the reader's reactions.

When considering the effect of a text, good readers step back and give an **overview** of what the writer has achieved and how they felt at different points in the text.

Activity 1

Read the following sentences. Look closely at the words used in them. What is the writer trying to make you feel in each example?

The nation weighs up the cost of obesity.

Can you imagine walking for five hours to collect fresh water?

friends of the earth
see things differently

British teenagers awarded European top spot for charitable donations.

NO ONE SHOULD FACE CANCER ALONE
WE ARE MACMILLAN. CANCER SUPPORT

Renewable energy policies will cost the average household in Britain a total of £400 a year by 2020.

Kira Salak is a woman who completed a solo kayak voyage, travelling 600 miles on the Niger River. This extract gives a brief snapshot of a section of her adventure.

Extract from *The Cruelest Journey* by Kira Salak

I wake up with dysentery. Still, I won't give up. Hunched over and faint, I get in my kayak, paddling off down the hottest, most forbidding stretch of the Niger to date. My thermometer reads 112 degrees. The sun burns in a cloudless sky that offers up no hint of a breeze. Great white dunes rise on either side of the river, pulsing with heat waves, little adobe villages half-buried beneath them. [...]

I stick to the very middle of the Niger. An island splits the river, creating a narrow channel on either side. The narrower the river, the more vulnerable I am. There is less opportunity for escape. All I can do is paddle as hard as I can, following my new guideline: don't get out of the boat—*for anything*. Some men onshore leap into their canoes and chase after me, demanding money. One man comes close enough to hit my kayak with the front of his canoe, nearly grabbing my lead rope with his hand. I'm able to see his face and his wild eyes as I strain to get away. I know one of us will have to give up—him or me. I pace my strokes as if it were a long-distance race, and he falls behind.

Exhausted and nauseous, I squint at the Niger trailing off into the distance, looking as if it's being swallowed by the Sahara. I don't know how much farther I can go on like this.

Activity 2

Summary skills are required to give an effective overview of a text. Re-read the extract *The Cruelest Journey*. Then follow the steps below, which will help you to produce an overview of the content and its effect on a reader's emotions.

1. In no more than 15 words, summarize the main information from each paragraph, for example:

    > The author is unwell and has a fever.
    > The weather is very hot.

2. Write down two or three words to summarize how you feel about the information given in each paragraph.

3. Now look at the information you have written down. Can you give a brief overview of this text in no more than 50 words? Remember to summarize the main information and also reflect how you feel.

Stretch

In an exam you may be asked to consider *how* a writer achieves an effect in their text. Look at the exam-style question below and write a brief plan of what you would include in an answer.

How does the author make the reader feel concerned about her health and safety?

To answer this question you should think about:

*   what she says to make you feel concerned
*   any words or phrases that support your ideas and points
*   briefly explaining why you are concerned (*this suggests… this shows…*)
*   any techniques used for effect.

Key term

Overview: a general summary, explanation or outline

11 Persuasive writing techniques

Learning objective

- To understand and explore a range of different techniques that a writer may use for effect

Alongside the language and content of a text, you need to think about the techniques used to create an effect.

Activity 1

1. In pairs, make a list of any persuasive techniques you know. Write down a definition of each of these.

2. Now look at the list you have made and write down why each of these techniques would be effective. (How do they work? What do they do? Why are they persuasive or effective?)

Tip When analysing a text, try to avoid writing vague statements. 'The writer uses short sentences to make me read on' is vague. Always give evidence to support your point or technique, and remember to explain the effect. For example, 'The writer uses short eye-catching sentences like "It was mesmerizing" to give the reader the clear impression that the events were captivating.'

Read the following text from the travel company Extreme Adventures.

EXTREME ADVENTURES
FANCY AN ADVENTURE YOU'LL NEVER FORGET?

Last year 2.5 million young people took a gap year and we're here to help. If you are looking for exhilarating adventures and remote destinations, then look no further. If you fancy a foray into the Falklands or a trek to Timbuktu, we're here for you. Are you fascinated by cultures, mesmerized by magnificent wildlife or want to sample bizarre local cuisines? We're here to help.

If you're wild about wildlife we can offer a tailor-made camping trip on the Serengeti. If you're nuts about Brazil we can organize an amazing journey that weaves through South America and ends at the breath-taking top of Machu Picchu.

Travel expert, Terry Maskell, claims our trips, *'allow you to immerse yourself in inspiring journeys and unforgettable adventures'*. With 99.4% customer satisfaction and over 10,000 successful trips each year, you'll be guaranteed an adventure you'll never forget. Our guides are the finest in their fields. We believe we are the best adventure agents around. But don't take our word for it; check out the thousands of reviews from satisfied customers.

Activity 2

Extreme Adventures is trying to persuade potential travellers to embark on one of its adventures.

1. Which emotions does the company appeal to and why?

2. Some persuasive techniques have been listed here. Can you find an example of each of these in the text? Explain why the examples persuade the reader to embark on one of the adventures.

Lists – used to show a range of potential reasons.

Quotations – often given by an 'expert' to support a product. An expert's support also suggests reliability/respectability.

Statistics – information that is represented by data or numbers.

Direct appeal – often uses pronouns such as *we, us, our, you*. This appeals to the reader who may feel personally involved in the text and can imagine themselves doing what the text suggests.

Rhetorical questions – questions that are used for dramatic effect, not intended to get an answer. They can suggest there is no alternative course of action.

Proper nouns – give the name of a specific place, person or organization. They are often used to make an argument credible or realistic as they give us something 'real' to think about.

Activity 3

Ben Fogle, a TV presenter and explorer, entered a competition in 1999. The BBC was looking for volunteers to be marooned for a year on an island. Fogle was successful and spent one year on an island in the Outer Hebrides.

Task: A TV company is looking for school leavers and college students who are willing to live on an island for one year with other young people. Successful winners will be filmed as part of the project. You have decided to apply.

1. With a partner, list the qualities and skills that would appeal to the producers of the TV show described in the task above.

2. Make a list of any hobbies, interests and personal characteristics that will make you suitable for the show.

3. Make a list of any persuasive techniques that you will use to attract the attention of the producer.

Tip A lively and interesting response will certainly get you noticed, but careful planning, sensible structure and well-written sentences are also persuasive.

Support

Plan your response. Think carefully about the structure of your work. How will you start and how will you end? What details will you include?

Stretch

Write your application. Try to use a wide range of persuasive techniques and sentence structures. Your application should be at least four paragraphs in length.

12 The writer's method

Learning objective

- To explore a range of different methods that can be used by a writer
- To draw together the persuasive skills explored in this unit

The writer's method includes any other ways in which the writer tries to achieve effects. For example, a writer may structure their text in a specific way. They may use comparisons, stark illustrations, anecdotes and so on.

Activity 1

Below is a list of methods writers may use when writing persuasively. Match the methods with their definitions.

> **Stark illustration** **List/accumulate points** **Structure**
>
> **Dismiss opposing ideas** **Comparison** **Anecdote**

> **A** A short, often amusing, story about a real person or event. This is an interesting or light-hearted way of giving information.

> **B** Writers can use pictures, graphs, tables, charts or diagrams to support their ideas. Illustrations will make it easy to visualize a point.

> **C** The writer may show a different perspective of two things within a paragraph or even across an entire text. When a writer includes a contrast, readers need to consider why.

> **D** Writers list arguments within a sentence or may choose to build up several across a whole text. Including a range of ideas adds to the strength of an argument.

> **E** Writers organize their arguments to maximize their effect. Texts may be structured in a certain way, for example, to build up tension.

> **F** Writers may be critical of the opposing or counter ideas and use this criticism to further support their own views.

Throughout this unit we have covered a range of different areas that a reader can consider when analysing a text. The real trick is to approach every text individually and think carefully about what each writer is trying to achieve and what/how they have written to achieve it.

Look at the extract on page 41, which has been taken from a description of the book *Great Outdoor Adventures*, Bear Grylls' guide to the best outdoor pursuits.

The writer uses a range of questions to…

Picture of well-known adventurer who looks like he is involved in…

A direct appeal 'you' is used throughout and this attracts readers because…

Lists a range of outdoor pursuits, attracting readers because…

Gives a problem … and then a solution … which attracts readers because…

Mentions the writer's name and tells us he is an 'intrepid survival adventurer' because…

Great Outdoor Adventures by Bear Grylls

Do you long for adventure without being quite sure how to find it? Do you want to sleep under the stars and experience the wonders of the natural world? More of us than ever are spending weekends and holidays climbing mountains, surfing waves or simply walking in the wilderness, as well as indulging in many other more extreme activities. But how can we use our time out in the open to the full? Now, Bear Grylls, one of the most intrepid survival adventurers of our day, shares his years of experience of the world's most extreme terrain to help you get the most from the great outdoors. So, if you've always been intrigued by kite surfing, now's the time to learn how to do it! Find out how to make a tree house or what dangers to watch out for when you're skiing or paragliding. And if you're planning a hike, discover how to navigate across the hills without ever getting lost and what to pack in your rucksack to keep you safe. Whether you're a novice mountaineer looking to graduate from the climbing wall to real rocks or a weekend camper in search of a little more adventure, this is the book for you.

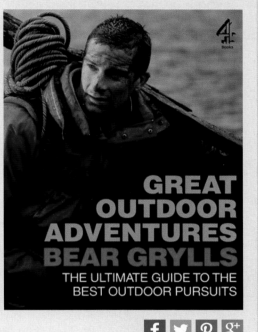

Gives a range of different activities to…

Subheading gives more information so we know what the book is about.

Activity 2

How does the writer try to attract readers to the book?

1. It is useful to annotate texts so you can have a visual record of your ideas. Some of the extract above has been annotated, but the student has not completed their annotations or included arrows to link the annotations with examples. See if you can match up and complete the information for them.

2. Can you find any other techniques in the text that might help to attract readers?

Exam link

When you are preparing to answer a question like this in an exam, ask yourself how the writer is trying to attract you by:

- what they say (language and content)
- the techniques used
- their methods.

When writing up an answer:

- keep referring back to the question
- support every point you make with evidence from the text
- state the effect of every technique used.

Assessment

Reading and understanding

Learning objectives

- To identify information within a text
- To explain and comment on how writers use language and structures to achieve effects and influence readers, using some linguistic terminology

Introduction

In this assessment you will have an opportunity to work through a piece of text and answer some questions. Think carefully about the skills you have developed throughout this chapter and make sure you incorporate these into your answers.

The number of marks alongside each question should give you some indication of how much information you need to include. Read the leaflet on pages 43 and 44 very carefully before you begin answering the questions.

Tip Question 1 has asked for five obstacles, so make sure you include at least five examples from the text. A list can be written in bullet-point format.

For Question 2, make sure you look for five different groups of people.

For Question 3, remind yourself of the work completed on the writer's perspective. The writer of this leaflet clearly thinks this is an excellent activity as they have used a wealth of positive language to describe the place and the activities.

For Question 4, remind yourself of the work completed on the layout and structure of a text.

To answer Question 5, you need to pick out what the writer says about the course, persuasive examples of language, techniques or methods used by the writer.

For each example, you need to write down an example from the text and then explain *why* that specific example is effective in persuading readers to visit Aerial Extreme. You may wish to use the phrases *this suggests...* or *this shows...* to help you explain the effect.

1. List five obstacles that you may face on a high-wire adventure. **[5]**

2. List five groups of people, mentioned in the text, who can enjoy the activities on offer at Aerial Extreme. **[5]**

3. List ten examples of positive language used by the writer to persuade people to try out Aerial Extreme. **[10]**

4. Make a list of the different features used by the writer of this text to appeal to a reader. **[5]**

5. How does the writer try to persuade people to enjoy themselves at Aerial Extreme? **[10]**

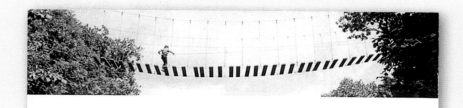

HIGH WIRE ADVENTURE

Aerial Extreme's High Ropes Adventure Courses are an action-packed day out involving a series of challenging obstacles set at varying heights above the ground.

You'll find yourself tackling extreme obstacles such as rope bridges, scramble nets, zip wires, swinging logs and balance beams, plus many more!

JUNIOR ADVENTURE

Once connected by instructors to an overhead safety line, that's it! You remain connected throughout the aerial journey allowing you to concentrate on enjoying yourself.

This means that five out of our six locations are perfect for youngsters as little as six years old!

Plus, no experience or skill is required, so all the kids need is a great sense of adventure.

ADVENTURE PACKAGES

Are you planning a birthday party? Or perhaps an extreme corporate day out?

For an exciting group day out, head for Aerial Extreme and enjoy our challenging and fun obstacles. We can cater for groups from 15 to over 100 but pre-booking is essential.

We've also created a whole host of brilliant birthday, corporate, stag and hen packages aimed at all ages.

PRE-BOOKING IS ESSENTIAL FOR LARGE GROUPS. FOR MORE INFORMATION CALL 0845 652 1736

SCHOOLS AND GROUPS

Experience the excitement of clambering and conquering our high ropes courses and find your inner leader and ultimate team-player when you upgrade to our interactive team-building challenges.

As well as having courses right on your doorstep, our programmes are designed to inspire, motivate and educate students of all ages (and even some teachers!).

Led by experienced and enthusiastic course instructors, we work with schools and community groups to create bespoke programmes which suit individual budgets and requirements.

FIND OUT MORE

We know that it's impossible to fit everything in about Aerial Extreme on one tiny leaflet, so why not check out our website for more? As a bonus, we occasionally pop mouth-watering offers and discounts on there, so it's definitely worth the trip...

SCAN THIS QR BARCODE WITH YOUR SMART PHONE TO GET STRAIGHT THROUGH TO OUR WEBSITE:

Self-assessment

Now look at your answer to Question 5, and use the advice below to help you to **evaluate** your answer.

1. Underline each separate piece of evidence you have used.

2. If you have linked a piece of evidence to the question by explaining how it persuades you to visit Aerial Extreme, place an 'E' above your explanation.

3. If you have mentioned a technique or explained the writer's method by suggesting how the quotation contributes to the overall persuasion, then give yourself a tick.

Support

Would you visit Aerial Extreme? If so, why?

Stretch

Think about the lessons on effect. Do you think this is an effective leaflet? Why?

Tip

- If a question asks for a list, remember to write in a bullet point list.

- When copying points down for a list, do not shorten them so they no longer make sense.

- Check how many marks each question is worth to help you calculate how much detail to include in your answer.

Assessment

Writing

Learning objectives

- To plan and write a letter
- To review and proofread your own writing

Introduction

In this assessment you will have the opportunity to plan and write a formal letter. Think carefully about the skills you have developed throughout this chapter and make sure you incorporate these into your writing.

You see the following letter in a local newspaper.

5 Grange Road
Dernham
DH2 3RG

16th December 2014

Dear Editor,

I recently read an article in your newspaper which seemed to celebrate extreme sports. I have to say that I was appalled when I read your views on these ridiculous activities. From bungee jumping to body boarding, skateboarding to skiing, these sports all carry extreme risks.

Young people are, by nature, risk takers. Young people need no encouragement to get involved in ridiculous activities that threaten their lives and worry their families. I appreciate your negative stance on some of the more dangerous sports like tombstoning, but encouraging young people to give free running a go is, to my mind, utterly irresponsible. I am not the type of parent who wishes to wrap my children in cotton wool, but I feel that urging them to try out new and exciting activities will only cause broken bones and broken hearts.

So what's wrong with a game of chess or a stroll around the park? What's wrong with badminton or bowling? I believe…

Activity 1

Task

The letter on page 46 appeared in a local newspaper. You feel very strongly about the letter and decide to write a response.

Write your letter.

Planning

Spend five minutes planning your work. If you wish, use the prompts opposite to help you.

Go through the letter and underline any of the words or phrases that you wish to discuss or follow up in your response.

Make a list of words or phrases to describe how you feel about the letter. This will help you to determine the tone of your letter.

Points to consider before you start:

- Remind yourself of the layout for a formal letter by studying the letter opposite.

- Who will you address your letter to?

- What will your opening sentence be?

- Plan four or five topic sentences that will begin each paragraph in your writing.

Share your plan with a partner. Make notes on each other's plans if you can think of any ideas or points that they could include in their work.

You now have 30 minutes to write your letter.

Do you agree or disagree with the writer of the letter?

What do you think and feel about extreme sports?

What do you think about the writer of the letter?

Do you have any experience of extreme sports?

Support

Remind yourself of the work completed on sentence types on pages 26–27. Try to include a range of sentence types in your work. Use the letter on page 46 to remind you how to vary your sentences.

Activity 2

Now that you have completed your work, spend two or three minutes reading it to ensure it makes sense.

Tips for proofreading:

- Check your work a sentence at a time and make sure each sentence makes complete sense.

- Highlight any spellings you are uncertain about and check them in a dictionary.

- Swap your work with a partner and ask them to annotate your work (in pencil) with suggestions or corrections.

Tip You can either agree or disagree with the views in the letter, but make sure you have clear, supported opinions.

2 CONFLICT

In this chapter you will be developing your ability to read and write narrative fiction based on the theme of conflict. You will encounter a range of activities that will build on what you already know to enable you to become a more effective reader and writer. Conflict is a common human experience and a key ingredient in fictional writing. You will have the opportunity to enjoy reading texts on this theme and complete activities that will support you in writing fiction of your own. This chapter is divided into three more targeted areas which are integral to the theme of conflict: problems, dialogue and resolution.

'Fiction reveals truth that reality obscures.'
Ralph Waldo Emerson

'Fiction is to the grown man what play is to the child.'
Robert Louis Stevenson

'Action is the pulse of any good story, but the character is the heart. If the action has no consequence to the character, the story loses heart.'
Linda Yezak

What is fiction?

For our purposes, fiction can be defined as:
● prose writing, such as novels, that describes *imaginary* people and events

or

● something produced by the *imagination*.

Fictional writing may be based in part on real events or memories but may contain details that have been imagined or invented by the author. For example, historical fiction often features real people and events from the period in which it is set, even though many of the details relating to plot and character are, in part at least, invented by the author.

Reading fiction

Reading fiction, first and foremost, is something most of us do for pleasure. Wanting to know what happens in a story and engaging with a character, a different world or an ideal is enjoyable. Fiction can provoke a range of emotions in a reader, but it can also teach us things. It can make us think; it can challenge our own views and assumptions; and it can put forward ideas that we may never have previously considered. You will have encountered many different types of fictional writing. Short stories, novels and scripts, for example, often include imaginary events and people.

Writing fiction

You will have produced many fictional pieces of writing during your years at school. You may have been asked to write a story or to imagine a scene and describe it. Autobiographical writing can also form the basis of fictional writing. Perhaps you have written about something that has happened to you or to someone you know well. If you have changed the story to embellish it or developed what happens, then you have made it, in part at least, into a fictional piece.

Exam link

Exam relevance

The study of fiction is very important for GCSE English Language. One of the exams you will sit at the end of your course is largely based on this type of reading and writing. In the first section of the exam you will be asked to read an extract from a fictional text and answer questions on it. In the second section you will be asked to write a story or recollect something that has happened to you. The information and activities you will encounter in this chapter aim to introduce and develop some of the skills that you need in preparation for this part of the exam.

Exploring conflict

Learning objectives

- To consider the theme of conflict
- To explore your own experiences relating to conflict

Key terms

Abstract noun: a noun which identifies things that cannot be physically touched or seen, such as a state, idea, process or feeling

Verb: a word like *eat*, *think* or *walk*. Some identify an action; others identify thoughts and feelings

Activity 1

1. Think about your own experiences of conflict. Have you disagreed with a parent over what to wear? Perhaps you wanted to go swimming but you should have been visiting a grandparent? Maybe your brother or sister borrowed a favourite t-shirt?

    a. Make a list of the different ways you have experienced conflict.

    b. Keeping your own experiences in mind, write down words or phrases you would associate with the idea of conflict.

2. The word 'conflict' does not just refer to two people having a fight. Discuss with a partner how the word 'conflict' can be used in different ways. Make a list of your ideas.

3. Using the ideas you have discussed, write a definition for this term in your own words.

Introduction

How does conflict begin? At its simplest level, there is a problem. In their broadest sense, problems are things that are 'difficult to deal with or understand'. Problems are often the cause or catalyst for conflict, which seems an appropriate place to begin.

It is important when you are asked to respond to an idea that you understand what you are being asked to do. In this case, there is an expectation that you know what the word 'conflict' means. An idea can have more than one meaning and it might mean slightly different things to different people. An expert reader would consider more than one way in which something can be interpreted.

Conflict can be defined in two ways:

1. As an **abstract noun** it can mean:

    - a fight or struggle

    - a disagreement between people having different ideas or beliefs.

2. As a **verb** it can mean:

    - to fight or struggle

    - to have a disagreement.

Activity 2

Look at the images below. What words or phrases would you use to describe the conflicts pictured in them?

Activity ③

You will have come across conflict in fiction in more ways than you have probably realized. Consider:

- Have you read a story, or part of a story, where there was conflict?

- Have you watched a TV drama or a film which focused on imagined conflict?

- Have you listened to a song where the lyrics responded to conflict?

Design and complete a table to show your recent experiences of conflict in fiction. For example:

Source	What happened	My reaction
Reading *The Hobbit*	Bilbo tries to steal from the trolls he has been sent to investigate. The trolls grab him and fight each other about how to interrogate him. The trolls seem naturally argumentative and are looking for conflict.	I felt tense as Bilbo tried to sneak in and then afraid for his safety. I was also eager to find out how he would escape. The conflict was also a little funny, because Tolkien presented a humorous contrast between the stupid trolls and the intelligent Bilbo.
Watching *Avatar*		
Listening to…		

How does conflict start?

There are many different reasons for the start of conflict, but it often revolves around a particular problem or issue. It can be something specific to individuals, such as an argument over the height of a neighbour's hedge, or something of wider concern, such as a conflict over religious beliefs. Conflict can also be something that is experienced internally, for example, someone worrying about something they think they should have done differently. One thing is certain: there is no shortage of reasons for conflict.

Activity ④

1. List at least five different times when you have observed or experienced the beginnings of conflict.

2. Share your experiences with a partner. Discuss whether any of them are similar.

3. Look at the list you have made. Do you think any of these experiences could form the basis for a story? Choose two of your experiences and answer the following questions:

   a. What title would this story have?

   b. How many characters are involved in the conflict?

   c. What would the reader need to know about the main characters?

   d. What is the most dramatic part of the conflict?

Revealing problems

1 Identifying explicit information

Learning objectives

- To understand the difference between explicit and implicit information
- To practise identifying explicit details

Key term

Interpretation: an explanation or understanding of something

Introduction

Problems present themselves in a variety of ways. This is particularly the case with problems that affect people. In this unit you will look at some of the ways problems are revealed by a writer and begin to explore techniques you can use in your own writing.

As readers, we process information. In a narrative piece this can be information on character or setting, or it can be information that moves the plot along. Some of the information that we gain is explicit, which means that it is clearly and openly expressed, and there is no room for doubt or **interpretation**. For example, if you read in a story that 'Jack is a 16-year-old boy', you explicitly learn that the character is called Jack, is 16 and a boy.

Through reading we can also receive information and ideas that are implicit. This means that the writer might suggest or imply something but that it is not openly stated. In literature you have read, you will have drawn conclusions from suggestions that a writer has made. For example, if you read that 'Jack sat hunched on the sofa, his arms wrapped tightly around his legs', the writer could be implying a number of things: Jack may be cold or upset or angry. As a reader you can infer these things from the description of his body language, 'hunched' and 'tightly'.

Read the following extract from *The Boy in the Striped Pyjamas*. Bruno, the main character, is a child who is about to be introduced to 'the Fury', an important visitor of his father's.

Extract 1 from *The Boy in the Striped Pyjamas* by John Boyne

The Fury was far shorter than Father and not, Bruno supposed, quite as strong. He had dark hair, which was cut quite short, and a tiny moustache – so tiny in fact that Bruno wondered why he bothered with it at all or whether he had simply forgotten a piece when he was shaving. The woman standing beside him, however, was quite the most beautiful woman he had ever seen in his life. She had blonde hair and very red lips, and while the Fury spoke to Mother she turned and looked at Bruno and smiled, making him go red with embarrassment.

Activity 1

1. Write down at least two explicit details you learn about the appearance of 'the Fury' and his female companion.

2. Write down two of the things that Bruno is explicitly thinking.

Next, you will read a paragraph taken from slightly earlier in the novel before the arrival of 'the Fury'.

Extract 2 from *The Boy in the Striped Pyjamas* by John Boyne

An hour before the Fury was due to arrive Gretel and Bruno were brought downstairs, where they received a rare invitation into Father's office. Gretel was wearing a white dress and knee socks and her hair had been twisted into corkscrew curls. Bruno was wearing a pair of dark brown shorts, a plain white shirt and a dark brown tie. He had a new pair of shoes for the occasion and was very proud of them, even though they were too small for him and were pinching his feet and making it difficult for him to walk. All these preparations and fine clothes seemed a little extravagant, all the same, because Bruno and Gretel weren't even invited to dinner; they had eaten an hour earlier.

Activity 2

Imagine you are helping a younger student with their reading. List ten simple questions you could ask to help them identify some of the explicit details provided by the author in Extract 2.

For example, you could begin as follows:

1. When were Gretel and Bruno brought downstairs?

Now read the following passage, taken from the novel *Winter in Madrid*. The main character has just arrived at Victoria railway station in London. Think about what explicit information you learn about Victoria station and its surroundings.

Extract from *Winter in Madrid* by C. J. Sansom

At Victoria it had been as busy as a normal Monday; it seemed the reports that London was carrying on as usual were true. As he walked on through the broad Georgian streets everything was quiet in the autumn sunlight. But for the white crosses of tape over the windows to protect against the blast, you could have been back before the war. An occasional businessman in a bowler hat walked by, there were still nannies wheeling prams. People's expressions were normal, even cheerful. Many had left their gas masks at home, though Harry had slung his over his shoulder in its square box. He knew the defiant good humour most people had adopted hid the fear of invasion, but he preferred the pretence that things were normal to reminders that they now lived in a world where the wreck of the British army milled in chaos on a French beach, and deranged trench veterans stood in the streets happily forecasting Armageddon.

Activity 3

1. Answer the following questions to locate explicit details from this extract.

    a. What immediate information are you given about the atmosphere at Victoria station?

    b. What made the houses look different from the way they had looked before the war?

    c. What additional details do we learn to convince us that it is an 'occasional businessman' or a nanny who walks past Harry?

    d. What was Harry carrying 'slung over his shoulder'?

    e. What did Harry think most people 'hid' with their 'defiant good humour'?

2. Swap your answers with a partner to see whether you agree with each other.

Activity 4

Now think about your own writing. Imagine you are going to be writing about yourself or someone you are close to. Don't worry about the details of the story, instead think about what explicit information you would like to present about one of the people involved. Use the framework below to help you.

Appearance	Typical mannerisms/ expressions	Personality	Words or phrases often used

Support

Proofreading is an important skill that you can practise. When your list is complete, underline any words that you think might not be spelled correctly. Using a dictionary, check them and change any that are incorrect.

Stretch

Re-read your list and identify five words that you could change to make your meaning more precise. Use a thesaurus to find an alternative for each of the five words.

2 How writers reveal information

Learning objective

- To investigate some of the implicit ways writers reveal information

> **Tip** When writing about implicit meaning, you will usually be putting forward your ideas as a suggestion about what the writer might mean. Here are some useful words and phrases that you could use as part of an answer to show that you are engaging with implied meaning: *This shows…, this suggests…, this implies…, this gives the impression that…, perhaps the writer…, the writer may be inferring that…*

A lot of the information we receive as we read comes through implicit ideas. When your teachers have talked to you about your own creative writing you may have heard them say, 'Show me, don't tell me.' This is what writers try to do – to show you a picture of a character or a setting through their words. You must then infer what they mean from that picture. A writer sows the seeds of an idea in your head, giving you clues and hints about the direction they would like you to take, but it is up to you to make up your mind about it.

Read the following extract from a story called 'Faith and Hope go shopping'.

Extract from 'Faith and Hope go shopping' by Joanne Harris

I'm not saying it's a bad place here. It's just so *ordinary* – not the comfortable ordinariness of home, with its familiar grime and clutter, but that of waiting-rooms and hospitals, a pastel-detergent place with a smell of air freshener and distant bedpans. We don't get many visits, as a rule. I'm one of the lucky ones; my son Tom calls every fortnight with my magazines and a bunch of chrysanths – the last ones were yellow – and any news he thinks won't upset me. But he isn't much of a conversationalist. *Are you keeping well then, Mam?* and a comment or two about the garden is about all he can manage, but he means well. As for Hope, she's been here five years, even longer than me – and she hasn't had a visitor yet.

Activity 1

1. The narrator is describing the nursing home she lives in. Read the extract again, thinking carefully about how you visualize this place and what it is that leads you to those conclusions.

2. Copy and complete the table below. Some of the boxes have been filled in as examples, but you could add to these with thoughts of your own.

Evidence	Initial thoughts	Development of ideas
'I'm not saying it's a bad place'	It's okay.	...but she's not saying it's a good place either. Is there something wrong?
'not the comfortable ordinariness of home, with its familiar grime and clutter'	She likes home.	'Familiar grime and clutter' suggests it is her own grime and clutter and at least that is personal to her.
'a pastel-detergent place'	The place is defined by its colour and smell.	
'a smell of air freshener and distant bed-pans'		
'We don't get many visits, as a rule'		
'I'm one of the lucky ones; my son Tom calls every fortnight'		
'any news he thinks won't upset me'		
'As for Hope, she's been here five years, even longer than me – and she hasn't had a visitor yet.'		

Read the following extract from *The Saturday Big Tent Wedding Party*. Mma Ramotswe, the main character, is a private detective in Botswana.

Extract from *The Saturday Big Tent Wedding Party* by Alexander McCall Smith

Mma Ramotswe's van had served her well, and she loved it. Its life, though, had been a hard one. Not only had it been obliged to cope with dust, which, as anybody who lives in a dry country will know, can choke a vehicle to death, but its long-suffering suspension had been required to deal with persistent overloading, at least on the driver's side. That, of course, was the side on which Mma Ramotswe sat, and she was, by her own admission and description, a traditionally built person. Such a person can wear down even the toughest suspension, and this is exactly what happened in the case of the tiny, white van, which permanently listed to starboard as a result.

Mma Ramotswe's husband, Mr J. L. B. Matekoni, that excellent man, proprietor of Tlokweng Road Speedy Motors and widely regarded as the best mechanic in all Botswana, had done his best to address the problem, but had tired of having to change the van's shock absorbers from side to side so as to equalise the strain. Yet it went further than that. The engine itself had started to make a sinister sound, which grew in volume until eventually the big-end failed.

'I am just a mechanic, Mma Ramotswe,' he had said to his wife. 'A mechanic is a man who fixes cars and other vehicles. That is what a mechanic does.'

Mma Ramotswe had listened politely, but her heart within her was a stone of fear. She knew that the fate of her van was at stake, and she would prefer not to know that. 'I think I understand what a mechanic does, Rra,' she said. 'And you are a very good mechanic, quite capable of fixing a – '

She did not finish. The normally mild Mr J. L. B. Matekoni had raised a finger. 'A mechanic, Mma,' he pronounced, 'is different from a miracle-worker. A miracle-worker is a person who... works miracles. A mechanic cannot do that. And so when the time comes for a vehicle to die – and they are mortal, Mma, I can assure you – then he cannot wave a wand and make the car new again.' He paused, looking at her with the air of a doctor imparting bad news. 'And so...'

The extract on page 58 uses **metaphors** and **personification**. As an effective reader you do not just need to identify that a writer has used **literary techniques**; you need to explain *how* they have been used and what *effect* they have had on the narrative.

Activity 2

1. How is personification used in this extract?

2. Why does the personification work well here? Think about how it makes you feel about what is being personified and what it shows about the characters' feelings.

Stretch

Choose any fictional book from the library. Read the first couple of chapters and note down examples of metaphors and personification that you think work well. For each example you have selected, explain *why* you think it works well.

Activity 3

Re-read the extract and answer these questions.

1. Why has Mma Ramotswe's van had a hard life?

2. Can you explain how Mma Ramotswe contributed towards the van's problems?

3. What do you think the writer means by saying that the van 'permanently listed to starboard'?

4. How do you think Mma Ramotswe is feeling when her heart is described as 'a stone of fear'?

5. What literary technique has the author used in the description 'a stone of fear'?

6. What is the effect of Mr J. L. B. Matekoni raising his finger?

7. Why does Mr J. L. B. Matekoni explain the difference between a miracle-worker and a mechanic?

8. What do you think Mr J. L. B. Matekoni is about to tell Mma Ramotswe at the end?

Key terms

Metaphor: a figure of speech in which a word or phrase is used to describe an object or an action without using *as* or *like*, e.g. 'There's daggers in men's smiles' (from Shakespeare's *Macbeth*)

Personification: the attribution of a personal nature or human characteristics to something non-human

Literary technique: a method used by a writer to convey his or her message

(3) Writing in the first person

Learning objective

- To write about yourself in a narrative

Some of the best narratives written by students come from direct experience. Using yourself as a character in a story makes sense because you know a lot about yourself and will find it easy to write convincingly and in detail on the subject. Also, your writing will feel more authentic and realistic because you will be writing about things that have happened (or could happen) to you in places you are familiar with. The other characters in your story are likely to be based on people you know well, which will add to the success of your story.

Activity 1

Imagine you are writing an account of something that has happened to you. You will want the reader to **empathize** with you and be on your side. Make a list of the key information a reader will need to know about you. For example, details to do with your appearance, your personality or your relationships with family and friends.

Activity 2

You will be able to tell your reader some of the information about you explicitly. However, it would not be interesting or engaging if you took that approach with all of the information. Take three points from your list and write two or three sentences to implicitly convey the information. Use real experiences to help you where you can.

For example, 'I am quite shy around people I don't know' might become:

> I stood back, not quite knowing what to say. Although Mrs Rose smiled encouragingly, this was the first time I'd met her and I could do little more than shuffle my feet and look at the floor. Glancing up nervously, I gave a tentative half-smile and quietly cleared my throat.

Key terms

Empathize: to share or understand another person's feelings

Figurative language: a word or phrase that shouldn't be taken literally, for example, 'the drying clothes waved like proud flags'. Figurative language requires the reader to use their imagination to complete the writer's meaning and almost always takes the form of either metaphors or similes

Activity 3

The extract on page 61 provides mostly explicit information about a person – 'The student'. It is quite straightforward but would not interest a reader. Rewrite this to reveal more of the information implicitly. In other words, show the reader some of the details – perhaps using **figurative language** – without directly telling them.

The student

Mark lived in a shared house with three other students. He attended college in the nearby town. He came from a wealthy family. He did not need to work while at college. His housemates did not like Mark. He was quite a mean person. He thought about money a lot. He secretly turned the settings down on the heating in order to save money. He even did that in the middle of winter. Even though he lived in a shared house, Mark did not share the work. He did not help to keep the house clean or do his share of the jobs.

Activity 4

Write a short character description of someone you know well, paying attention to both explicit and implicit information.

Progress check

a. Ask a partner to read your work, and then complete the first two columns of the table below with five things that they learn about your character. Two of these details must be implicitly learned.

Details discovered about the character	Is it explicitly or implicitly presented?	What else could the writer have included here?	Your response
1.			
2.			
3.			
4.			
5.			

b. Next, ask your partner to complete the third column of the table to help you improve your writing. They should think about how you could make your ideas clearer or provide more detail.

c. In the fourth column of the table you should indicate which of their comments you find helpful and why. Explain how you would use them to help you improve your writing.

Developing dialogue

4 Exploring dialogue

Learning objective

- To explore the idea of dialogue

Key term

Direct speech: words quoted in the form in which they are or were actually spoken

---

Introduction

Speech, discussion and dialogue are all terms used to describe the way we communicate. It is through speech and dialogue that problems can be presented, discussed and potentially resolved. In this unit you will look at what these terms mean and think about how they work in fiction.

You will begin by exploring how dialogue is used – in everyday life and in writing.

For our purposes, dialogue can be defined in two ways:

- the words spoken by characters in a play, film or story

or

- a conversation or discussion.

The first definition is fairly straightforward and refers to the way conversations are usually presented in fiction. In a story, for example, dialogue is often represented through the use of **direct speech** and any additional description of the characters who are speaking. For example, *'What are you doing?' asked Seb in astonishment.*

The second definition is more open to interpretation, but generally involves a discussion between two or more people or groups, and is usually entered into to gain some sort of resolution. For example, a head teacher may need to engage in a dialogue with parents in order to resolve a problem with unsafe car parking at his or her school. Similarly, a police officer who has been injured in the line of duty may have a dialogue with senior officers about how they can support his or her return to work.

Activity 1

Write down at least three or four examples of when you have entered into a dialogue with someone in order to resolve something.

If we return to the idea of dialogue in fiction – or the conversations that take place in a story – it is important to think about how this is often different from the speech that takes place between two or more people in real life. Think about your own conversations; there will be pauses, repetition of ideas, **fillers** such as 'erm' or 'ah' and **false starts**. Your language use may also be very different from the way a character in a story would speak.

Key terms

Filler: a word or sound that fills a pause in an utterance or conversation (e.g. *er, well, you know*)

False start: an unsuccessful attempt to begin something

Activity 2

Record a conversation with a partner. Choose a topic you are familiar with and record what you say for two or three minutes. Use this recording and attempt to write down the beginning of your conversation as direct speech (you should aim to write at least half a side in continuous prose, but you don't need to write down the entire conversation). Apart from speech tags (e.g. *he said* or *Mark replied*), don't add in anything that is not in the recording and make sure you don't miss out any of the speech or sounds that either of you make in the part of the conversation you are writing about.

Support

For example, a typical conversation might begin:

> I said to Michael, 'Err. Did you watch the match last night then?'
>
> Michael yawned. He said, 'Mmm. Yeah. Thought I was going to miss it. I — I got back late from the gym.'

Activity 3

1. Read through your written conversation. Compare it with your partner's. Have you missed any of the content of the conversation that needs to be added in? When you feel that your conversation is a good representation of what took place, read it through for a final time.

2. Write down as many reasons as you can why this would not be an effective way to write dialogue in a story.

The truth is that if we write down all the content of our conversations, it is not very interesting. There are lots of pauses and some stumbling for words; we often restart what we are saying and don't always follow through to the ending we intended. Dialogue in narrative is very different. Read the following extract, which features the characters of George and Lennie from *Of Mice and Men* by John Steinbeck.

Extract from *Of Mice and Men* by John Steinbeck

Lennie looked timidly over to him. 'George?'

'Yeah, what ya want?'

'Where we goin', George?'

The little man jerked down the brim of his hat and scowled over at Lennie. 'So you forgot that awready, did you? I gotta tell you again, do I? Jesus Christ, you're a crazy bastard!'

'I forgot,' Lennie said softly. 'I tried not to forget. Honest to God I did, George.'

'OK – OK. I'll tell ya again. I ain't got nothing to do. Might jus' as well spen' all my time tellin' you things and then you forget 'em, and I tell you again.'

'Tried and tried,' said Lennie, 'but it didn't do no good. I remember about the rabbits, George.'

'The hell with the rabbits. That's all you ever can remember is them rabbits. OK! Now you listen and this time you got to remember so we don't get in no trouble. You remember settin' in that gutter on Howard Street and watchin' that blackboard?'

Lennie's face broke into a delighted smile. 'Why sure, George. I remember that ... but ... what'd we do then? I remember some girls come by and you says ... you says...'

'The hell with what I says. You remember about us goin' into Murray and Ready's, and they give us work cards and bus tickets?'

'Oh, sure, George. I remember that now.' His hands went quickly into his side coat pockets. He said gently: 'George ... I ain't got mine. I musta lost it.' He looked down at the ground in despair.

'You never had none, you crazy bastard. I got both of 'em here. Think I'd let you carry your own work card?'

Lennie grinned with relief. 'I ... I thought I put it in my side pocket.'

Dialogue within a story has to do more than represent the speech that is taking place. It is also one of a writer's tools for developing the story. We find out information about the characters of George and Lennie and what is happening to them through what they say and the way they say it.

Activity 4

1. Use a table like the one below to list what you find out about the characters of George and Lennie and their situation. First, look for information you are given directly, and then try to analyse both the explicit and implicit meanings.

Dialogue	How words are spoken	What this tells you	What we can deduce
'Yeah, what ya want?'		George can be quite short in the way he speaks to Lennie.	George might just be rude, or Lennie frustrates George, perhaps asks a lot of him and George is weary of this.
'George?'	timidly	Lennie is nervous about George's reaction to what he is about to say.	Lennie has done something wrong, or something he knows George won't be happy about. This suggests he cares about what George thinks.

2. Once you have completed your table, write up character profiles for both Lennie and George. Imagine you are a director who will be giving instructions to actors who are auditioning to play the parts of George and Lennie in a new film adaptation. Write a paragraph which summarizes the key information you want the actors to know before auditioning.

3. Compare your profiles with a partner. Were they similar? Did you do anything differently? Discuss any differences and explain why you made the choices you did, using evidence from the extract to support your arguments.

Activity 5

Look back at the written conversation that you produced for Activity 2. Using a highlighter pen, highlight a few lines of the conversation that you think could be used as a starting point for dialogue in a story. This time you should add descriptive detail and edit the content in order to engage a reader.

Stretch

5 Writing speech

Learning objective

- To revise the presentation of direct speech in fictional prose

Below is a reminder of how speech should be set out in writing and an extract from *The Hobbit* demonstrating the use of speech.

Key information

✓ Speech marks or inverted commas are used when writing direct speech. It is fine to use either double (" ") or single inverted commas (' '), but make sure that you consistently use the same ones.

✓ The punctuation that goes at the end of the words that are spoken always appears *inside* the final set of speech marks. The first word that is spoken by a character always begins with a capital letter, even if it follows a comma.

Extract from *The Hobbit* by J. R. R. Tolkien

'Now we are all here!' said Gandalf, looking at the row of thirteen hoods – the best detachable party hoods – and his own hat hanging on the pegs. 'Quite a merry gathering! I hope there is something left for the late-comers to eat and drink! What's that? Tea! No thank you! A little red wine, I think for me.'

'And for me,' said Thorin.

'And raspberry jam and apple-tart,' said Bifur.

Activity 1

Copy out the sentences below and insert the necessary speech punctuation.

1. The weather has been dreadful this week, commented Mrs Phillips.
2. I want to go first! demanded Max.
3. The doctor replied, The news isn't good, I'm afraid.

If direct speech is broken up by information about who is speaking, you need to remember the following things:

You should use punctuation to end the first piece of speech.

If the second part of the speech is still part of the same sentence, it should also begin with a lower-case letter.

There should also be either a comma or a full stop before the second piece of speech.

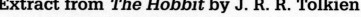
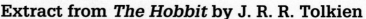

'Looking back,' I said, 'we should have guessed there was something wrong.'

'I can't believe it!' Jack said. 'He was lying all along.'

'Please don't give me that,' she said. 'I can't stand mashed potato.'

Activity 2

Copy out the sentences below and insert the necessary speech punctuation.

1. That's the doctor, said the woman behind the desk. He's back now and will be with you soon.

2. Let go of the rope, warned the leader, or you will hurt yourself.

3. What time is it? I asked. Can we have dinner yet?

Every time a new speaker says something you should start a new paragraph. For example:

'It's not possible,' said James.

'That's what I said,' agreed Harry, 'but he is convinced he can do it.'

'We've got to stop him,' James urged.

Activity 3

Copy out the following text and correct the punctuation and paragraphing.

How are you getting into town? asked my mum. I'm going to catch the bus with Sam, I replied. I'm going shopping myself later, she said, It won't be for a while but I can give you both a lift back if you like? Maybe, I said, I'll see what time we're thinking of setting off and give you a ring. No problem, I'll have my phone on me. Mum replied. Don't leave it in the car like you usually do, I joked. As if I would! she smiled.

Stretch

Find a piece of your own writing where you have used direct speech and highlight any mistakes you made. Next, rewrite the incorrect speech accurately.

6 The purpose of dialogue in fiction

Learning objective

- To investigate the use of dialogue in fiction

Dialogue in fiction fulfils a number of important roles:

- It appears to be like a conversation.
- It develops what the reader knows about the characters in the story.
- It develops the plot of the story.
- It is realistic.
- It takes hold of and keeps the attention of a reader.

In 'Revealing problems' (pages 52–61), you will have explored the necessity to 'show' as well as 'tell' a reader what you want them to know. Writing can often involve the 'telling' of information, but a writer can also use what a character does or says to show the reader what they want them to know. Read the following extract and notice how the author uses action to inform you.

Extract from *The Hunger Games* by Suzanne Collins

When I am done with instructions about fuel, and trading and staying in school, I turn to my mother and grip her arm, hard. 'Listen to me. Are you listening to me?' She nods, alarmed by my intensity. She must know what's coming. 'You can't leave again,' I say.

My mother's eyes find the floor. 'I know. I won't. I couldn't help what – '

'Well, you have to help it this time. You can't clock out and leave Prim on her own. There's no me now to keep you both alive. It doesn't matter what happens. Whatever you see on the screen. You have to promise me you'll fight through it!' My voice has risen to a shout. In it is all the anger, all the fear I felt at her abandonment.

She pulls her arm from my grasp. Moved to anger herself now. 'I was ill. I could have treated myself if I'd had the medicine I have now.'

That part about her being ill might be true. I've seen her bring back people suffering from immobilising sadness since. Perhaps it is a sickness, but it's one we can't afford.

'Then take it. And take care of her!' I say.

'I'll be alright, Katniss,' says Prim, clasping my face in her hands.

In the narrator's first spoken words the writer shows us the urgency of her message.

- We see the action of her gripping her mother's arm and that it's 'hard'.

- The use of the **imperative** 'Listen…' followed by the question 'Are you listening to me?' shows the importance of what she will say.

- No words are wasted.

Key term

Imperative: expressing a command, e.g. *come* in *'Come here!'*

Activity 1

Write down in your own words how the writer 'shows' us that what the narrator is saying is urgent. You can use anything you have learned in this section, in addition to your own ideas, to help you with this.

Activity 2

Complete the following table to show how the dialogue in the extract helps to develop what the reader knows about the characters and plot. Then complete the boxes to explain whether the speech seems realistic and helps to keep the reader's attention.

Example	Knowledge of character	Knowledge of plot	Is it realistic?	Does it keep the reader's attention?
'Listen to me. Are you listening to me?'		What she has to say will be important.	Brief sentences are used to show urgency. These work with the command and are convincing.	Tension is created as the reader anticipates what she has to say.
'You can't leave again,'	We now know that her mum has left in some way before.			
'I know. I won't.'		We know that her mum intends to be there and do the right thing.		
	Her mum had her reasons for what happened last time.		The narrator (Katniss) cuts off her mum — giving the sense that there is little time.	

7 Using and developing dialogue

Learning objectives

- To consider how you can use dialogue as a device in writing
- To develop planning skills in writing

The next few activities will build towards planning a narrative scene which develops using dialogue. You will then use your plan to help you write a scene containing dialogue.

The plan

Activity 1

Imagine you are involved in an argument with a friend or family member. It can be as simple or complex as you choose to make it. Decide who will be involved and what you will be arguing about. Write this down.

Activity 2

Using a spider diagram, write down as many words as you can to describe the kinds of emotions the people involved in the argument might be feeling.

Activity 3

You know the sorts of things you say and the way in which you might say them. You have also probably listened to the person involved in the argument many times during your life and are familiar with the kinds of phrases they might use. Make a list of any words or phrases that you might expect to hear in an argument, for example, a parent might use your full name in an argument – 'Stephen James Watson!' – whereas a friend might use the nickname 'Stevie'.

Activity 4

Answer the following questions.

1. How will the argument begin?
2. What are the viewpoints of the people involved in the argument?
3. Will someone win the argument or will it reach a stalemate?
4. How will the argument end?

Activity 5

You have enough information now to help you begin. Write a short dialogue in which two or more characters are having an argument. This is not supposed to be a complete story; you don't need to set the argument in context or demonstrate what happens next – you are only concerned with the scene of the argument.

Progress check

Exchange your piece of writing with someone else's. You are going to check each other's work and see if you can improve it. Make notes on the following:

1. Is what happens clear? Could this be improved upon?

2. Do you get enough detail about the speakers and their emotions? If not, what else would you want to know? Could more specific vocabulary have been used?

3. Is the speech realistic? How could it be made more so?

4. Does the writer use opportunities to 'show' the reader what is happening rather than telling them? Can you suggest how this could be improved?

5. Does the argument end convincingly?

6. Is the speech written accurately? Check the layout and punctuation, and mark any errors.

7. Now look at your own work and the suggestions that have been made. Redraft your work in light of the feedback you have received.

Resolving conflict

8 Exploring resolution

Learning objective

- To consider the idea of resolution

Introduction

Resolving issues that have caused conflict is not always easy. A resolution does not always bring happiness or peace, although sometimes it might. This unit will focus on some of the ways problems are resolved in fiction and encourage you to think about how you would show the resolution of problems in your own writing.

For our purposes, resolution can be defined as:

- a firm decision to do or not to do something

or

- the action of solving a problem or contentious matter.

If we apply these definitions to the theme of conflict, they might work in slightly different ways. A firm decision to do or not to do something or the action of solving a problem could result in a difficult situation ending in entirely opposite ways – for example, by attempting to resolve political unrest, a government could decide to go to war or invest in a peace treaty. Either would be a resolution of sorts.

Activity 1

Look up the word 'resolution' in a dictionary. You will probably see more definitions than are mentioned here. Use this information to help you write five different sentences which all contain the word 'resolution'.

When discussing fiction, the term 'resolution' can take on a slightly different meaning. Resolution can occur where some of the events and issues of the story are resolved for the reader. This does not necessarily mean that the reader gains closure and has all of their questions answered, but that some of the issues that have been most important to the story will be resolved.

Activity 2

Think about a story, film or TV programme you have encountered recently where an issue was resolved. Answer the following questions in relation to that issue.

1. What was the initial problem?
2. What happened as a result of this problem? Did it create additional issues?
3. How was the problem resolved?

Tip The more you read, the better you will be at English. It will exercise your brain and challenge you to think in different ways, and can also help you relax.

Reading more than the texts you are given in your English lessons is very important to your development as a student of English. Through reading you will become accustomed to a wider vocabulary and gain awareness of how to use it. You will regularly be exposed to writers who know how to punctuate, spell and construct sentences well. Reading will make some of the more fundamental techniques of writing really obvious to you.

Activity 3

Stretch

Make the resolution that you will read more.
Discover really good books that will appeal to you.
Whether you are interested in mysteries, science fiction or stories from other cultures, there are plenty of books to choose from. Read book reviews on the Internet or in newspapers to find books that might appeal to you. Make a list of five books that you would like to read and set yourself a time limit in which to read them. Why not try the list of recent winners of the Carnegie Medal as a starting point?

9 Identifying tension

Learning objective

- To identify tension in fiction

Tension in fiction is concerned with the creation of situations or atmosphere that can cause a reader to react with emotion. It is the ingredient that makes a story interesting and keeps us turning the pages. Good writers handle the creation of tension with some caution and employ many different techniques to both build and reduce tension effectively.

In the following extract, a group of soldiers are about to go into battle. Read the first paragraph carefully.

Extract 1 from *The Ghost Road* by Pat Barker

The barrage was due to start in fifteen minutes' time. Prior shared a bar of chocolate with Robson, sitting hunched up together against the damp cold mist. Then they started crawling forward. The sappers, who were burdened by materials for the construction of the pontoon bridge, were taking the lane, so the Manchesters had to advance over the waterlogged fields. The rain had stopped, but the already marshy ground had flooded in places, and over each stretch of water lay a thick blanket of mist. Concentrate on nothing but the moment, Prior told himself, moving forward on knees and elbows like a frog or a lizard or like – like anything except a man.

Activity 1

1. In the first sentence, which word tells you what is going to happen? What does that word mean?

2. What do you learn about the movement of the men in the extract?

3. Which route is more difficult: 'the lane' taken by the 'sappers' or the 'fields' taken by the 'Manchesters'?

4. What do you know about the weather conditions? How will this affect the soldiers?

5. Re-read the last sentence. How does the description of Prior as 'like a frog or a lizard' link back to what the writer has already told us?

Now read the second extract.

Extract 2 from *The Ghost Road* by Pat Barker

There is to be no retirement under any circumstances. That was the order. They have us tied to the stake, we cannot fly, but bear-like we must fight the course. The men were silent, staring straight ahead into the mist. Talk, even in whispers, was forbidden. Prior looked at his watch, licked dry lips, watched the second hand crawl to the quarter hour. All around him was a tension of held breath. 5.43. Two more minutes. He crouched further down, whistle clenched between his teeth.

Prompt as ever, hell erupted. Shells whined over, flashes of light, plumes of water from the drainage ditches, tons of mud and earth flung into the air. A shell fell short. The ground shook beneath them and a shower of pebbles and clods of earth peppered their steel helmets.

Activity 2

Rewrite the second paragraph of Extract 2 in the **first person** as if you were there and experiencing what was taking place. Read the support box below to remind yourself of what to consider in your writing.

SPAG

Support

To write in the first person you need to show what your thoughts and feelings would be. In a scene such as this you might also pay attention to your **senses** and how they are affected by what is happening.

Key terms

First person (*I/we*): using first-person narrative allows you to tell a story from the perspective of a character in the text. In non-fiction texts it can be seen as a biased view because it only tells one side of the story

Senses: the ability to see, hear, touch, taste or smell

10 Responding to a text

Learning objective

- To evaluate the way a text can make you feel

Resolution can lead to a writer answering some of a reader's questions and making sure that the outcome for a character is satisfying to us. It can mean that there is a moral to the story and that the main character learns something significant through the events of the narrative. These types of endings are amongst the first we are exposed to as readers – children's stories and fairy tales often follow this path.

The following extract is from *Billy the Kid*, a story written for children. The story is told from the perspective of Billy, an 80-year-old man looking back on his life. As a youngster he was a star striker for Chelsea Football Club until the outbreak of war, when he became a soldier. Football is his passion and helped him through the war, but his injuries left him unable to play on his return. His life was then one of a vagrant until he is befriended by a family who move him into a shed in their garden. The extract begins towards the end of the story.

Extract from *Billy the Kid* by Michael Morpurgo

It was on Christmas Day that Maddy told me she was going to have a baby. I was so happy, happy for them, happy for me. […] They called him Sam, and I bought him a football. As soon as he was up and running I could see he was going to make a footballer. Before he was three I was kicking a tennis ball around with him in the garden. By five he could trap and turn and shoot. […] He called me Uncle Billy and I thought the world of him.

Thinking about it now, I know it was Sam who stopped me drinking, Sam and Maddy. One day I did the unforgiveable. Sam was about seven or eight by now, and at school down the road. One afternoon I found myself outside the school gates. I was drunk as a lord. I saw Sam and he saw me. He waved and began to run across the playground towards me, and then he stopped. He saw the state of me and turned, and ran back indoors. I'd seen him recoil from me once or twice before. I'd promised myself I wouldn't ever get drunk when Sam was around. But I had. […]

That evening sitting around the kitchen table Maddy and Jamie came to an agreement with me. They were both very stern. They would let me stay, but only under certain conditions. I would be allowed two beers a day, one in the morning and one in the evening. They would bring it to me. I was never ever to buy a drink for myself again. I had to do my teeth twice a day, have a bath once a day and keep my clothes clean. I agreed, and I stayed.

Best thing I ever did. I kept the garden tidy for them, looked after the house, even did a bit of cooking – I wasn't bad either. And little Sam was my pride and joy. Every day we'd be out in the park practising. I taught him all the skills I knew, trained him so he could run as fast as a whippet – he was small like me. I taught him to be tough as a terrier too. He was soon scoring goals for his school. […] At seventeen he was playing in the Chelsea Reserves, and I was there seven years ago with Maddy and Jamie when he ran out for Chelsea for the first time. Proudest day of my life that was. Chelsea lost, but I didn't care. […]

Who knows what causes these things – too much excitement maybe, but the next day, I had a bit of a stroke. Nothing much, the doctor said, but I'd have to take it easy. It affected my eyesight more than anything else – all the peripheries are still a bit fuzzy. I'd have been quite happy staying where I was in the cabin, but it was winter and Maddy wouldn't hear of it. For a while I found myself living again in the basement in Jamie's studio. But we all knew that couldn't go on for ever. It was Jamie who found a way out of it, a way that suited us all perfectly – the Royal Hospital Chelsea: a sort of retirement home for old soldiers. […]

'You're an old soldier,' he said. 'And you've got a disability pension, so you'd qualify. I've checked. All you have to do is have an interview.'

To be honest I wasn't all that happy with the idea at first. But when I saw the place I changed my mind. I'd have my own cubicle, three good meals a day and everything provided. And best of all, it wasn't that far from Chelsea Football Club. I had my interview with the Adjutant Colonel and the Captain of Invalides. I liked them and they seemed to like me. I had a three-day stay, sleeping there and eating there, just to see how I got on. I loved every minute of it. […]

Within a month I moved in and became a Chelsea Pensioner. I'd seen them about in their scarlet coats – some of them always come to watch Chelsea – and always thought how fine they looked. Now I'm one of them. And what a life of Riley I have. I paint a bit, when my eyes aren't too fuzzy, and I play a lot of bowls. […]

I eat like a horse, go home every Sunday for lunch to see the family, and do just what I like – but I never ever have more than two beers a day. And every home game I'm there down at the Shed End at Chelsea watching Sam play.

Activity 1

Re-read the extract and complete the following table to chart your thoughts and feelings. Try to put these down in the order in which they appear in the story.

Evidence	Thoughts and feelings
'… on Christmas Day that Maddy told me she was going to have a baby.'	Pleased for them – being on Christmas Day makes it seem like an extra present
'… the next day I had a bit of a stroke.'	Concern for Billy's health and what would happen to him now

It is important that you show the ability to track through a text. The most sensible way to answer a question on a piece of writing is to comment about what happens **chronologically**. This provides natural structure to your work and will prevent your answer becoming confused. It will also show that you are aware of the **context** of what has been written. If you write about part of a story out of context it can lead to misunderstanding.

Activity 2

Use three pieces of evidence from your table to answer the following question:

What are your thoughts and feelings about how Billy's life has turned out?

(11) Planning your ending

Learning objective

- To plan for an ending

Ending a story is not easy. Ultimately, it comes down to you and what you want your reader to go away knowing and feeling. Do you want all the loose ends tied up neatly? Do you want to leave your reader guessing? Perhaps you want to surprise your reader? If you are writing about something that has actually happened to you it can be easier because you already know exactly what happened and can build upon that.

Activity 1

The following writing tasks are similar to the types of task you might see in an exam. Choose one of them and think about three different ways in which you could end that narrative. Don't think about what happens during the story or how it develops – just think about what ending you would want to get to. For example, 'The Argument' might end with both people learning to see the other person's point of view.

a. Write a story called 'The Argument'.

b. Write a story that begins with the words, 'It wasn't my fault. I am not accepting the blame for this...'.

c. Write about a time when you felt very worried about something.

Activity 2

Choose one of the endings you have suggested and think about what would happen in the story to get you to that point. Make bullet-point notes of how the story will begin and the key events that will take place.

Progress check

Find out what someone else thinks about your work. Swap plans with a partner and aim to give them three constructive suggestions about ways to improve their plan.

Complete the following table for your own work and that of your partner.

What do I think about the ending?	My partner's work	My work
Is it a good ending to a story?		
What improvements could be made to the ending?		
Is there anything you would change about the events that lead up to the ending?		
Can you find any spelling errors?		

Compare what you have said about your own work with the advice from your partner. Highlight the suggestions which you think are most helpful.

Support

Learning to give constructive criticism is a skill that will always be useful. Sometimes it's easy to see a problem, but constructive criticism means a) finding a solution and b) communicating that solution tactfully. Feedback is a two-way process – your partner may want to discuss your solution, so be ready to explain why something isn't working. Is the meaning unclear? Has something important been missed or has an instruction with the task been misinterpreted, for example?

Stretch

Keep a notebook you can add to when you encounter a good ending – you might be reading a book or watching a film or a play. Endings are not always easy to write, but we can learn what works well (and what doesn't) by our own responses to other people's stories.

Assessment

Reading and understanding

Learning objectives

- To practise identifying and interpreting implicit and explicit ideas
- To begin to explain how writers use language and structure to influence

Introduction

During this chapter you have learned and practised a number of techniques that will help you investigate and explore a text. The following extract and questions will help you to put some of these into practice.

Read the following extract about a young foster girl called Liesel, living outside Munich in Nazi Germany.

Extract from *The Book Thief* by Markus Zusak

When school broke up briefly for *Weihnachten*, Liesel even afforded Sister Maria a 'merry Christmas' before going on her way. Knowing that the Hubermanns were essentially broke, still paying off debts and paying rent quicker than the money could come in, she was not expecting a gift of any sort. Perhaps only some better food. To her surprise, on Christmas Eve, after sitting in church at midnight with Mama, Papa, Hans Junior and Trudy, she came home to find something wrapped in newspaper under the Christmas tree.

'From Saint Niklaus,' Papa said, but the girl was not fooled. She hugged both her foster parents, with snow still laid across her shoulders.

Unfurling the paper, she unwrapped two small books. The first one, *Faust the Dog*, was written by a man named Mattheus Ottleberg. All told, she would read that book thirteen times. On Christmas Eve, she read the first twenty pages at the kitchen table while Papa and Hans Junior argued about a thing she did not understand. Something called politics.

Later, they read some more in bed, adhering to the tradition of circling the words she didn't know and writing them down. *Faust the Dog* also had pictures – lovely curves and ears and caricatures of a German Shepherd with an obscene drooling problem and the ability to talk.

The second book was called *The Lighthouse* and was written by a woman, Ingrid Rippinstein. That particular book was a little longer, so Liesel was able to get through it only nine times, her pace increasing ever so slightly by the end of such prolific readings.

It was a few days after Christmas that she asked a question regarding the books. They were eating in the kitchen. Looking at the spoonfuls of pea soup entering Mama's mouth, she decided to shift her focus to Papa. 'There's something I need to ask.'

At first, there was nothing.

'And?'

It was Mama, her mouth still half full.

'I just wanted to know how you found the money to buy my books.'

A short grin was smiled into Papa's spoon. 'You really want to know?'

'Of course.'

From his pocket, Papa took what was left of his tobacco ration and began rolling a cigarette, at which Liesel became impatient.

'Are you going to tell me or not?'

Papa laughed. 'But I *am* telling you, child.' He completed the production of one cigarette, flipped it on the table, and began on another. 'Just like this.'

That was when Mama finished her soup with a clank, suppressed a cardboard burp, and answered for him. 'That *Saukerl*,' she said. 'You know what he did? He rolled up all of his filthy cigarettes, went to the market when it was in town, and traded them with some gypsy.'

'Eight cigarettes per book.' Papa shoved one to his mouth, in triumph. He lit up and took in the smoke. 'Praise the Lord for cigarettes, huh, Mama?'

Mama only handed him one of her trademark looks of disgust, followed by the most common ration of her vocabulary. '*Saukerl*.'

Liesel swapped a customary wink with her papa and finished eating her soup. As always, one of her books was next to her. She could not deny that the answer to her question had been more than satisfactory. There were not many people who could say that their education had been paid for with cigarettes.

Activity 1

Answer the following questions. Try to make sure your answers are clear, and detailed where they need to be. Make sure you use evidence from the text to support what you say.

1. Reading it in context, what do you think the word *Weihnachten* means?

2. Can you find any clues to suggest what sort of school Liesel goes to?

3. In the first paragraph, what do you find out about the Hubermann family?

4. What did Papa and Hans Junior argue about?

5. How does the writer show us that *Faust the Dog* is probably a children's book?

6. How do you think the introduction of dialogue helps to develop the story?

7. How do Papa's answers add tension to the story?

8. What impressions do you get of Papa throughout the extract?

9. You might not know what *Saukerl* means, but how do you think Mama uses this word?

10. What are your thoughts and feelings about how Papa managed to obtain the books for Liesel?

11. How do you think Liesel and her papa feel at the end of this exchange? Write about each character separately.

Assessment

Planning to write

Learning objective

- To think about the content of a story and plan how it will unfold

What does this have to do with the story? It's not relevant and sounds like something rehearsed that has been put in because the writer is determined to use it.

Neither word is used accurately. What meaning was the writer intending with 'restly'? Would someone be kneeling with 'rest' if they had just broken their mum's favourite photo frame?

Is this the perfect moment to introduce a bit of character detail on a younger brother who may become a key player shortly?

Introduction

A class was set a story-writing assignment to respond to the task 'The Argument'. Below is one student's opening paragraph. It has been annotated to show you some areas that could be improved on.

A drift of white clouds was floating in sky. The rays of bright sun light were dazzling the not yet sun-kissed skin of pedestrians. I kneeled on the brown parquet floor restly, looking frighteningly at the remains of my mum's favourite photo frame. I could still make out the gemstone hearts amongst the bits of glass.

'Oooh! No! That's Mum's favourite frame gone. She's gonna kill me.' I groaned to myself. My brain began to spin frantically, trying to figure out what to do next. I could tell her the truth and hope that in her great merciful mood, she would forgive me. Or I could blame my younger brother, though he's never a suspect when anything goes wrong.

Show us, don't tell us!

Use this opportunity to show the character's despair. What is he or she doing?

Activity 1

Using the suggestions above and your own ideas, rewrite and improve these opening paragraphs.

Activity 2

Write a detailed plan explaining how you would develop this story. Opposite is a sample plan to give you an idea of what another student wrote for this story.

Support

- Aim to write around a side of A4.
- Think about what characters will be involved in your story. Think about the ending of your story. What would take place in order to get to that ending?
- Split your plan into sections.

Title: The Argument

Characters: Me, brother Jacob and a cross
old lady

What happens:
— I break Mum's favourite photo frame.
— Jacob comes in, sees what has happened
and tries to run off to tell Mum.
— I stop him and persuade him to help me
shop for a replacement.
— I clear up the debris and we head into town.
— We eventually find an identical frame.
— As we check we've got enough money an
old lady tries to buy it.
— We argue about who it belongs to.
— Jacob bursts into tears and the old lady
takes pity on us.

Where story takes place:
Our lounge, full of mum's treasured things

Bus	— detail on the length of bus journey, passing too many housing estates, panic of not going to get to town before shops shut
Department store	— detail of looking at store plan, add pace by running up escalators. Some description of finding right floor and the search through shelves of frames — glass, silver, wood

Ending:
Get home, get frame into place before Mum
any the wiser. Just sit down in relief, realize she
has been sitting in the room watching us!

Character detail needed:

Characters

Me
— quite feisty/argumentative
— good with a plan
— clumsy
— in a world of my own

Jacob
— a bit wet but does well in
a crisis
— goody two shoes, tells me
off before agreeing to help
— typical brother, needs
bribing to stop him telling
in first place

Old lady
— quite grumpy
— makes lots of comments
on 'youth of today'
— pinched mouth and eyes
— quite shrunken in height
— softens at end

3 CHANGE

In this chapter you will explore both fiction and non-fiction texts that were written before 1900. You will explore a number of exciting and challenging source materials, all based around the theme of change. The activities will help you build up a set of reading strategies to develop your ability to understand both the obvious or explicit meanings in a text, and those implicit meanings that often lie hidden just beneath the surface. Throughout this chapter you will need to employ the skill of empathy in order to think about the ideas in a text from the viewpoint of a character who lived in a different time from you. In considering how a character might view events in a story, you will deepen your understanding of the meanings behind the texts.

'Isn't it funny how day by day nothing changes but when you look back everything is different...' *C. S. Lewis*

'Nothing happens until the pain of remaining the same outweighs the pain of change.' *Unknown*

'Nothing is so painful to the human mind as a great and sudden change' *Mary Wollstonecraft Shelley*

Reading texts

You will cover a range of different reading materials in this chapter including fictional prose and non-fiction texts such as posters, autobiography, journals, travel writing and essays.

Writing

This chapter will largely focus on developing your reading skills but there will be opportunities to write both fiction and non-fiction responses using the reading texts as stimulus.

Through the texts and activities you will explore the following topics:

- Facing changes: how the context of writing shapes our views of its subjects; methods writers use to present change, such as extended metaphor; how changes in setting can reflect character changes. You will also be introduced to the skill of evaluation as a means of deepening your response to a text.
- Crossing boundaries: how changing ideas, scientific development and the supernatural have influenced writers of non-fiction and fiction. You will look at how writers craft their texts carefully to create multiple meanings or messages. You will also enhance your skills of comparison through study of extracts which follow change in one particular character.
- Strength in adversity: How real people can show admirable strength in the face of difficult changes to their lives. The activities and texts selected will focus on how text and images can be used to reflect different messages about characters or figures, and will also help you to understand the devices writers use to build tension.

Exam link

Exam relevance

One of the English Language exams you will sit (Component 2) is solely focused on non-fiction texts. Some of these will have been written or published before 1900. Therefore, developing strategies to help read these texts with confidence is essential to ensure you succeed in the exam. The skills you gain in reading pre-1900 fiction will also assist you with your English Literature course.

Exploring change

Learning objectives

- To consider why change is often an interesting topic for writers
- To explore the ideas of perspective and context, and how they affect our reading of a text

Introduction

There's no denying that life can be pretty fast-paced sometimes, and changes can happen to us without us even noticing. The people who often notice us changing are those who we don't see for a period of time. Writers are interested in how these changes happen too. They can use their characters or settings to explore what happens when things change.

Activity 1

Discuss with a partner anything that has happened recently and changed you. It might be something positive like passing a test or your team winning a really important game. It might be something which made you feel sad, like finding out that something you had been looking forward to was now not going to happen. It could be something where you had mixed emotions, like moving house. What emotions might we feel when things change?

Stretch

Look back at the quotations on page 84 which introduce this section. Two of them comment on pain. Why do you think pain is often an emotion associated with change?

Activity 2

The two extracts on page 87 give views about what it was like to be 15 in 1960. In what ways are these experiences of teenage life similar to and different from yours?

Stretch

Find out about what life was like for your own parents, guardian or grandparents when they were your age. Ask them to focus on similar things to the extracts opposite and then list the main changes in teenage life between then and now.

Extract 1

Having left a sheltered school environment one month earlier, and facing up to a real adult world, I accepted the first job I was offered, which I regretted. Not having passed any exams, I decided to attend college. My evenings were spent studying: I went to college three evenings per week, taking lessons in shorthand, typing and English (O Level), and had one extra shorthand lesson. I attended church on Sundays, visited grandparents and did homework. Occasional cinema visits and cycling with friends filled some time at weekends. I didn't have much money as I was on a low wage. What I did have I put towards clothing and shoes. Being a teenager I felt lonely at times – not an adult – not a child. It was hard work with a job and college. I was always wanting something better!

Extract 2

Aged 15, I was still travelling 9 miles on the bus to the grammar school, so I was up fairly early in the morning and home later than some. My family were fairly poor so I didn't live a lavish lifestyle. In the evenings, I did my school homework and watched some TV at an aunt and uncle's house as we didn't own one! I played tennis and football on the local Miner's Welfare facilities at weekends, went cycling and coarse fishing in the local canal. My Saturday job doing a baker's round meant I worked from early morning to evening. I spent my money on model railway sets, AIRFIX kits and model gliders. I had a few really good local friends so time passed quite quickly.

It is important to think about who you are and what you value when you read a text. The words of a text don't change according to who reads it, but a reader might see different meanings according to their own **values** or mood. For example, being religious might make you see references to God or heaven which another reader might not notice; being in a good mood might make you see the positive things in a text.

In Activity 2, you were looking at the world from the **perspective** or viewpoint of another person. Throughout this chapter you will read texts which have been written in a different time. **Contextual** information can help you understand how the writing has been shaped by issues surrounding the writer or the topic. Your initial response to the text might change once you see what was important to the writer at the time.

Key terms

Values: standards or principles considered important in life

Perspective: a particular way of thinking about something

Contextual: relating to the circumstances or background in which something happens

Activity 3

Write down definitions of 'perspective' and 'change'. In your own words, and using information on these pages, explain how these ideas are going to be important through your reading of pre-1900 texts.

Personal change

1 Changing perspectives over time

Learning objective

- To consider how the time when a text is written affects the views/ideas within it

Key terms

Imagery: the use of figurative language or other special language to convey an idea to an audience

Purpose: something you intend to do or achieve; an intention or aim. All writers will have a clear aim or purpose when they produce a text. The purpose of a text is what the writer deliberately sets out to achieve. They may wish to persuade, encourage, advise or even anger their reader, or a mixture of these

Society: an organized community of people in a particular country or region

Introduction

As the world changes, so do people's views about the world. This might seem like a philosophical idea that belongs in a literature textbook. However as the texts you will study in this chapter are essentially from a different time to the one you live in now, it is sensible to begin by thinking about how the changing world shapes the words and **imagery** a writer uses to present their ideas. In this unit, you will consider how writers can change or add to a reader's ideas about something by presenting it using a group of words with a similar meaning or through extended metaphor.

Over time, many things have changed the way adults treat children. You might have heard the expression 'children should be seen and not heard'. This seems like an odd concept to us today, with many families putting their children at the forefront of their lives. This change in the way children are viewed is evidenced in the text you will study on page 89.

Activity 1

1. With a partner, role-play a conversation where one of you is a child who has a bad habit and the other is an adult trying to reform the child's behaviour. First, decide on what the bad habit is and then think about what tactics the adult might use.

2. After you have carried out your role-play, judge which were the most successful tactics used by the adult and give some reasons why.

The extract on page 89 is from *Mrs Beeton's Book of Household Management*, published in 1859. The audience for the text is the mistress of a fairly wealthy house. The **purpose** of the book is to give advice about how she should run her home to maximize 'the happiness, comfort, and well-being of a family'.

Activity 2

1. Before you read, discuss whether you think a book with this purpose might exist today. Give reasons why or why not.

2. Where do people turn now for help or advice? Do you think anything has changed in **society** to make you have these views? Think about servants, roles/expectations of men and women, the influence of newspapers, the Internet and TV, for example.

Extract from *Mrs Beeton's Book of Household Management* by Isabella Beeton

Most children have some bad habit, of which they must be broken; but this is never accomplished by harshness without developing worse evils: kindness, perseverance, and patience in the nurse, are here of the utmost importance. When finger-sucking is one of these habits, the fingers are sometimes rubbed with bitter aloes*, or some equally disagreeable substance. Others have dirty habits, which are only to be changed by patience, perseverance, and, above all, by regularity in the nurse. She should never be permitted to inflict punishment on these occasions, or, indeed, on any occasion. But, if punishment is to be avoided, it is still more necessary that all kinds of indulgences and flattery be equally forbidden. Yielding to all the whims of a child, – picking up its toys when thrown away in mere wantonness, would be intolerable. A child should never be led to think others inferior to it, to beat a dog, or even the stone against which it falls, as some children are taught to do by silly nurses. Neither should the nurse affect or show alarm at any of the little accidents which must inevitably happen: if it falls, treat it as a trifle; otherwise she encourages a spirit of cowardice and timidity. But she will take care that such accidents are not of frequent occurrence, or the result of neglect.

*bitter aloes – the juice from aloe plants, which has an unpleasant taste

Activity 3

After you have read the extract carefully, complete the following tasks. They will help you practise a key exam skill: finding specific information in a text.

1. A mistress of the time would have decided how the nurse, the equivalent of a modern nanny, should look after the children in her care. List five types of behaviour a nurse should show to help a child break a bad habit.

2. What advice is given about accidents that children might have? What do you think about this advice? Would you give the same advice? Give reasons for your answers.

Stretch

Other topics covered in Mrs Beeton's book concern how the household budget should be spent, employing and managing servants, food storage and recipes. This advice on how to change the bad habits of a child is included towards the end of the book. What might this say about how children were viewed or valued at this time? Give evidence for your ideas.

2 Changing the ordinary to the extraordinary: extended metaphors

Learning objectives

- To explore layers of meaning in extended metaphors used in pre-1900 non-fiction texts
- To evaluate possible reasons for metaphor choice

Key terms

Metaphor: a figure of speech in which a word or phrase is used to describe an object or an action without using *as* or *like*, e.g. *The clouds are taking the sun away to bed* (a child's description of a sunset)

Extended metaphor: a longer or more detailed metaphor, often with a description that extends over several sentences

You will be familiar with **metaphor** from your study of literary texts at Key Stage 3, especially poetry. Here you will study non-fiction extracts that use similar **extended metaphors** to create an image which simultaneously concentrates on a number of different features. You will also consider how writers use metaphors to make readers change their thoughts about something that initially seemed fairly ordinary or simple.

Activity 1

Read the two extracts from Mrs Beeton and Florence Nightingale (below and on page 91), and identify the subjects or things being compared. What are the links between the subjects and the images that the authors create?

Support

Use the structures below to help you explain your ideas.

- Mrs Beeton compares _____ with _____. She says that the _____ is like the _____ because _____. Moreover, the _____ can be linked to the _____ as _____. This is an interesting way of looking at _____ because _____.

Stretch

For each metaphor, try to add another feature to the image which illuminates a further detail about the subject.

Extract from *Florence Nightingale on Public Health Care: Collected Works of Florence Nightingale*, originally published in 1845

Nursing is an art; and if it is to be made an art, requires as exclusive a devotion, as hard a preparation, as any painter's or sculptor's work; for what is the having to do with dead canvas or cold marble compared with having to do with the living body, the temple of God's Spirit? It is one of the fine arts; I had almost said, the finest of the fine arts.

Extract from *Mrs Beeton's Book of Household Management* by Isabella Beeton

The human body, materially considered, is a beautiful piece of mechanism, consisting of many parts, each one being the centre of a system, and performing its own vital function irrespectively of the others, and yet dependent for its vitality upon the harmony and health of the whole. It is, in fact, to a certain extent, like a watch, which, when once wound up and set in motion, will continue its function of recording true time only so long as every wheel, spring, and lever performs its allotted duty, and at its allotted time; [...] or till it has run down.

Activity 2

Explaining the metaphor is a good way of helping you understand what the writer might be trying to say about the subject.

1. Before you read on, write down a few ideas which show your view of the human body and of nursing.

2. Now discuss the metaphors in the extracts with a partner: consider why Mrs Beeton chose a watch as an effective way of imagining the human body, and why Florence Nightingale chose to compare nursing with art. Use the prompts below and the images on this page to help you.

   • What might people have thought about watches/art at the time?

   • What kinds of ideas do the watch/art metaphors make you think about?

   • What values become attached to the body and nursing as a result of these metaphors?

   • In what ways do these metaphors change your way of thinking about the body and nursing? Do they make you consider them as something more special than you first thought?

Activity 3

To conclude your discussion, try to decide which is the most effective metaphor and why. Write up your evaluation of these metaphors, giving as clear an explanation for your view as possible. Use the structure below to start you off.

> I think the metaphor of _____ is most effective in explaining _____ because _____

Activity 4

Try to come up with your own extended metaphor. Decide what you want to explain, then consider what would be a good metaphor to use. Write your metaphor and obscure the subject so you can test whether a partner can work out what you are comparing.

③ Metaphors and prediction

Learning objectives

- To consider how impressions and layers of meaning are created by extended metaphor
- To consider how description and metaphor can aid a reader in making predictions

Change is always happening to someone, somewhere. One way fiction writers can show these changes is by using descriptive techniques such as metaphor. The layers of meaning created by metaphors can make reading a pre-1900 text more difficult, but also more rewarding. The activities on pages 92–95 will help you consider how these techniques shape the way you, the reader, might view characters and settings.

Activity ①

The extract opposite is taken from the novel *Great Expectations* by Charles Dickens. It is **narrated** by a young boy named Pip, whose life changes after he meets a wealthy old lady, Miss Havisham. Here he is telling us what he sees as he is being shown around her house.

1. Before you read the extract, make a list of features you think a welcoming room might have.
2. As you read the extract, tick off any features on your list that Pip describes.
3. What do you notice? How do you think these things have changed over time?

Extract from *Great Expectations* by Charles Dickens

I crossed the staircase landing, and entered the room she indicated. From that room, too, the daylight was completely excluded, and it had an airless smell that was oppressive[1]. A fire had been lately kindled[2] in the damp old-fashioned grate, and it was more disposed[3] to go out than to burn up, and the reluctant smoke which hung in the room seemed colder than the clearer air – like our own marsh mist. Certain wintry branches of candles on the high chimneypiece faintly lighted the chamber: or, it would be more expressive to say, faintly troubled its darkness. It was spacious, and I dare say had once been handsome, but every discernible[4] thing in it was covered with dust and mould, and dropping to pieces. The most prominent object was a long table with a tablecloth spread on it, as if a feast had been in preparation when the house and the clocks all stopped together. An epergne[5] or centre-piece of some kind was in the middle of this cloth; it was so heavily overhung with cobwebs that its form was quite undistinguishable[6]; and, as I looked along the yellow expanse out of which I remember its seeming to grow, like a black fungus, I saw speckled-legged spiders with blotchy bodies running home to it, and running out from it, as if some circumstance of the greatest public importance had just transpired in the spider community.

[1] oppressive – worrying and difficult to bear, or cruel or harsh
[2] kindle – to set light to something, to start a fire burning
[3] disposed – willing or inclined to do something
[4] discernable – capable of being recognized or perceived clearly
[5] epergne – an ornamental centrepiece for a dining table
[6] undistinguishable – not able to be seen clearly

Activity 2

1. Some of the descriptions in the passage use **adjectives** to shape what you think about what has happened in the room. In the list of phrases below, explain what you think is meant by each adjective.

   - airless, oppressive (smell)
   - damp old-fashioned (fire grate)
   - wintry (branches of candles)

2. Once you have thought about the meaning of the adjectives, consider possible deeper layers of meaning. For example, 'wintry' is fairly obvious in its dictionary meaning, but what could the writer be trying to say about how the passage of time affects the items in the room? Discuss your ideas with a partner. Think about:

   - What happens in nature at wintertime – what changes take place?
   - Are there different possible meanings?
   - Which meaning seems the best fit for the changes that are described?

Support

You could use a dictionary to help you. For example, *wintry* is defined as 'characteristic of winter, especially in being very cold or bleak'. By going on to look up *bleak*, you will be able to see further layers of potential meaning intended by an author. Not every meaning will be relevant, but a dictionary can help you broaden your understanding.

In the writing exam, the accuracy of your writing is very important. It is important to remember that, for each writing piece, 40% of the marks are allocated to assess the quality of your vocabulary, sentence structure, spelling and punctuation, so make sure you look at the spelling of new words in a dictionary, as well as their meaning.

It is likely that you have already formed some opinions about the room described in the extract and how it has changed over time. Dickens has used a variety of comparisons to help focus his description on concrete things, like the spiders and, in turn, shape the way a reader thinks about these things and Miss Havisham.

Activity 3

1. Read the sample student answer on the right. This explanation suggests how readers might view the image of the spiders as a way of seeing the changes that are happening. Discuss your response to these ideas with a partner.

2. Do you agree with the ideas suggested? Are there other ways of interpreting the image?

In the extract, the spiders are said to make the table centrepiece their 'home', which might give us the impression that they have lived there a long time because they have had long enough to spin a web. The movement of the spiders is compared to 'a black fungus'. This simile allows the writer to focus our attention on the growth and collection of unhygienic things on the dining table like mould, dust and cobwebs, which might make us feel repulsed or disgusted. Yet it also makes us wonder what has happened to this woman for her to allow these things to take place. What changed this room from being the scene of a celebratory 'feast' to a cold, cobwebbed place, paused in time?

Activity 4

1. What question do you think the student writing above was answering?

2. Make a list of other questions you might have thought of while reading about Miss Havisham's dining room.

3. Try to suggest answers to your questions and then judge which answer is most likely by supporting it with evidence from the extract.

Asking questions of a text is something which informs your reading because you want to find the answers as you read on. In Activity 4, you might have asked, 'What changes might happen later in the story?' or 'How might Miss Havisham have been changed too?' Therefore, metaphor is not only something which helps you to imagine a scene – it also invites you into the story to predict or question what is to come.

Activity 5

1. Draw the room as it is described on page 93 and label it with quotations from the extract. Try to summarize how you feel about the room and what creates that feeling.

2. In this extract, apart from the table centrepiece which is explored on page 94, there are three other main images: the fire, the candles and the table. Choose one of these and explain what you think it means. Look at the explanation of the spiders in Activity 3 to help you. What does your image make you feel or think about Miss Havisham's room and the changes taking place within it?

3. Share your explanations with a partner and see if there are any similarities or differences in what you have said.

Support

Use the stages listed below to help you explore your chosen image.

1. Say what you see. The fire is described as...
2. Give a dictionary meaning for the key words in the image. The word... means...
3. What does this make you think about? This might make a reader think about...
4. Now think about the impact of this image. What are the main messages or meanings? The writer is perhaps trying to show how...
5. Finally, think about the item as part of the whole extract. What links of similarity or difference can you draw? A reader might draw links with...

Progress check

What have you learned in this unit about the ways writers use imagery to change our ideas about something? Work through the following prompts to consider how much you have understood. For each prompt, decide which statement most applies to you.

	I need to look back over this or ask for help.	I think I'm OK with this.	I feel fairly confident with this.	I feel really confident with this and could happily explain it to someone else.
I can spot when an extended metaphor/imagery is being used in a text.				
I can use a structure to explain how the imagery makes me read the item being described.				
I can comment on how an image might say something about the values held at the time when the text was written.				
I can evaluate the effectiveness of an image.				
I can read imagery as a tool to help me predict what will happen in a text.				

Crossing boundaries

4 Thinking about differences

Learning objectives

- To introduce the theme of crossing boundaries
- To consider what makes someone stand out as being different or 'freaky'

Key terms

Boundary: a line that marks a limit
Autobiographical: to do with a writer's story of their own life

Introduction

In this unit you will look at a number of texts that present something different from what is considered to be normal. Crossing **boundaries** can mean different things, and this unit will make you consider the boundaries around how we view or respond to others, how we behave and the decisions we make. In **autobiographical** texts, you will explore how writers show the impact of the unusual. You will also consider and compare how writers present the same subject in different ways, and transformations in real or imaginary characters. Comparison is an exam skill which many students find difficult, but you will learn some techniques to guide you to produce a purposeful and well-structured response.

Activity 1

1. Work in a pair or small group to create a spider diagram of things that make people different. Try to group differences that might be experienced in real life, like unusual tastes in fashion or music, or cultural differences. Then think about differences you might find in fiction, for example, the ability to talk to the dead or see ghosts. You might find this grouping causes some discussion if people have different ideas about what is 'normal' and therefore also what is 'different'.

2. Do you think there are boundaries around what is normal or acceptable? What happens if people cross these boundaries?

Stretch

What makes us consider certain people different from us? In what ways are our perspectives on what is normal and different shaped by our own experiences or values?

In the Victorian era many people were interested in the physical differences of some people's bodies. They would go to look at them in freak shows, just as people today might go to the theatre or a museum.

Activity 2

1. Write a list of things that you think are meant by the noun 'freak' or the adjective 'freaky'.

2. Share your ideas with a partner and discuss the similarities and differences on your list.

3. Now compare your ideas with the dictionary definition below.

> **Freak** *noun* **1** a person or thing that is unusual or abnormal in form. **2** something very unusual or irregular: *a freak storm*. **3** a person who is obsessed with a particular thing: *a fitness freak*.

Activity 3

How might you feel if you were called a freak? Write a short paragraph or a poem in a form of your choice explaining your feelings. You might choose to start your writing with the following:

> *Today they called me a freak...*

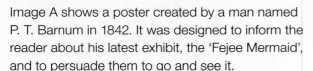

5 Presenting difference

Learning objectives

- To consider how things that are 'different' are presented in graphic form
- To explore and compare the messages or perspectives shown through different presentations of the same subject

Key term

Interpretation: an explanation or understanding of something

Many people take and show photos on a daily basis using cameras on mobile phones and apps such as Instagram, Snapchat or Vine, but have you ever thought about the messages which the image might send to its viewers?

If you are going to take a photo of a person you have a number of choices to make, for example:

- Do you want your subject to do something consciously with their facial expression like smiling, laughing or frowning which shows a particular emotion? Or do you want to capture them in a more natural position, not even looking at the camera?
- Do you want them dressed in particular clothes like a suit or fancy-dress outfit which might show their role or interests? Or do you let them choose their own clothes?
- Do you want to take the shot outside in a field to suggest freedom and a love of nature? Or do you choose a studio setting for a more posed image?

When you examine a poster like the one opposite, you need to be aware that the same kinds of choices have been made about the images that have been selected. A different choice will probably produce a change in your response.

Activity 1

Image A shows a poster created by a man named P. T. Barnum in 1842. It was designed to inform the reader about his latest exhibit, the 'Fejee Mermaid', and to persuade them to go and see it.

1. Work with a partner and focus only on the image, not the words. Write down, in as much detail as you can, what you see. Consider who or what is included, how the people are dressed, where they are looking, their facial expression or body language, the scale of the different parts of the image, the setting, and how the parts of the image are arranged or located in relation to each other.

2. Compare your list with another pair, or the list in the support box here. Add any details you missed. Are there any parts of the image which you had different ideas about? Why might this be? Which **interpretation** might be most interesting and why?

Support

You might have noticed some or all of the following details:

- The three mermaids are positioned centrally in the image, which shows a scene at sea.
- The mermaids appear to be floating on a calm sea but could be sitting on an unseen rock.
- They are all white skinned and naked from the hips up, with long hair or arms covering their breasts.
- The body language of the three mermaids is different: the one on the left is looking towards the men on the boat; the central figure is leaning slightly to one side but appears upright and strong; the one on the right is looking towards the central figure and has her arms outstretched with the palms of her hands facing up.
- The small boat is in front of a larger sailing ship and is being rowed towards the group of mermaids by men in hats.
- The men are all looking towards the mermaids and three of the five pictured men are standing up.
- In the background are what could be clouds or a sunset.

Image **A**

EGYPTIAN MUMMIES,
and ancient Sarcophagi, 5000 years old ; and an entire
Family of Peruvian Mummies ;
the DUCK-BILLED PLATYPUS, the connecting link between the BIRD and BEAST, being evidently half each ;—the curious half-fish, half-human

FEJEE MERMAID,

which was exhibited in most of the principal cities of America, in the years 1840, '41, and '42, to the wonder and astonishment of thousands of naturalists and other scientific persons, whose previous doubts of the existence of such an astonishing creation were entirely removed ;

Now you have got a good sense of the features of the presentation, you need to consider what messages might be sent and how they suit the informative and persuasive purposes of the poster. For example, you probably noticed that the central mermaid figure is looking straight at 'the camera' or audience. Maybe the creator of the poster wants to put the audience into the shoes of the person who might go and view the mermaid, to be intrigued and invited by her stare. This links to the persuasive purpose of the poster: it is trying to encourage the audience to pay to see the exhibited mermaid in order to find out more about her.

Exam link

In an exam you can be asked to comment on the presentation of an image. This means that you need to consider what messages are present in the image, and what decisions may have been made to shape that image and its presentation. The activities on pages 98–101 will help you understand how to do this.

Activity ②

Choose three or four other details from the list in the Support panel in Activity 1 and then discuss what messages the audience might receive from this style of presentation. Explain your ideas clearly in your writing.

Support

To help you explain your ideas, choose one feature of the presentation which you think is interesting. Next, write down a reason why this particular feature was chosen: focus on what the audience might think. Then link this to the persuasive and informative purposes of the poster.

Stretch

Barnum clearly made lots of decisions about how to present the mermaids in the image. Which do you think was the most significant? Give reasons for your choice.

Activity ③

Now look at the words below the picture in Image A. How did the people who saw the mermaid respond or feel? Pick out words and phrases to support your ideas. Why do you think these responses are presented on a poster which is advertising the mermaid?

Activity ④

Would you be convinced by claims like this on a poster today? Why or why not? What kinds of developments in thought or science have taken place over the last 170 years which might have shaped your view?

Activity ⑤

Now look at the images here, which also depict 'mermaids'.

1. For each image, list the details you see, as you did in Activity 1.

2. What similarities and differences strike you between the presentation of the 'mermaid' in these images and in the poster?

3. What kinds of messages do these images send and in what ways do they differ from Barnum's poster? Give reasons for your ideas and refer to the details of the images as evidence.

Image B

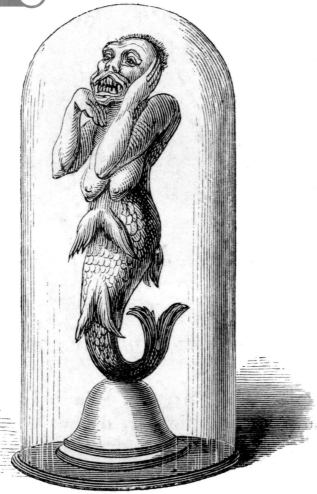

Image C

Activity 6

Stretch

Look again at all three images.

1. Consider your own response to each presentation of the mermaid. The people who went to see the exhibit expected 'wonder and astonishment', but the mermaid they saw was something like the creature presented in the second and third images.

2. How might these people have felt?

3. Look up the words 'wonder' and 'astonishment' in a dictionary. Can they be used to accurately describe people's response to the grotesque image of the mermaid, as well as to the enchanting image on the poster?

4. What might this tell you about Barnum's skill as an advertiser?

5. List words which might *only* be used to describe the possible responses to Image B *or* Image C. Why might your words not have been chosen for the poster?

6 Tracking changes in presentation and responses

Learning objectives

- To explore impressions of a character and our possible responses
- To explore and compare how the written styles of texts are shaped by the context in which they were produced

Key term

Impression: effect produced on the mind, ideas

Tip This kind of language focus can help you improve your response in the exam.

When you meet someone for the first time, you can make a decision about them based on your first impression. Sometimes these **impressions** turn out to be misguided or not a true reflection of the person's character. Here you will be exploring a number of different texts, both visual and written, all of which present the same famous figure: Joseph Merrick, who was known as 'the Elephant Man' because of his extraordinary features.

Activity 1

1. Look at the two photos below and write down reasons why Merrick was 'exhibited like a monstrosity' and 'shunned like a leper; housed like a wild beast'.

2. Consider the three similes above. What impressions do they give about how Merrick was treated?

3. What kinds of response do you have towards him, based on these photos?

4. How do you view the similes when you learn that they were written by Dr Treves, who rescued Merrick from being imprisoned and displayed as a freak, and became his friend?

Activity 2

1. The four short extracts on pages 103–104 were all written by Dr Treves following his first meeting with the Elephant Man. Track through them carefully and pick out two or three key quotations from each which show Treves' response to what he encounters.

2. In what ways do his responses change as he learns more about Merrick?

3. What might be the reasons for these changes?

Stretch

Track through the words and phrases used to refer to Merrick; you might have quoted some of these as evidence to support your ideas in Activity 2. For example, in Extract 1 he starts off as 'the Elephant Man… a frightful creature' and is later 'the perverted object'. In Extract 2, he is 'a bent figure' but also 'it'. There are lots more to find. When you have listed all these labels for Merrick, decide:

a. what they show about how Treves responds to him

b. how these differ in order to match Treves' changing feelings about Merrick.

Extract 1: seeing the poster of the Elephant Man, before the examination, from *The Elephant Man and Other Reminiscences* by Frederick Treves

Painted on the canvas in primitive colours was a life-size portrait of the Elephant Man. This very crude production depicted a frightful creature that could only have been possible in a nightmare. It was the figure of a man with the characteristics of an elephant. The transfiguration[1] was not far advanced. There was still more of the man than of the beast. This fact – that it was still human – was the most repellent attribute of the creature. There was nothing about it of the pitiableness of the misshaped or the deformed, nothing of the grotesqueness of the freak, but merely the loathing insinuation[2] of a man being changed into an animal.

[1] transfiguration – transformation
[2] insinuation – a hint at something unpleasant or offensive

Exam link

In the exam you can be asked to describe either your impressions or your responses. Remember that giving impressions means saying what something is like, whereas giving your response means forming an opinion or saying what you think or feel about something. Both need to be supported by evidence from a text. Your impressions and responses may change towards a character or topic as you read and this is important to explain in your analysis.

Extract 2: Treves views the figure under a blanket, from *The Elephant Man and Other Reminiscences* by Frederick Treves

The showman pulled back the curtain and revealed a bent figure crouching on a stool and covered by a brown blanket. In front of it, on a tripod, was a large brick heated by a Bunsen burner. Over this the creature was huddled to warm itself. It never moved when the curtain was drawn back. Locked up in an empty shop and lit by the faint blue light of the gas jet, this hunched-up figure was the embodiment of loneliness.

Extract 3: Treves' first sighting of Merrick's body, from *The Elephant Man and Other Reminiscences* by Frederick Treves

The showman – speaking as if to a dog – called out harshly: 'Stand up!' The thing arose slowly and let the blanket that covered its head and back fall to the ground. There stood revealed the most disgusting specimen of humanity that I have ever seen.

A poster which might have been the one described in Extract 1 by Dr Treves

Extract 4: Treves' reflections on Merrick and the poster, from *The Elephant Man and Other Reminiscences* by Frederick Treves

From the intensified painting in the street I had imagined the Elephant Man to be of gigantic size. This, however, was a little man below the average height and made to look shorter by the bowing of his back. The most striking feature about him was the enormous and misshapen head. From the brow there projected a huge bony mass like a loaf, while from the back of the head hung a bag of spongy, fungous-looking skin, the surface of which was comparable to brown cauliflower. On the top of the skull were a few long lank hairs. The osseous* growth on the forehead almost occluded one eye. The circumference of the head was no less than that of the man's waist. From the upper jaw there projected another mass of bone. It protruded from the mouth like a pink stump, turning the upper lip inside out and making the mouth a mere slobbering aperture. This growth from the jaw had been so exaggerated in the painting as to appear to be a rudimentary trunk or tusk. The nose was merely a lump of flesh, only recognizable as a nose from its position.

*osseous – bony

Merrick's deformities are described in both Extract 4 and Merrick's own account, which is given below. What is interesting about these extracts is that their written styles are quite different and this shapes our response to what is being described. Comparing the style of writing is something you can be asked to do in the exam; you will be guided through how to do it in the activity which follows and the support feature on page 105.

Extract from *The Autobiography of Joseph Carey Merrick* by Joseph Merrick

The measurement around my head is 36 inches, there is a large substance of flesh at the back as large as a breakfast cup, the other part in a manner of speaking is like hills and valleys, all lumped together, while the face is such a sight that no one could describe it. The right hand is almost the size and shape of an Elephant's foreleg, measuring 12 inches round the wrist and 5 inches round one of the fingers; the other hand and arm is no larger than that of a girl ten years of age, although it is well proportioned. My feet and legs are covered with thick lumpy skin, also my body, like that of an Elephant, and almost the same colour, in fact, no one would believe until they saw it, that such a thing could exist. It was not perceived much at birth, but began to develop itself when at the age of 5 years.

Activity 3

Re-read Extract 4 and Merrick's account carefully and then list the things that make the doctor's written style different from Merrick's. Do they share any features of written style? Why might they share some and not others?

Support

Knowing what kind of things to look at when you compare writers' styles will give some structure to your answer. Look at the student's work below, which has been annotated with some guidance on how to write a thorough comparison.

> *Treves' text is written from a third-person perspective as he is an outsider looking in at Merrick, whereas Merrick is talking about himself.*
>
> *Treves uses labels for Merrick like 'a little man' or 'the man', and third-person pronouns as in the examples 'him' and 'his back'. He also says 'the brow' or 'the head', rather than 'his head'. In contrast, Merrick's writing uses some first-person pronouns to refer to some of his features such as 'my head', 'my feet and legs' and 'my body' but, similar to Treves, uses the **definite article** 'the' to describe others, as in 'the face', 'the right hand' and 'the other hand'.*
>
> *As a doctor Merrick keeps a professional distance from his patient and writes about him as a medical subject. The third-person references and use of 'the' help him to do this. On the other hand, the mixture of Merrick's perspective — sometimes first person and sometimes as if he is an outsider looking on — might suggest that he is torn between telling the story of who he is as a man, while also considering himself of interest to medical people who want an **objective** account of his interesting body. Alternatively, the use of 'the' to describe his body parts might suggest some sense of shame or disgust, almost as if he does not want to own these peculiar features by using the first person pronoun 'my'.*

First, make a point which gives a judgement or observation about each text.

Find evidence from the texts to support your comments.

Use a group of examples to show that there is a pattern or repeated use of certain features.

Use comparative vocabulary to link your points.

Try to give contextual reasons, like writer and purpose, why they are like this. You might be able to suggest more than one.

Key terms

Definite article: a grammatical term for *the*, as in *the head*
Objective: not influenced by personal feelings or opinions

The questions below will help you to consider other features of the writers' styles. Use the annotations above to help you answer them.

1. What information is presented as fact and what as opinion?

2. How precise or vague are the descriptions?

3. What kind of vocabulary is used (for example, scientific, simple, emotive)?

4. What kinds of comparisons or references are made (for example, previous experience, household or countryside items, animals, family)?

7 How characters are transformed

Learning objective

- To explore and compare how changes in a character are presented and the possible responses a reader might have

When a person changes, people around them often want to talk about it. Documenting changes in real people or characters can be an interesting task for writers too.

The two extracts (below and on page 107) both present a moment of transformational change. The first is an account written by Dr Treves following an encounter between Joseph Merrick (see pages 102–105) and a young lady. The second is taken from a story by Robert Louis Stevenson. In this extract the respectable Dr Jekyll first takes a potion which changes him into a different character, the evil Mr Hyde.

Activity

Read both extracts carefully. Draw up a table like the one below to allow you to compare the features of the texts and your responses to them as you read.

	Merrick's transformation	Jekyll's transformation
Who tells the story?		
What causes the change?		
What changes in the character?		
What are the key words/phrases that describe the change?		

Extract from *The Elephant Man and Other Reminiscences* by Frederick Treves

I asked a friend of mine, a young and pretty widow, if she thought she could enter Merrick's room with a smile, wish him good morning and shake him by the hand. She said she could and she did. The effect upon poor Merrick was not quite what I had expected. As he let go her hand he bent his head on his knees and sobbed until I thought he would never cease. The interview was over. He told me afterwards that this was the first woman who had ever smiled at him, and the first woman, in the whole of his life, who had shaken hands with him. From this day the transformation of Merrick commenced and he began to change, little by little, from a hunted thing into a man. It was a wonderful change to witness and one that never ceased to fascinate me.

Extract from *The Strange Case of Dr Jekyll and Mr Hyde* by Robert Louis Stevenson

The most racking pangs[1] succeeded: a grinding in the bones, deadly nausea[2], and a horror of the spirit that cannot be exceeded at the hour of birth or death. Then these agonies began swiftly to subside, and I came to myself as if out of a great sickness. There was something strange in my sensations, something indescribably new and, from its very novelty, incredibly sweet. I felt younger, lighter, happier in body; within I was conscious of a heady recklessness[3], a current of disordered sensual[4] images running like a millrace in my fancy[5], a solution of the bonds of obligation, an unknown but not an innocent freedom of the soul. I knew myself, at the first breath of this new life, to be more wicked, tenfold more wicked, sold a slave to my original evil[6]; and the thought, in that moment, braced and delighted me like wine. I stretched out my hands, exulting[7] in the freshness of these sensations; and in the act, I was suddenly aware that I had lost in stature[8]. [...]

I stole through the corridors, a stranger in my own house; and coming to my room, I saw for the first time the appearance of Edward Hyde.

[1] racking pangs – sudden sharp feelings of pain
[2] nausea – a feeling of sickness or disgust
[3] heady recklessness – a sense of ignoring risk or danger, giving feelings of happiness or drunkenness
[4] sensual – to do with the physical senses
[5] fancy – imagination
[6] original evil – in Christianity, original sin is the condition in which all human beings live since Adam and Eve first disobeyed God
[7] exulting – rejoicing or feeling triumphant
[8] stature – a person's natural height

Activity 2

What are the main similarities and differences in these transformations? Use the headings in your table to structure your writing into paragraphs that summarize your ideas.

Activity 3

What are your responses to the changes in these characters? Which character would you like to read more about and why? What influences your decision?

Progress check

List the methods you used to compare how characters are presented. Rate your understanding of each one on a scale of 1 to 3, where 1 is the one you would feel most confident in using again and 3 is the least.

Heroic behaviour in testing times

8 Exploring what makes a hero

Learning objectives

- To explore definitions and views about heroism
- To formulate and present opinions, listening to and challenging the views of others

Introduction

The texts you will study in this unit emphasize the power of a person's environment to control the way they respond to what is happening to them, and maybe even turn them into heroes. You will be guided through a number of reading skills, such as retrieving information from a text and focusing on how a writer uses particular language to build excitement and tension. You will also be given opportunities to use some of these skills in your own writing and respond to the themes of heroism and change.

Activity 1

What is a hero like? Think of words that describe their physical, emotional and personal qualities. Discuss this question with a partner and try to explore the reasons for similarities and differences in your views. Can there be only one definition of a hero?

Activity 2

Look at the dictionary definition below and compare it with your ideas. Do you agree with this definition?

> **hero** *noun* **1** a man who is admired for his brave or noble deeds. **2** the chief male character in a story, play or poem.

Activity 3

The image here represents a popular view of a 'hero'.

1. What do you think this says about our associations with the word 'hero' in the early 21st century? Think about what is being suggested about who and what a hero is, as well as the presentation of the figure in terms of their gender, clothes, pose and facial expression.

2. Discuss your ideas with a partner or in a small group. Make sure you listen carefully to views that are different from your own, and challenge them with a reasoned argument.

Activity 4

The heroic individuals you will explore in this unit are real people who were written about in the 19th century. How do you think ideas about what makes a hero might change according to the time or society in which the label 'hero' is used?

9 Considering how everyday heroes are presented

Learning objectives

- To select specific information from source texts
- To explain or analyse the meaning and effects of similes and topic words within their historical context

The extract on page 111 considers the life of a fireman in London in 1857, as reported by a novelist, R. M. Ballantyne. You will use this text to practise your skills in finding information and commenting on the meaning and effect of the language used by a writer; both these skills are tested in the English Language exam.

Activity 1

Before you read the extract on page 111, look at the images here. They will give you some historical context for the extract. Note down things that strike you about the appearance and equipment of a fireman living and working in the 1850s.

Activity 2

Much of the extract opposite is giving information to support Ballantyne's view that the life of a London fireman is amongst the most 'trying' and 'thrilling' possible. Complete the three tasks below, which ask you to find information from the text. Remember to:

- use the part of the text which the question instructs you to
- use the key words from the question to help you search
- only give the information that is asked for in the question.

1. List three things from paragraphs 2 and 3 which show that a fireman must always be 'on alert'.

2. Re-read paragraph 4 carefully. What two types of fire might the fireman be called to?

3. Re-read paragraph 5 carefully. Why does the fireman get 'no respite' (little rest)?

MOLYNEUX SERIES

SUN ST. FIRE BRIGADE
WOOLWICH (COPYRIGHT)
GREENWICH COUNCIL

Extract from 'Nights with the fire brigade' by R. M. Ballantyne

There are few lives, we should think, more trying or more full of curious adventure and thrilling incident than that of a London fireman.

He must always be on the alert. No hour of the day or night can he ever count on as being his own, unless on those occasions when he obtains leave of absence, which I suppose are not frequent. If he does not absolutely sleep in his clothes, he sleeps beside them – arranged in such a way that he can jump into them at a moment's notice.

When the summons comes there must be no preliminary yawning; no soft transition from the land of dreams to the world of reality. He jumps into his boots which stand invitingly ready, pulls on his trousers, buttons his braces while descending to the street, and must be brass-helmeted on the engine and away like a fiery dragon-gone-mad within three minutes of 'the call,' or thereabouts, if he is to escape a fine.

Moreover, the London fireman must be prepared to face death at any moment. When the call comes he never knows whether he is turning out to something not much more serious than 'a chimney,' or to one of those devastating conflagrations[1] on the river-side in which many thousand pounds' worth of property are swept away, and his life may go along with them. Far more frequently than the soldier or sailor is he liable to be ordered on a duty which shall turn out to be a forlorn[2] hope, and not less pluckily does he obey.

There is no respite for him. The field which the London Brigade covers is so vast that the liability to be sent into action is continuous – chiefly, of course, at night. At one moment he may be calmly polishing up the 'brasses' of his engine, or skylarking[3] with his comrades, or sedately reading a book, or snoozing in bed, and the next he may be battling fiercely with the flames. Unlike the lifeboat heroes, who may sleep when the world of waters is calm, he must be ever on the watch; for his enemy is a lurking foe – like the Red Indian who pounces on you when you least expect him, and does not utter his warwhoop[4] until he deems his victory secure. The little spark smoulders while the fireman on guard, booted and belted, keeps watch at his station. It creeps while he waits, and not until its energies have gained considerable force does it burst forth with a grand roar and bid him fierce defiance.

Even when conquered in one quarter it often leaps up in another, so that the fireman sometimes returns from the field twice or thrice in the same night to find that the enemy is in force elsewhere and that the fight must be resumed.

[1] conflagration – a large and destructive fire
[2] forlorn – left alone and unhappy
[3] skylarking – playing about light-heartedly
[4] warwhoop – a savage, hostile yell

Activity 3

Writers choose their words carefully so they can present their subject in a specific way. One way they can do this is to use imagery. In paragraph 3, Ballantyne uses the simile 'like a fiery dragon-gone-mad' to describe the way the fireman speeds away on the fire engine to answer an emergency call. What do you think he means by this? Use the structure below to help guide you in your exploration.

What features do a dragon and a fire engine share?

What does this suggest about the movement of the fire engine?

like a fiery dragon-gone-mad

A mythical beast – what does this suggest about the firefighters, and why is it interesting?

Activity 4

1. Another way a writer uses language to give a certain presentation of a subject is by using a collection of words that behave like an extended metaphor. During your reading of the extract, you might have spotted words to do with a certain topic in paragraphs 4–6. Look at the list of quotations below and see if you can identify the topic each one belongs to.

'on duty'   'action'   'battling fiercely'

'on the watch'   'warwhoop'   'victory'

'pounces when you least expect'   'on guard'

'conquered'   'keeps watch at his station'

'the enemy is in force'   'his enemy is a lurking foe'

'the fight must be resumed'

2. The writer clearly chooses a number of words and phrases that draw links between a fireman fighting a fire and a soldier fighting a war. Use the questions below to prompt you in your exploration of why he links them.

   a. What features link the soldier and the fireman?

   b. Look at other phrases like 'prepared to face death at any moment', 'when the call comes' and 'ordered on a duty'. Why might the writer want to emphasize these features?

Stretch

Read the Context box on page 113. The writer is relying on his readers responding to the fireman with similar emotions as they might to a soldier. What kinds of emotional responses get attached to the fireman because of the writer's comparison? Think especially about the way both soldiers and firemen risk their lives to save others.

In your writing it is often best to build your story on what you already know. For example, basing settings and characters on places and people you know will give you lots of ideas, as you already have clear images of what these places and people are like.

Activity

You are going to choose a subject for the following task:

Write a short but lively article on someone you consider to be a hero.

Think carefully about who you will choose as your inspiration. You should be able to describe them clearly, relate stories about them or comment on the effect they have had on you.

Support

Use interesting vocabulary and similes or metaphors when you describe your hero. Give clear reasons to explain why you think they are heroic. What have they done and why is this heroic?

Stretch

As you begin to plan your writing, consider ways to make it more entertaining and emotive.

- What techniques have you seen other writers use to make their writing more entertaining?
- What kinds of words could you add to achieve a more emotional response from a reader?

Context

The Crimean War, which had claimed 25,000 British, 100,000 French and up to a million Russian lives, had ended a year before this extract was written. It was the first war where journalists had been on the front line, sending back first-hand reports and photographs. The British people had an immediate sense of the war and an intimate view of a soldier's life.

10 Making and presenting a heroine

Learning objectives

- To consider how women are presented as heroines compared to men as heroes
- To consider the methods used to build the tension or danger of a situation

There are very few well known 19th-century heroines. Florence Nightingale, a pioneer for higher standards of care in nursing, see page 90, is probably the most legendary. You may also have heard of Grace Darling. She helped to rescue the passengers of the *Forfarshire*, a ship that was wrecked just off the coast near the lighthouse where she lived in north-east England. She became celebrated for this act of courage, which challenged 19th-century ideas about gender and showed that women can be just as brave, strong and skilful as men.

The following account of Grace Darling's actions comes from an anthology entitled *Tragedy of the Seas*. You join the rescue narrative as the remaining survivors cling to the front part of their wrecked ship, which is stuck on a rock. Grace hears their cries for help and alerts her father, who is the lighthouse keeper. The pair battle through the storm in a rowing boat to rescue the men.

Activity 1

As you read the extract below, decide what impressions the writer wants his reader to gain of the sea. Write down evidence to support your ideas.

Tragedy of the Seas by Charles Ellms

The fore-part of the vessel[1], in the mean time, remained fast on the rock, and to it still clung the few passengers who remained, every instant expecting to share the fate of their unfortunate companions, whom they had seen swept away by the raging element. In this dreadful situation, their cries attracted the notice of Grace Darling, the daughter of the keeper of the Outer Ferne lighthouse. With a noble heroism, she immediately determined to attempt their rescue, in spite of the raging of the storm, and the all but certain destruction which threatened to attend it.

Having hastily awakened her father, he launched his boat at daybreak, and with a generous sympathy, worthy of the father of Grace Darling, prepared to proceed to their rescue. The gale, in the mean time, continued unabated[2], and the boiling of the waves threatened a speedy destruction to their frail boat. It was, therefore, with a heart full of the most fearful forebodings, that he undertook the perilous enterprise. After watching the wreck for some time, they discovered that living beings were still clinging to it; and the gallant young woman, with matchless intrepidity[3], seized an oar and entered the boat.

Those unacquainted with the tempestuous state of the Ferne Islands, during a storm, will be unable to appreciate the praiseworthy deed of daring performed by Mr Darling and his daughter, Miss Grace Horsely Darling. By a dangerous and desperate effort, her father was landed on the rock in the frail coble[4]. To preserve it from being dashed in pieces, it was rapidly rowed back among the awful abyss of waters, and kept afloat by the skilfulness and dexterity of this noble-minded young woman. They succeeded in saving the lives of the nine persons; and, by the assistance of some of the crew, they were enabled to bring the coble and its burden to the Longstone lighthouse; otherwise return and aid would have been impracticable, from the state of the current. This perilous achievement stands unexampled in the feats of female fortitude[5].

[1] vessel – a ship or boat
[2] unabated – not dying down or becoming less
[3] intrepidity – fearlessness and bravery
[4] coble – a traditional open fishing boat from north-east England
[5] fortitude – courage in bearing pain or trouble

Activity 2

The writer repeatedly emphasizes the danger involved in the rescue mission. Select five short quotations from the extract and explain how you think each one emphasizes the danger.

Stretch

Explore how the focus on danger is sharpened by the writer's choice of adjectives. Answer the questions below to help you.

a. Why is the 'destruction' described as 'all but certain'?

b. What suggestions does the word 'unabated' add to 'the gale'?

c. Why describe the destruction as 'speedy'?

d. What is emphasized by saying that the forebodings are 'the most fearful'?

e. Why describe the effort as 'dangerous and desperate'?

f. Why is the boat (coble) personified as 'frail'?

g. Why is the enterprise described as 'perilous'?

h. Why describe the waters as an 'awful abyss'?

Activity 3

1. What are your impressions of Grace and her father? Draw a spider diagram to record your thoughts, supporting each impression with a quotation from the text.

2. How does the presentation of the sea as a fierce enemy shape our impressions of Grace and her father?

Activity 4

Find evidence in the text which suggests that both Grace and her father are heroes. Write the quotations in three columns, headed 'Grace', 'father', 'both'. Alternatively, you could produce a Venn diagram, like the one here.

Grace

Both

Father

'...she immediately determined to attempt their rescue'

'They succeeded in saving the lives of nine persons'

'It was, therefore, with a heart full of the most fearful forebodings, that he undertook the perilous enterprise'

Activity 5

Images A and B opposite are both fictionalized presentations of Grace Darling. Image A is a poster from an 1838 theatre dramatization of the rescue and Image B is from the cover of George Lindley's sheet music to his 'Grace Darling Ballad'.

1. Pick out details from the images to describe these two visual presentations of Darling.

2. Now pick out quotations from the extract on page 114 which you think match each image.

3. Which picture do you think best represents the heroine as depicted in the extract? Discuss your ideas with a partner and give reasons for your view.

Stretch

Up to this point you have considered Grace as a heroine – a woman who has behaved heroically. Today, would you call her a heroine or a hero?

Activity 6

Consider how these images show a similar conflict in terms of how to present a woman as a hero. Image A depicts her as rowing the boat strongly, with arguably masculine-looking forearms and angular features. In Image B she is presented as a romanticized maiden in a flowing white gown, standing in the boat holding her oar, while her father looks on and she looks out over the sea.

a. How might these presentations send different messages about what a female hero might be like?

b. How might they be shaped by ideas about gender in this period?

Image **A**

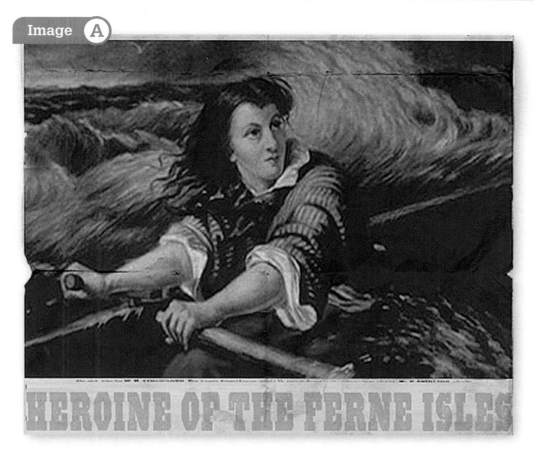

HEROINE OF THE FERNE ISLES

Image **B**

11 Creating a quieter type of hero

Learning objectives

- To use some interesting choices in sentence grammar and words to develop variation and interest in descriptive writing
- To explore how impressions of a character are created through presentation

Just as some people are artists with paint or a camera lens, writers are artists with grammar and word choices. The annotated extract below is taken from a non-fiction travel book written by Wilkie Collins in 1850–51. It describes his response to an area of Cornish coast called the Lizard Peninsula, known for its dramatic rocky landscape. The annotations focus on how Collins uses both words and grammar to encourage the reader to see his perspective and, like him, be impressed or even slightly scared by the power of the sea.

Activity 1

Read through the annotated extract and discuss the annotations with a partner or in a small group. If you notice any other things about the writer's use of certain grammatical techniques or word patterns, note them down and discuss their effect.

Use of prepositions at start and/or end of sentences focuses reader's attention, like a camera angle or pointing finger.

The repeated noun-preposition-noun structure mimics layers of precipices and caverns in the landscape. It draws the reader's eye, as a photographer might, from foreground to distance.

Extract from *Notes in Cornwall Taken A-foot* by Wilkie Collins

The 'great cliffs' are personified as strong protectors of the land where the writer is standing. This in turn personifies 'raging sea' as an angry enemy threatening the writer's (and reader's) safety.

The verbs are active and give a sense of movement in the scene. Even the least active verb – 'perched' – is made active by dynamic 'flapping' and might suggest only momentary stillness before flight.

On each side of us, precipice over precipice, cavern within cavern, rose the great cliffs protecting the land against the raging sea. Three hundred feet beneath, the foam was boiling far out over a reef of black rocks. Above and around, flocks of sea-birds flew in ever lengthening circles, or perched flapping their wings and sunning their plumage, on ledges of riven stone below us. Every object forming the wide sweep of the view was on the vastest and most majestic scale.

Language to do with getting bigger or going further uses the superlative -est and most, emphasizing huge scale of scene.

Like the prepositions and the sense of scale created by the superlatives, this phrase summarizes the idea that the whole view is impressive or possibly daunting. 'Sweep' draws the reader's eye to the movement of the writer's view around the scene.

Activity 2

Using carefully chosen grammatical techniques, Wilkie Collins created a piece of writing that draws in the reader and helps you see the scene as he saw it.

SPAG

Choose one of the images on this page and write four or five sentences describing it. Try to achieve the same effect: communicate what you see to your reader.

This doesn't mean copying the words or phrases Collins used, just the techniques, such as prepositions to focus attention, verbs that work together to create a theme like movement or speed or scale, and **personification** to add life to a scene. Concentrate on editing and redrafting a small number of lines, focusing on the impact each word or phrase makes, rather than writing a long paragraph.

> **Key term**
>
> **Personification:** the attribution of a personal nature or human characteristics to something non-human

Activity **3**

The extract below describes Collins's descent from a specific rock on the Lizard Peninsula called 'Devil's Throat'. Before you read, consider your first impressions of a rock face which has been given this name.

- What kind of shape might this rock be?
- What does the name make you think of?
- What might be the response of those who see it?

Extract from 'Descending from a rock called "Devil's Throat"' by Wilkie Collins

It is settled that we shall descend again to the beach. Stimulated by the ease with which my worthy leader goes down beneath me, I get over-confident in my dexterity[1], and begin to slip here, and slide there, and come to awkward pauses at precipitous[2] places, in what would be rather an alarming manner, but for the potent[3] presence of the guide, who is always beneath me, ready to be fallen upon. Sometimes, when I am holding on with all the necessary tenacity[4] of grip, as regards my hands, but, 'scrambling my toes about' in a very disorderly and unworkmanlike fashion, he pops his head up from below for me to sit on; and puts my feet into crevices for me, with many apologies for taking the liberty! Sometimes,

I fancy myself treading on what feels like soft turf; I look down, and find that I am standing like an acrobat on his shoulders, and hear him civilly entreating[5] me to take hold of his jacket next, and let myself down over his body to the ledge where he is waiting for me. He never makes a false step, never stumbles, scrambles, hesitates, or fails to have a hand always at my service. The nautical metaphor of 'holding on by your eyelids' becomes a fact in his case. He really views his employer, as porters are expected to view a package labelled 'glass with care'.

[1] dexterity – skill in performing physical tasks, especially with the hands
[2] precipitous – steep, like a cliff face
[3] potent – having a powerful effect
[4] tenacity – the act of holding or clinging firmly to something
[5] entreating – requesting something earnestly or emotionally

Activity 4

1. Collins refers to his guide as 'my worthy leader'. Find one piece of evidence each to show where you have an impression of the guide as: helpful, supportive, apologetic, careful, prepared and thoughtful.

2. Discuss with a partner or in a small group whether you think the guide is a hero.

Activity 5

You are now going to describe an exciting or dangerous journey. Plan your writing carefully.

- What key things do you want your reader to see/experience and what kind of response do you want them to have?

- Do you want to present yourself as a hero?

- Just as Wilkie Collins showed the character of his guide using carefully chosen language and examples of action, so must you.

- Think about how you will reveal your personality. What do you want a reader to see? Then consider what vocabulary would best show those personal characteristics.

- What situation will you find yourself in?

- How will you react?

As well as the two extracts by Wilkie Collins, re-read your own practice writing from Activity 2 to help you make your style interesting and varied for the reader.

Support

For each thing you want to say, consider ways you can show it rather than say it. Think about how you can send hidden or implicit meanings to the reader by your presentation, without explicitly telling them things. Look back at pages 56–59 to help you.

Progress check

1. A good way of assessing whether you have made your reader think or feel the things you intended is to ask them. First, answer the following questions yourself.

   a. What impressions do you get of the main character? What is your evidence for this?

   b. Is the main character a hero? Why? Where is this shown in the writing?

   c. What is the most interesting part of the writing? What makes it interesting?

   d. Find one or more specific examples in your writing which could be amended to make it clearer or more engaging for the reader. If you could make just one change, what would it be and why?

2. Now swap your writing with a partner and ask them to answer Questions 1a–d about your writing. Do not show them your answers. Read their writing and answer the same questions for them.

3. When you have both finished, compare the intentions (the writer's answers) with the results (the reader's answers). What differences are there between intentions and results? Why might this be the case?

4. Finally, edit your writing using any helpful feedback this activity has created.

Assessment

Reading and understanding

Learning objective

- To test confidence in the reading and writing skills taught in this chapter

Introduction

The assessment materials here will help you judge how successfully you can use the reading and writing skills that have been taught in this chapter.

Can you:

- select information from a text and present it clearly?
- comment on the impressions you get of a character or subject?
- comment on the presentation of a character, subject or text?
- explain how the presentational methods used shape your response to a character, subject or text?
- write about an event in a way that will engage your reader and show your own response to the characters or events?

Conditions in the polar seas can change very quickly, as the following first-hand account will show. The paragraph that introduces the extract is written by R. M. Ballantyne, a novelist who was researching this topic for his next book. The rest is written by a survivor describing how the polar ice destroyed the ship he was on.

Extract from 'The Loss of the *Breadalbane*' in *The Ocean and its Wonders* by R. M. Ballantyne

Before passing from the subject of risk to navigators to the consideration of other forms and aspects of polar ice, let us take a glance at an effectual case of nipping. There have been many partial and severe nips[1], the descriptions of which are all more or less graphic; but few ships have come so suddenly to the end of their career as did the Breadalbane, *a small vessel that was used as a transport ship to the expedition in search of Sir John Franklin in 1852. One who was on board when it occurred thus describes it:*

Sunday, August 21st – About ten minutes past four, the ice passing the ship awoke me, and the door of my cabin, from the pressure, opened. I hurriedly put on my clothes, and on getting on deck found some hands on the ice endeavouring to save the boats; but the latter were instantly crushed to pieces. They little thought, when using their efforts to save the boats, that the ship was in so perilous a situation.

I went forward to hail the *Phoenix* (another ship that was fortunately near) for men to save the boats; and whilst doing so, the ropes by which we were secured parted, and a heavy nip took us, making every timber creak, and the ship tremble all over. I looked in the main hold[2], and saw the beams giving way. I hailed those on the ice, and told them of our critical situation, they not for one moment suspecting it. I then rushed to my cabin, hauled out my portmanteau[3] on deck, and roared like a bull to those in their beds to jump out and save their lives. The startling effect on them might be more easily imagined than described. On reaching the deck, those on the ice called out to me to jump over the side, that the ship was going over. I left my portmanteau, and jumped over the side on the loose ice, and with difficulty, and with the assistance of those on the ice, succeeded in getting on the unbroken part, with the loss of the slippers I had on when quitting the vessel, with wet feet, etcetera. The cold was little thought of at the exciting moment – life, not property, being the object to be saved.

After being on the ice about five minutes, the timbers, etcetera, in the ship cracking up as matches would in the hand, it eased for a short time; and I, with some others, returned to the ship, with the view of saving some of our effects.

Captain Inglefield now came running towards the ship, and ordered me to see if the ice was through it. On looking down into the hold, I saw all the beams, etcetera, falling about in a manner that would have been certain death to me had I ventured down there. But there was no occasion for that (I mean to ascertain the fact of the ice being through), it being too evident that the ship could not last many minutes. I then sounded[4] the well[5], and found five feet in the hold; and, whilst in the act of sounding, a heavier nip than before pressed out the starboard[6] bow[7], and the ice was forced right into the forecastle[8]. Every one then abandoned the ship, with what few clothes they saved – some with only what they had on. The ship now began to sink fast, and from the time her bowsprit[9] touched the ice until her mast-heads[10] were out of sight, did not occupy above one minute and a half!

It was a very sad and unceremonious way of being turned out of our ship. From the time the first nip took her, until her disappearance, did not occupy more than fifteen minutes.

[1] nip – a sharp bite or pinch, here by the ice on the ship
[2] hold – a space for carrying cargo on a ship
[3] portmanteau – a large travelling bag
[4] sound – to test the depth of water using a line with a lead weight on one end
[5] well – an enclosed space in the bottom of a ship
[6] starboard – the right-hand side of a ship
[7] bow – the front end of a ship
[8] forecastle – the forward part of a ship below the deck
[9] bowsprit – the foremost part of a ship
[10] mast-head – the highest part of a ship's mast

Re-read the first paragraph beginning 'Before passing from the subject of risk...' and answer the following questions in full sentences.

1. What is the name of the small transport ship which gets 'nipped' or caught in the polar ice? **[1]**

2. Who is the expedition searching for? **[1]**

3. **a.** What clue does this introductory paragraph give about the speed with which the shipwreck happened? **[1]**

   b. What impression does this give of the power of the polar ice? **[1]**

Re-read the second paragraph beginning 'Sunday, August 21st...' and answer the following questions.

4. At what time is the narrator of the anecdote woken up? **[1]**

5. What happens due to the pressure of the ice? **[1]**

6. After he puts on his clothes, what does the narrator find the men on the ice doing? **[1]**

7. What does the word 'perilous' mean and what impression does it give of the situation they are in? **[2]**

Re-read the third paragraph beginning 'I went forward to hail the *Phoenix*...' and answer question 8 below.

8. Comment on your response to the presentation of activities in the third paragraph.

    • What are the activities being described?

    • What techniques does the writer use to present each of these activities? You might comment on the words used, use of simile, sentence structure, **narrative perspective** and anything else you feel is important.

    • What is your response to his presentation in this paragraph? **[5]**

Re-read the fourth paragraph beginning 'After being on the ice...' and answer question 9 below.

9. **a.** What simile is used to describe the timbers in the ship 'cracking up' or breaking up? **[1]**

    b. What impressions do you get of the ice because of this simile? Explain your ideas clearly. **[3]**

Re-read the last two paragraphs beginning 'Captain Inglefield now came running towards the ship...' and answer question 10 below.

10. Select and comment on some of the ways the writer presents the danger of their situation. Remember to quote from the text and explain the effects of the words and phrases you are commenting on. **[5]**

Assessment

Planning to write

Learning objective

- To write using interesting presentational features to entertain your reader and shape their response to characters, subjects and situations

Introduction

In this chapter you have read extracts which cleverly crafted characters and subjects to entertain the reader and control the way they respond. Now you are going to do some writing of your own.

Activity 1

Choose one of the writing tasks below. Remember that one which will allow you to draw on personal experience can often make your writing more vivid.

EITHER:

Write about a time when you had to react quickly or when you were in danger.

OR:

Write a story which ends with the words '... and I declared I would never take such a big risk again.'

Questions to consider at the planning stage

What will be the key elements of the plot?	Select your ideas carefully and write them in a way that will help you order and link them.
Important information	Is there information you will need to communicate or to withhold from your reader so your narrative makes sense?
Openings and closings	The beginning and end need particular attention. How will you tackle them? You might start in the middle of the action or use a flashback. You could end on a cliffhanger or with a personal reflection. What other options might you choose?
Main character	What impressions do you want to give of your main character's personality? How will you show these? Do you want your reader to feel sympathy or that your character made a foolish error and deserved the consequences?

Further preparation work on style

Re-read some of the extracts in this chapter. Think carefully about what in particular made them interesting. Could you use any of their presentational methods to entertain your audience and shape their response? What style does your writing need to use to appeal to your audience?

As you write

Keep looking back at the task and your plan. Check that you are communicating your ideas clearly to the reader. Review how successfully your word choices and presentational devices will shape your reader's thoughts or feelings.

Checking

Check the accuracy of your spelling and grammar, and your punctuation of sentences and direct speech. Check that your writing is paragraphed carefully and that the reader will be able to follow the ideas as they develop. Have you covered everything in your plan?

'If thought corrupts language, language can also corrupt thought.' *George Orwell*

'I have been a believer in the magic of language since, at a very early age, I discovered that some words got me into trouble and others got me out.' *Katherine Dunn*

'If you talk to a man in a language he understands, that goes to his head. If you talk to him in his language, that goes to his heart.' *Nelson Mandela*

In this chapter you will explore the theme of language through careful study of a range of fiction and non-fiction extracts. These all express different points of view about language: its development, its use and its future. The activities surrounding these extracts will help you improve your reading, writing and discussion skills. You will read in order to understand the points of view expressed in the articles and focus on them as models of good writing. You can then apply the persuasive power of language when you come to write your own response. There will be lots of opportunities to discuss your ideas too, so you will also be improving your speaking and listening skills.

Through the extracts and activities in this chapter, you will explore the following topics:

- Changing language: influences and opinions on language change; how an article can be persuasive; how differences in arguments are presented. You will also consider the impact of context on an argument and write a well-structured argument which engages and persuades your reader.
- Dialect and variety: perceptions on accent and dialect; how using factual information and an objective or sympathetic tone can affect the way a reader views an argument. You will also: track the arguments given to support a controversial decision; infer the argument in a literary text; write a persuasive speech for a class debate.
- Language learning: views about learning languages. You will consider: how writers use a number of techniques which affect the way an argument is styled and structured including the use of scientific research; references to knowledge or literature; emotional appeals; balancing and counter-arguments.

Reading texts

You will cover a range of online non-fiction reading materials in this chapter, including extracts from news articles, language-school websites, blogs, online advice and magazine-style websites.

Writing

This chapter will help you improve your persuasive writing skills by applying the techniques demonstrated in the extracts in your own fiction and non-fiction responses.

Exam link

Exam relevance

In the Component 2 exam you will be tested on your ability to follow a line of argument, comment on the way an argument is presented and to compare and contrast arguments or ideas. This chapter will help you build these skills in readiness for the exam.

Exploring language

Learning objectives

- To consider the overall theme of language
- To explore your own use and experience of language

Introduction

Language means the words we use and hear every day – words of joy, words of despair, words to our friends, enemies and loved ones, words to do with telling someone how we feel or just saying thank you for lunch in a café. Sometimes language can be a barrier when we don't really understand what someone else is saying, because the words they choose might be different from ours or because they say words in a different way. Because language changes all the time and some people consider their language to shape who they are, many people hold strong views about it. This chapter will allow you to analyse, discuss and compare some views about language, while considering the language used to present these views.

What is language? The dictionary defines it first as 'communication by the use of words' and then as 'any method of expressing or communicating meaning'.

To many people the second definition is crucial: language is much more than simple words. It is a powerful form of communication that enables us to express ourselves, to understand others, to share ideas, to form personal relationships – the list is almost endless. Language can express emotion or create new worlds through literature, yet most of the time it simply serves us in everyday life in the most ordinary ways – asking for a bus ticket, greeting friends, answering questions in English lessons.

Activity 1

1. **a.** Make a list of all the people you might speak with or write to (text, email, tweet, etc.) in a day, for example, parents, teachers, friends, other relations. Quote an example of something you might say to each of them.

    b. Do you think you use the same language with each of them, or does your language differ according to whom you speak with?

    c. What other things affect the language you use, apart from just the audience?

2. **a.** If you were to use only one of these language styles or varieties, which one would you choose and why?

    b. What difference do you think this would make to the way you communicate with others?

Activity 2

Look carefully at the quotations about language on page 128.
What do they suggest about the power of language?

Activity 3

Some people believe that every word counts, while others think we
have such a wide vocabulary available that it's a shame not to use it.

1. **a.** Describe your best friend in five words.

   b. Now describe them again in three sentences.

2. How did you feel as you wrote each description? Which was more
   difficult to do, and why?

A limitation on what you write, whether it is the number of words you
can use, or the purpose or audience for which you are writing, can
make a writing task more challenging. However, those limitations
can also mean you focus more closely and think more about what you
say and how you say it. In the pages that follow you will read extracts
where every word contributes to the overall message or argument of
the piece. Identifying how a writer has used language to achieve this
is what you will now learn.

Changing language

1 Following an argument

Learning objectives

- To identify the main argument in an article
- To comment on how an argument is convincing or persuasive

Introduction

Language is dynamic. Over time it has travelled, grown and mutated, absorbing and creating new vocabulary and diversifying into **dialect**. The extracts in this unit consider different elements of language development and each one presents its arguments using persuasion, style and other valuable techniques.

Although the purpose of the webpage below is to give information about how the Welsh language is used in Wales, it also expresses a particular point of view or opinion. Therefore, it serves a persuasive **purpose** as well as an informative one. You should be ready to notice multiple purposes of an extract in your exam.

Key terms

Dialect: vocabulary, grammar and pronunciation used in a particular area which differ from what is regarded as standard

Purpose: the purpose of a text is what the writer deliberately sets out to achieve. They may wish to persuade, encourage, advise or even anger their reader.

Activity 1

Read the webpage below. What is the main point of view expressed about the Welsh language?

Language
- Alphabet
- Place names
- Phrases

We all speak English in Wales but the Welsh language is thriving. It's spoken fluently by around half a million people in Wales, that's about 19% of the population.

It's called Cymraeg, and is a language with entirely regular and phonetic spelling. Our place names may look complicated but once you know the rules, you can learn to read and pronounce Welsh fairly easily.

Our Celtic language is closely related to Cornish and Breton and is one of Europe's oldest living languages; the Welsh we speak today is directly descended from the language of the sixth century.

Local councils and the Welsh Government use Welsh as an official language, issuing official literature and publicity in Welsh as well as in English. Road signs in Wales are in English and Welsh, including the Welsh versions of place names.

The Welsh people are keen to keep the language alive so Welsh is a compulsory subject for all school pupils up to the age of 16 in Wales. Welsh-medium schools are also increasingly popular.

We have a national Welsh language television channel, S4C, and a Welsh-language radio station, BBC Radio Cymru. There is no daily newspaper in Welsh, but there is a weekly national paper as well as Welsh-language magazines and regional monthly papers.

Now you know the main argument is that 'the Welsh language is thriving', you can start to look at how this argument is written to persuade you to believe it. A question in the exam might ask 'How does the writer try to convince you that the Welsh language is thriving?' The question word 'how' wants you to do two things:

- find information in the text which shows that you understand what the writer is saying

- explain how interesting language or techniques help to persuade you.

The paragraph below might form the beginning of an answer to the question above. Look carefully at the annotations to help you learn how to structure your own answer.

Giving the location of the quotation shows that the argument is obvious from the very first line.

Embedding the quotation in the sentence makes it clear the ideas are focused in the text.

The explanation is tied to the question and shows how the reader is convinced.

Picking out a single word allows the explanation to delve deeper into what the writer might be trying to say.

We don't know the writer's intentions, but 'might' shows that what we are saying is a possibility.

The writer states in the first line that 'the Welsh language is thriving', which makes the argument clear from the beginning. The word 'thriving' might make us think that the language is growing — we often think of a child or plant thriving in the right situation or conditions — and therefore this sends a positive and persuasive message about the state of the Welsh language.

Giving the meaning of the word helps us to explain why this word might have been used.

Giving an example helps to steer focus on to the impact of the word.

The impact of the word is given here with focus on the positive message.

Activity 2

Find other examples of how the writer convinces you that the Welsh language is thriving and explain each one. Use some of the methods in the annotated example above to help you structure your response and develop your comments.

Reading Tip To begin with, track through the argument from the start to make sure you don't miss any points. As you get more confident, you might be able to link up similar techniques scattered throughout a text to talk about them as a pattern.

② Opposing views

Everyone is entitled to their own point of view. That is one of the reasons why it is interesting to talk to people who have different ideas. The texts here will explore two opposing views. 'Opposing' means that the views expressed are not only different, but that they are opposite. A key exam skill is being able to comment on how views differ and pick out arguments that support each view.

The two extracts here express opposing ideas on the same topic: the influence of digital technology on language.

Learning objectives

- To consider different points of view expressed about the same issue
- To consider the supporting arguments for each point of view

Activity

Begin a table like the one below; allow yourself plenty of space to write. Track through each extract and note down what you think is being said about the influence of digital technology on language.

Support

Proofreading is an important skill that you can practise. When your table is complete, underline any words that you think might not be spelled correctly. Check them using a dictionary, and change any that are not correct.

What your favourite emoji says about you	Internet Linguistics – Q&A with David Crystal
700 emoji might be seen as proof that the written word could be becoming extinct.	Crystal has written how texting and tweeting is good for language.
Emoji being seen as modern hieroglyph might suggest that there is a whole language of signs and symbols, and that therefore a huge range of things can be said.	

Extract ①

What your favourite emoji says about you

With over 700 emoji characters now available, we could be watching the written word becoming slowly extinct. But what are you saying with that little cartoon?

Currently being touted as a modern day version of the Egyptian hieroglyph, emojis have come a long way since the simple smiley face.

With over 700 characters and rising now available in the core set of emojis we could be watching the written word becoming slowly extinct.

One small symbol is said to be capable of depicting a subtle range of messages all at once, and with the popularity of Botox, who wants to bother struggling with actual facial expressions when we can get our favourite little cartoon to do the emoting for us?

In fact the emoticon might even have surpassed the human body language repertoire. While US psychologists have recently discovered 21 different facial expressions that all humans use, the emoji appears to provide a core selection of over 40.

One symbol is said to be able to replace dozens of characters and there's nothing the modern communicator likes more than speed and precision.

◀ ▶ ⟳ 🖼 + | 　　　　　　　　　　　　　　　　　　　　　　 | ⌃ Q⁃

Internet Linguistics — Q&A with David Crystal

David Crystal is a world-renowned linguist.

You've written about how texting and tweeting are good things for language. Why is that?

Whenever new technology comes along people always get worried about it, as far as language is concerned. It's not just with the Internet. When telephones arrived in the 19th century, people panicked because they thought it was going to destroy language. Then broadcasting comes along in the 1920s and people panicked because they think everybody's going to be brainwashed.

Same with the Internet. People panicked because they thought the Internet was going to do devastating things to language.

In each particular case, what you see is an expansion of the expressive richness of language. In other words, new ways of talking and communicating come along. The Internet has given us 10 or 15 new styles of communication. Long messages like blogging, and then short messages like texting and tweeting. I see it all as part of an expanding array of linguistic possibilities.

 Email　　　🐦 Tweet

f Share　　　🗀 Save

Activity **2**

1. Look carefully at your table from Activity 1. Connect up the arguments which seem directly opposed to each other using highlighters or coloured pens.

2. Using your table as evidence, write a paragraph commenting on how the arguments contrast.

3. Which argument do you think is most convincing about the power of digital technology to change language, and why?

Writing Tip Make sure you signpost your ideas using appropriate connectives. When you comment on something being different from what has come before, you could say: *In contrast…, On the other hand…* or *However, ….* If you want to compare within a sentence you can use *whereas, although* or *but.*

3 The influence of context on an argument

Learning objectives

- To identify different views about a similar topic
- To consider the contextual reasons behind the different views

Key term

Context: the words that come before and after a particular word or phrase and help to clarify its meaning; the circumstances or background against which something happens. For a written text this might be when it was written, who wrote it or its purpose

We often talk about the importance of **context** to a piece of writing. This means the things that influence and shape the way a text is created. For example:

- the type of text (genre)
- the person who constructs the argument (the writer)
- the reason the text was written (the purpose)
- the people the text is written for (the target audience).

The extracts on pages 136–137 focus on the same topic, but because they have different contexts (genre, writer, purpose, audience), the arguments take a different course. The activities will help you explore how and why the context shapes their arguments.

Activity 1

Extract 1 is taken from the beginning of a *Guardian* online newspaper article and Extract 2 is from the website of a school which teaches English as a second language.

1. Look at the headlines of the two extracts. Make a prediction about what views they will express, and share it with a partner.

2. Read the extracts and judge whether your predictions were correct.

3. What helped you to make a prediction about the content? What might this teach you about the role of a headline?

Activity 2

Look at both extracts. Use the acronym GAWPS to help you focus on the context of each one. GAWPS stands for **G**enre, **A**udience, **W**riter, **P**urposes and **S**tyle. *To gawp* means 'to stare in a rude or stupid way' – this acronym might help you remember how to compare the contexts of arguments in an exam and prevent you 'gawping' at the exam paper! Copy and complete the table below.

	8 pronunciation errors that made the English language what it is today	How important is pronunciation?
Genre		
Audience		
Writer		
Purposes		
Style		

» 8 PRONUNCIATION ERRORS THAT MADE THE ENGLISH LANGUAGE WHAT IT IS TODAY

Mispronunciations are fairly common. The 20-volume *Oxford English Dictionary* lists 171,476 words as being in common use. But the average person's vocabulary is tens of thousands smaller, and the number of words they use every day smaller still. There are bound to be things we've read or are vaguely familiar with, but not able to pronounce as we are supposed to.

The term 'supposed' opens up a whole different debate, of course. Error is the engine of language change, and today's mistake could be tomorrow's vigorously defended norm. There are lots of wonderful examples of alternative pronunciations or missteps that have become standard usage.

In Norwegian, 'sk' is pronounced 'sh'. So early English-speaking adopters of skiing actually went *shiing*. Once the rest of us started reading about it in magazines we just said it how it looked.

Extract 2

Home ▶ Skills ▶ Pronunciation

How important is pronunciation?

🖨 Print   ✉ Email   ➕ Share

There's a simple answer to this too. It's the next most important after vocabulary. You need words first, but then you need pronunciation, because it's no use having words if people can't understand the words when you say them!

But people often get too worried about pronunciation, and want to pronounce English 'correctly', so here's an idea which may surprise you: there is no such thing as 'correct pronunciation'. It doesn't exist. Asking what is correct pronunciation is a bit like asking what the correct length for a book is. We all know that some books feel too long, others too short, and some are just right. So, with pronunciation: it depends what you want to do with your English.

But of course there is another side to pronunciation, which is that you want people to understand you. [...] Most countries have a more neutral form of their different accents or dialects – one that everyone can understand – often the form used on national television or radio – and usually it's the form that people from other countries can understand too. In Britain the form is the same as what used to be called 'Standard English'. So whatever English-speaking country you're in, take that form as your model, and don't worry if you put a bit (but not too much!) of your own accent on top of it. People will know better who you are.

The sample student paragraph below analyses how the context surrounding the writing shapes the argument in the *Guardian* article. It explores how the style or ideas are shaped by the type of writer and purpose.

The extract from the opening of '8 pronunciation errors which made the English language what it is today' is reporting a reason for language change, mispronunciation. Writing for a broadsheet newspaper, the writer refers to respected sources like the '20-volume Oxford English Dictionary' to give factual weight, '171,476 words in common use', to support their argument. The writing also seems to appeal to a target audience who already know something about the subject by using phrases like 'bound to be' and 'of course' to make the reader agree with their view. The style tries to persuade the reader in favour of a view that language change is a natural thing. The evidence for this is the positive adjectives such as 'wonderful' to describe 'alternative' pronunciation, rather than using 'incorrect'. Mispronunciation or 'error' is described as an 'engine' for language change, which seems to celebrate it as a welcome force to drive pronunciation change forward.

Activity 3

Look at how the student paragraph opposite uses quotations to support ideas and how the meaning of each quotation is suggested. Produce your own analysis of Extract 2, using quotations to support your work.

Support

Use the information on context in your table and the following opening sentence to start you off on your analysis:

> The article 'How important is pronunciation?' is shaped to help students make a decision about which language school to choose. It does this by giving advice about how important pronunciation is, for example...

Stretch

As you write about the website advice, include comments on how and why it differs from Extract 1. This will help you practise your skills on comparing arguments, which you will revisit later.

4 Sustaining your line of argument

Learning objectives

- To give and support a point of view using examples
- To develop clear and engaging arguments

A common writing task is one that asks for your views. Here you will be given some tips on how to make your argument clear and engaging for your reader. Many students just write as much as they can but planning helps you to decide what you think about a topic before you start writing, which in turn can make your argument better structured and more persuasive.

The activities on pages 140–143 are going to help you build up to answering the following task:

> **Write a blog entry, giving your views on whether technology is a positive or negative influence on the way teens communicate. You might consider TV, voice calls, video calls, texting, email, social-networking sites like Facebook, photo-sharing sites or apps, micro-blogging like Twitter or any other technologies you think are influential.**

Activity 1

Choose a planning format.

1. Work with a partner and decide who the audience will be for your blog, including age, gender, group. Will your writing need to be informal or formal? Write these key words at the top of your plan so you can keep looking back at them to check your writing will appeal to and convince your audience.

2. List planning methods you might use, for example, lists, spider diagrams, tables. Discuss their advantages and disadvantages.

For a task where you need to consider whether you are going to argue for negatives or positives, a table forces you to organize your thoughts in this way.

Activity 2

Gather information.

Complete the table below with your ideas about how technology can be both a positive and negative influence on teens' communication. Add more examples or use these as a springboard for your own ideas.

> **Tip** Try to make your ideas specific to a technology and its impact on communication.

Positive influences of technology on teens' communication	Negative influences of technology on teens' communication
Teens can communicate easily with each other to organize their social lives through technology, e.g. group texts or Facebook.	Teens often spend less time actually talking to each other when they meet face-to-face as they are distracted with phones and TV.
Micro-blogging such as Twitter encourages teens to write and respond to groups of friends; any writing is developing teens' literacy skills.	Facebook can be a target for abuse; this can lead to all sorts of social and emotional problems for the victims.
Video calling...	Social networking sites encourage teens to hide behind a 'perfect' online self...

Activity 3

Prepare your arguments.

1. Decide whether you will argue that technology is positive or negative. Which side had the most arguments or seemed strongest? Highlight your choice.

2. What is the best order for your arguments? Do any lead on from one another, consider the same type of issue or have a similar effect? Consider using your best argument first to have a strong impact. Mark numbers on your plan to show your order.

3. Now look at the arguments that support the other side. Link up opposing arguments with numbers or colour coding. For example, in the table above, video calls and getting distracted by technology are linked as video calling uses technology to make social connections, whereas mobile phones break social connections if they distract teens from building bonds with the people they are with. Use a form like 'It has been argued that... but...' to link counter-ideas.

As you know from articles and blogs, the heading is a good guide to the topic and direction of the argument and can interest your audience. Using techniques like alliteration or puns can make it catchy. For example, if your article was largely about the negative impact of Facebook, you might have a title like 'Faceless friends, 'cause they're all on Facebook'.

Activity 4

Write a heading.

Write a number of headings and choose the best. Get your classmates to help you decide which is the best and why.

Your opening also needs to grab your readers' attention and clearly show the direction of your writing. Remember that you are writing a blog, not an essay – your tone needs to be lively to engage your readers. You could start with a question such as: 'Ever considered why…?', or a clear statement: 'There is no question that technology has improved the way teens communicate.' Make your introductory paragraph short – two or three sentences – which are on-topic and interesting.

Activity 5

Write an introduction.

Write your introductory paragraph following the advice above.

Writing Tip

Remember to hook your arguments together like the links of a chain.

You will need to structure each paragraph of your argument to make it clear and persuasive. The steps below will help you.

1. Make a clear statement about the issue.

2. Give an example of the technological influence on teen communication.

> Think carefully about your language choices and their impact. For example, use:
> - superlatives for emphasis/exaggeration
> - a simile/metaphor to create imagery
> - a joke to get your reader laughing with you.

3. Consider using fact or opinion to help explain the example's impact.

> Go further than re-stating your original point. Emphasize why this argument is important in your view.

4. To end, signpost where your argument is going next.

> A hook to the next paragraph helps your reader follow your argument and shows you control its direction.

5. To start your next paragraph, join to the previous hook.

> Use words that refer back to the previous paragraph to join up your argument. Continue by repeating steps 1 to 4 with a new point.

Activity 6

Write your argument.

Write three or four argument paragraphs following the structure on page 142 and making at least three points from your planning table.

End on a strong note to signal that your writing is finished by summing up your key ideas. You could use a 'group of three': three points in support of your argument which make a powerful impact when listed together, for example: 'Technology brings teens closer to their friends, closer to information and closer to the future.'

There may be a rhetorical question that will make your reader consider the impact of your arguments or a change you can propose, such as: 'Why complain about a development that is here to stay and whose influence will only increase? We should embrace the power of technology to improve our relationships, our studies, our lives.'

Activity 7

Write a conclusion.

Using a rhetorical question and/or a group of three, write your own concluding paragraph.

Progress check

Once you have proofread your work, swap with a partner to give each other feedback. Use the following questions/prompts to target your comments:

1. How well have they followed or adapted the structure above?

2. How strong or well structured are their arguments? Put a ☺ next to any that work well and say why. Put a '?' next to any you can't follow and make sure you suggest an improvement.

3. Highlight or circle two word choices or techniques that you think work well and give a reason why. Highlight one that you think might need to change to be more appropriate for the task or be more specific, and suggest an improvement.

Dialect and variety

5 The impact of factual information and opinion

Learning objectives

- To follow a line of argument
- To consider the impact of fact and opinion on the way you read an article

Introduction

Dialects are an important part of language and can be a vital part of a person's regional or social identity. This unit will explore different attitudes towards dialect, expressed using a range of persuasive techniques.

In Chapter 1 you learned the difference between factual and fictional writing, including description, speculation and opinion. Writers use these devices to support their arguments. Now you will practise selecting facts and opinions, and consider how they affect the way you view information.

Activity 1

With a partner, agree and write down definitions for the terms 'fact' and 'opinion'. Check your definitions in a dictionary, then write down two things each that will help you identify factual information or opinion.

Activity 2

The extract on page 145 is taken from the news section of a magazine-style website for call-centre workers. Read it and list the facts and opinions it contains.

Activity 3

1. Look at your lists of facts and opinions from Activity 2. Do you have more facts or more opinions? Why do you think this is and what is the effect?

2. Were the facts and opinions concentrated in certain areas of the article? Why might the writer have done this? Discuss your ideas with a partner.

Consumers reject regional accents

The way a brand or business 'sounds' could be as important as how it 'looks', according to new research into voice branding[1].

With 56% of Britons stating that they are more inclined to listen to a special offer or promotion if it comes from a voice that they find appealing, businesses cannot afford to ignore the growing importance of voice within promotion and customer service.

The research, conducted by YouGov, reveals that over half (52%) of British consumers find a 'Queen's English' accent appealing when speaking with someone in a call centre[2]. The Scottish accent remains popular, coming in as the second most pleasing accent to listen to (with 34% of consumers finding it appealing), while a North East 'Geordie' accent is the third most popular accent with 26% of consumers finding it appealing. The least popular regional UK accents are from Liverpool 'Scouse' (9%) and Birmingham 'Brummie' (9%). […]

Leading brand expert James Hammond believes this may be explained by the power of celebrity.

'With personalities such as Cheryl Cole and Ant and Dec dominating the media, it's no surprise consumers have become familiar with the Geordie accent and currently favour it above more traditionally perceived call-centre accents. However, these accents may only work well in their respective contexts. An effective voice is a consistent and authentic one. The voice that you use to attract footfall must also chime with the customer's experience of the company. If it doesn't, you could be in trouble.'

Ian Turner, Northern European General Manager at Nuance Communications, said: 'It is human nature to react differently to varying types of voices, based on accent, gender and tone. What this survey highlights is exactly how important it is for businesses to recognize the impact that brand has at every customer touch point[3]. Some of the world's biggest companies invest millions of pounds each year ensuring that the way their brands 'look' and 'feel' reflects the values and beliefs of the brand. Yet very few organisations actually think about how their brand 'speaks', despite the fact that the vast majority of customer service communication and advertising is based on listening.'

[1] voice branding – the personality/voice heard in a company's communication
[2] call centre – a customer service office handling telephone calls
[3] touch point – the physical or virtual places where a customer and business meet

Activity 4

Look at the statements below about the use and effects of facts and opinions in the extract. Discuss them with a partner and decide whether they are true or false. Discuss and write down the reasons for your views.

1. The writer uses the factual 'survey' information at the beginning of the article as concrete evidence that accents shape the way a consumer sees a business.

2. The writer names who conducted the survey to show his information is authentic.

3. Ian Turner mixes fact and opinion to argue that companies should invest as much money in how they 'speak' as in how they 'look' and 'feel'.

Stretch

Summarize how fact and opinion are used in the extract to help argue that businesses should think carefully about the voices of the people who represent them.

6 Sympathetic and objective tones

Learning objectives

- To understand the difference between a sympathetic and an objective tone in an article
- To consider the effects of objective and sympathetic tones on the way a reader views the arguments

When you ask someone you know for advice, you often know the type of response you will get. Some people will respond sympathetically to your feelings. Other people focus on the facts and make you step back from your emotions, giving an objective **perspective**. You are going to consider how these two techniques are used in two extracts exploring why regional accents cause confusion for voice-recognition technology, and how they shape the way a reader responds to the views presented. Extract 1 is taken from a *Daily Mail* article and Extract 2 is from the technology section of a website called fastcompany.com.

Activity 1

1. Using the information above, write down a definition of 'sympathetic' and 'objective'. Check your definitions in a dictionary and amend them as necessary.

2. As you read both extracts, identify which one relies heavily on research to maintain a more objective tone and which one connects with the feelings of people who have experienced problems in order to create a more sympathetic tone.

Extract 1

How regional accents cause confusion for call-centre technology

Speech-recognition technology used by call centres fails to understand regional accents, according to a study unveiled today.

The University of Birmingham discovered northerners and those from the Midlands with strong accents are frequently misunderstood when dealing with call centres for anything from paying a bill to booking cinema tickets.

Scousers, Brummies and Glaswegians suffered when on the phone, possibly because most voice-recognition technology uses Americanised English, said the researchers.

Professor Martin Russell, head of the university's Electronic, Electrical and Computer Engineering department, is heading the research and he pointed out that the technology generally worked best for people with 'standard British southern accents'.

He said: 'There's lots of anecdotal evidence of accents not working well with voice recognition, with people experiencing certain problems.'

Extract 2

HOME   FEATURES   BLOG   CONTACT

Siri, Why Can't You Understand Me?

Siri still struggles with accents. When, and how, will it get better?

There are many indignities involved with having an accent. To begin with, many strangers will say they can never understand you. Added to the list, in our modern world, is the inability of those with accents to get the most out of their voice recognition technology. Shortly after Siri launched on the iPhone 4S, Scottish users took to the Internet to protest that she couldn't understand their accents.

The good news, according to several experts, is that Siri and other voice recognition software will inevitably get better at understanding accents. Though understanding accents poses a particular problem for voice recognition, research is advancing, and the increasing stores of data on accents means that Siri will improve with time. 'All recognizers get better every year,' and Siri will be no exception, Dan Jurafsky, a professor of linguistics and computer science at Stanford, tells *Fast Company*.

Activity ②

1. Extract 1 refers to a study from the University of Birmingham. How many times is the research or researchers mentioned and how does this affect the way you read the information being presented?

2. In what ways does it help to explain the reasons that those 'with strong accents' 'suffered' when phoning call centres using voice-recognition technology?

Stretch

Extract 2 also uses an expert to give an authenticity to the ideas. However, the professor's view, stated in Extract 2, presents the solution to the problem, not the problem itself. What is the effect of this difference on the way the articles might be seen to present pessimistic or optimistic views for people with strong accents?

Activity ③

1. Look at the headline and first paragraph of Extract 2. List the **(SPAG)** techniques the writer has used to try to connect with those readers who might have experienced difficulty using Siri.

2. Comment on how these techniques might impact on readers with, and readers without, strong accents.

   Draw up your ideas in a table like the one below.

Key term

Perspective: a particular way of thinking about something

Writer's techniques	Quotation from Extract 2	Impact on reader with accent who has trouble using Siri	Impact on reader who doesn't have strong accent or trouble using Siri
Use of pronouns 'me' and 'you'			
Idea from someone with an accent			
Use of strong words like 'inability' and 'protest' to present anger at the situation			

Activity ④

1. Which do you think is the most persuasive extract?

2. Do you have a strong accent? In what way does this shape the way you view the two extracts?

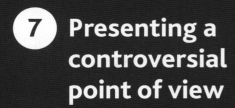

7 Presenting a controversial point of view

Learning objectives

- To follow a line of argument objectively
- To explore how a writer presents both sides of a controversial argument to demonstrate a considered point of view

Students often miss out on marks in exams because they give their own opinion of a subject when answering a question which is actually asking what a text says. Here you have to put your own opinions aside and look at how a writer structures an argument that you might not agree with.

Activity 1

The article opposite clearly lays out its argument in the headline and subheading. Just from reading these, say what kind of structure you think the article will have. Then read the article and see if you were right.

Support

What does the word 'defend' mean? The article says it is going to show how the school is going to 'defend' its actions of 'banning the local dialect from classrooms'. Predict what techniques it will use to do this.

Activity 2

The writer knows that the head teacher's decision is controversial, and gives the reasons for and against it. Make a table with two columns: 'Arguments for banning the dialect' and 'Arguments against'.
Track through the article carefully and list the arguments in your table. Do you think the writer supports one side or the other?

Activity 3

Look at some of the devices the writer of this article uses to make one point of view more persuasive:

- emotive language, for example, 'attack'
- dynamic verbs, for example, 'criticized'
- examples of words and phrases that have been banned.

Find examples of these devices and consider whether they make the reader agree with the head teacher.

Stretch

What other devices has the writer used to make their point of view more persuasive?

HOME   WORLD   REGIONAL   BUSINESS   SCIENCE   ARTS   SPORT

School defends Black Country dialect ban

The head teacher of a Black Country school has defended banning the local dialect from classrooms, saying it will help raise literacy standards.

Simon Green said the school had decided to ban the dialect from lessons or otherwise put at risk the future prospects of its 600 pupils.

The measure, which came into force [...] at the start of the term, is accompanied by a guide explaining to parents the reasons for the ban.

Some mothers and fathers have reportedly criticised the step as an attack on Black Country culture.

However, Mr Green said: 'Some have thought it might be a bit finger-wagging or patronizing, which we did not want to do and indeed we discussed that before we even introduced the ban.'

The list of ten banned words includes prohibitions on saying 'you cor' rather than 'you can't'. [...]

Other phrases on the banned list include the more widely-used 'somfink' instead of 'something'; 'gonna' rather than 'going to' and 'ain't' rather than 'are not'.

Mr Green said: 'We'd been looking at our literacy standards and we wanted to talk to parents about some of the confusion that happens when children are talking in slang to their mates in the playground.

'When it comes to phonics and English lessons it can be very confusing for the children.

'When they are reading phonics, it's incorrect, so we think it's better for them this way.' [...]

Mr Green added he was seeing an increasing number of pupils coming through nursery with little or no proper English, and put slipping standards of language down in part to 'a reduction of conversations around the dinner table' at home and too much time spent by children 'in front of television screens'.

'We're not stopping them talking to their friends in the playground how they want to,' he added.

'We're just saying that in the classroom we'll correct them.'

8 Inferring an argument from a literary text

Learning objective

- To use skills of inference to pick out an argument in a literary text

Willy Russell's play *Educating Rita* follows a woman called Rita from Liverpool who is studying Literature with the Open University as she wants to 'be educated'. She starts to feel a tension between her own Liverpudlian roots and her new-found ambition. Before this extract, she has explained to Frank, her lecturer, that she didn't attend the dinner party he invited her to as she felt awkward.

Extract from *Educating Rita* by Willy Russell (Act 1, Scene 7)

RITA   […] I'm a freak. I can't talk to the people I live with anymore. An' I can't talk to the likes of them on Saturday or them out there because I can't learn the language. I'm a half-caste. I went back to the pub where Denny was, an' me mother, an' our Sandra, an' her mates. I'd decided I wasn't comin' here again.

FRANK turns to face her

RITA   I went into the pub an' they were singin', all of them singin' some song they'd learnt from the juke-box. An I stood in that pub an' thought, just what the frig am I trying to do? Why don't I just pack it in an' stay with them, an' join in the singin'?

FRANK   And why don't you?

RITA   *(angrily)* You think I can, don't you? Just because you pass a pub doorway an' hear the singin' you think we're all OK, that we're all survivin' with the spirit intact. Well I did join in with the singin', I didn't ask any questions, I just went along with it.

But when I looked around me mother had stopped singin', an' she was cryin', but no one could get it out of her why she was cryin'. Everyone just said she was pissed an' we should get her home. So we did, an' on the way I asked her why. I said, 'Why are y' cryin', Mother?' She said, 'Because – because we could sing better songs than those.' Ten minutes later, Denny had her laughing and singing again, pretending she hadn't said it. But she had. And that's why I came back. And that's why I'm staying.

Activity 1

For Rita, being educated means changing her language to be more like the people at the university than her own family.

1. As you read the extract, consider how you think Rita feels about her situation.

2. Note down her feelings, using evidence from the text to support your ideas.

The term 'half-caste' is considered to be an unsavoury or racist label based on a prejudiced view that places black people as lower status, and therefore children who have one white and one black parent as being lower than all-white status. The word 'caste' actually means status or social group, and Russell doesn't intend Rita to use it to say anything derogatory about race or ethnicity.

Activity 2

1. What do you think Rita is trying to say about her own situation when she describes herself as 'half-caste'?

2. What methods does Russell use to help Rita support her argument that her language makes her feel caught between two worlds, like a 'half-caste'?

3. What impact does each of these techniques have on the way an audience might view Rita and her argument?

Support

Pick four of the following features that Russell uses in this extract. Comment on how each one makes you feel a certain way towards Rita. Make sure you are specific about how you feel and why you feel like this.

- Controversial labels like 'freak'
- Rita asking herself questions
- Frank asking Rita the same question she asks herself
- Rita's aggressive response to Frank
- Rita's mum crying because of the singing
- Rita's mum pretending she hadn't made a comment about singing 'better songs'
- The repetition in Rita's justification of her decision to return to Frank's classes

Stretch

Which technique do you think makes the audience most sympathetic to Rita's position, and why?

9 Class debate

Learning objectives

- To use persuasive strategies to present and defend a strong point of view
- To take a role in a class debate as speaker, chair or floor

The verb 'to debate' is defined as 'to discuss or consider something'. Your class is going to take up roles in a discussion about dialects. The roles you are given will shape the type of views you put forward and whether you agree with or 'oppose' (disagree with) the 'motion' that has been 'proposed' (put forward) for the debate. The 'motion' is the formal name given to the idea that is being discussed. The debate is going to centre around the following motion:

This class proposes that teachers and students who use dialects in classrooms should be punished.

Activity 1

In pairs or small groups, explore the possible arguments for and against this motion. You might like to work on a large piece of paper to help you present all your ideas. Make sure you consider supporting evidence for these arguments. You could also explore what kind of punishments might be possible and how these might work in practice.

Activity 2

Now look at the background/factual information opposite. Add these ideas where you think they support an argument you gave in Activity 1. You can also look back at the other extracts in this unit where dialects are considered.

Dialect is defined as 'the words and pronunciation used in a particular area which differ from *what is regarded as standard in the language as a whole*'
– Oxford Student's Dictionary

No one dialect is better at communicating meaning than another. The fact that some dialects and accents are seen to be more prestigious than others is a reflection of judgements based on social, rather than linguistic, criteria.
– *British Library website*

Dialects of a region are often preserved in the working classes. This is partly because members of the working class tend to live in the same place, so their language stays the same as the people around them. Research also shows that features of the standard language are more likely to be found in speakers who are of a higher social class or who are highly educated.
– *A Level English Language student*

Extract from *Telegraph* online article 'Facebook and Twitter "helping spread regional dialects"'

Dialects were traditionally passed on relatively slowly through spoken language. But social changes such as the speed of modern communication mean they are spreading much faster than they would have. Twitter, Facebook and texting all encourage speed and immediacy of understanding, meaning users type as they speak, using slang, dialect respellings and colloquialisms. The result is we are all becoming exposed to words we may not have otherwise encountered, while absorbing them into everyday speech.

Comment in response to an article about the United Nations Education, Scientific and Cultural Organization (UNESCO) list of endangered languages

People think that languages being lost is an issue for other people. These are the same people who think that deforestation only affects those in 'far flung tribes'. In reality, three languages native to our British shores: Welsh, Scottish Gaelic and Irish (not to mention Manx and Cornish) are also on the UNESCO endangered languages list and are at risk of dying out. Politicians need to do more to help protect these local languages of the UK before they're lost forever.

Activity 3

1. In your group, make a list of devices that writers can use to make their arguments persuasive.

2. Discuss which ones you think will be particularly persuasive when making a speech and why.

153

Activity 4

Now you are going to take up a role and write the speech from the perspective of that character or group. You will need to make sure that all four roles are covered by people in the class so that all views can be expressed when you have your debate. Alternatively, you might want to split into four groups as a class, with each group taking a particular role.

Discuss ideas for the speech in your group, work individually to produce a persuasive speech and then decide whose is the best to represent that point of view.

The four roles are:

1. a professor of language studying the decline of dialects

2. a student who speaks with a strong dialect

3. the spokesperson for an organization called Ditch the Dialect, set up to represent parents who believe that dialects are disadvantaging their children at school and socially

4. a head teacher who has banned dialects throughout their school, except in the staffroom.

Plan your speech carefully and remember that it needs to give a clear point of view for or against the motion.

Support

You might like to look back through this chapter for ideas on using facts, opinions, rhetorical questions, lists and a sympathetic or objective tone. Make sure you look at the advice in the numbered flowchart (page 142) on how to structure each paragraph using:

| Statement | ····▷ | Example | ····▷ | Impact | ····▷ | Signpost/hook | ····▷ | Link at the start of next paragraph |

Writing Tip Remember that you are writing for a listening rather than a reading audience. Tactics that will help you write an engaging speech include using personal pronouns, shorter-than-normal sentences and an increased number of connectives to signpost your ideas.

To make your debate a success you need to listen carefully as the other speeches are being presented. The chairperson introduces the speakers and invites questions from the floor (the listening audience) and from the other speakers. The questions you ask will need to be phrased carefully to uphold your side of the debate. For example, if the speaker you are questioning is on the same side of the debate as you, you might ask them to elaborate on a point supporting your side of the debate. If they are arguing the opposite point of view to you, you need to ask them a question to challenge what they said.

Activity

Finally, you need to vote on which side of the debate should win. Your chairperson might sum up the key arguments for and against the motion, or your teacher might ask you to **evaluate** the strength of the arguments put forward. Your decision in the vote should be based on which arguments were most persuasive, rather than voting for your friends or for the side you wrote a speech for originally. You can make the vote anonymous if you want to disguise any of these factors.

Key term

Evaluate: to form an idea of the state or value of something

Progress check

Now you have written your speech, possibly presented it and heard those of other people, how successful do you think it was in achieving its purpose? Answer the following questions to evaluate your speech:

1. What techniques did you use from this unit?

2. Which was the most and which the least successful technique? Why might this have been?

3. Overall, how successful was your speech?

   1 – very, 2 – partly, 3 – limited, 4 – not at all

   What are your reasons for this judgement?

4. How might you make improvements to your speech?

Now assess the other speeches you heard in the class debate against the questions above. Evaluate two of them and write a short summary explaining what you learned from both of these.

Language learning

10 Styling an argument to persuade

Learning objective

- To consider how the style of an argument contributes to its appeal and persuasive power

Introduction

You will now look at some of the different ways a writer can style their argument persuasively. Using a variety of methods is important, as it increases the text's appeal and therefore the chances that its argument will achieve its purpose: to persuade you to agree with it.

Activity 1

The extract below is trying to persuade you to learn a dead language (a language which is no longer spoken in everyday conversation). As you read, list the reasons given to learn a dead language.

news today

Search

Top Story

Why you should learn a dead language

Learning a dead language might not be as useless as it sounds

The British are the dumb men of Europe and it is embarrassing. So, go ahead – learn a modern language. If you want to be obvious about it.

But all sorts of 'dead' languages enjoy important existences today, albeit in quieter, more subtle ways. They're threaded almost invisibly through contemporary culture, kept in shape by a combination of tradition and devotion, like good hand-stitching.

There are practical reasons for learning an extinct language. It can make acquiring second, third, even fourth languages easier. Linguists map languages on to family trees. [...] So, according to the same principle that your great-grandfather had children and grand-children and great-grandchildren, learning a language that occupies a place farther up the family tree will mean that younger languages will have grown up out of it.

This argument is often used in defence of learning Latin, which is parent to French and Spanish, among others (it doesn't apply to Ancient Greek, however, whose offspring are few).

Some dead languages are more dead than others. Languages whose writings are beloved never really die. Old English will be with us as long as we treasure Beowulf. While our fascination with King Arthur rumbles on, Old English's inheritor, Middle English, survives. Middle English romance tales of the kings, queens and chivalric heroes of Britain are woven into the stories we still tell our children, while film studios seemingly never tire of adapting them. Show me a lover of televised dragons and I will show you a fan of medieval literature.

If you were asked the question 'How does the writer present her view that dead languages are worth learning?' then you've already done half of it in Activity 1, having identified the content that is presented: the reasons given in the article. The other part of a 'how' question focuses on language and style. This article uses some clever techniques, which make it interesting to read. You will analyse these now.

Activity 2

1. Complete the table below to find examples where the writer uses the following techniques, and comment on how they help to appeal to the readers and make the argument persuasive. The techniques are listed in the table in the order in which they appear in the article.

SPAG

Language technique	Examples or quotations	Reason it appeals to or affects the audience	Reason it persuades
Derogatory/insulting comment			
Command			
Conditional language – if			
Direct address			
Quotation marks around a word or phrase for emphasis			
Simile			
Making a link to a familiar situation to explain a technical idea (**analogy**)			

2. Which feature do you think is the most effective in persuading the reader to learn a dead language, and why?

Activity 3

Now it's your turn to try out a few of the techniques used in the extract. Choose three or four and use them in a paragraph of writing to persuade an audience to learn something new. It can be any subject of your own choice, from learning a language from *Lord of the Rings*, like Elvish, to the skill of knitting.

Writing Tip When you quote, make sure your quotation shows a technique at work. For example, to show an example of direct address, don't just quote 'you', which could come from any text! Instead, quote one clearly from this text, such as 'if you want to be obvious'.

11 Balancing and counter-arguments

Learning objective

- To consider how a writer can acknowledge opposing sides of an argument to strengthen their own argument

The chances are that if you've ever had an argument with someone, you didn't get far by just repeating your own view without considering theirs. One of the most effective ways you can argue your case is to try to knock down the opposing point of view. The extract on page 159 does just that. You will examine how the writer succeeds in doing this and you can practise doing it in your own writing.

Activity 1

There are a few words in this extract which you probably will not have come across as they are specialist vocabulary for this topic: anglophone, monolingualism, monoglot. See if you can work them out by drawing links with other words.

- First, write down any other words you can think of containing the affixes *anglo-*, *-phone* or *mono-*.
- Now see if you can define the affixes by what you know about those words.
- Next, find the three words above in the extract and see if you can work out their meaning from the surrounding ideas.
- Finally, check the definitions at the end of the article to see how close you were.

Activity 2

1. Look at paragraphs 1–3. In what ways does the writer argue that being an English-speaking country is a blessing? In what ways does he argue it is a curse?
2. Now look at paragraphs 4–5. When can it be a benefit to hear different languages rather than English, and why?

Activity 3

The writer starts off by celebrating knowing English. What techniques does he use to turn the argument round to show that knowledge of other languages is really valuable?

Home **Business** **World** **UK** **Sports**

Featured story

Will UK universities cope if English no longer rules the world?

Being an English-speaking country is a blessing – and a curse. It is a blessing to be native speakers of the language of Shakespeare – and the language of world science and popular culture (and financial capitalism … well, maybe not).

The success of UK science is built not just on its excellence but also its English, which since the decline of the Soviet Union[1] has been the only serious global scientific language. The success of UK universities in recruiting international students also owes a great deal to our language.

But it is also a curse. As the incentives to learn other languages decline year by year, we are increasingly locked into an anglophone[2] prison. It may be an advantage to travel almost everywhere and be 'understood'. But maybe our ability really to understand, to get inside, other cultures is also declining. The Chinese speak English; not many of us speak Mandarin. Who has the advantage?

There are glimmers that we recognise our loss. BBC4's success in importing foreign-language series may be because of the need for subtitles not in spite of them. It is appealing to hear Danish or Swedish. If they were dubbed, they would lose authenticity. Maybe there is a wider lesson here: monolingualism[3] inhibits[4] multicultural sensitivity.

This inhibition is expressed in a number of ways. Within the university the humanities, where such sensitivity is crucial, are hardest hit. Stem subjects[5] may be able to flourish as a monoglot[6] domain (because their language is as much mathematics as English). But that can never be the case with literature, philosophy, history – and even some of the less theoretical social sciences – without a narrowing of perspectives and creative possibilities.

[1] Soviet Union – a powerful group of Communist republics in the northern half of Asia and part of eastern Europe. Many of those republics regrouped as the Russian Federation when the Soviet Union broke up in 1991
[2] anglophone – English-speaking
[3] monolingualism – speaking only one language
[4] inhibits – restrains or prevents
[5] stem subjects – science, technology, engineering and maths
[6] monoglot – using or speaking only one language

The writer gives the other side of the argument first, that speaking English is a blessing, in order to counter this argument with his own view: that speaking only English is actually more of a curse. A mistake some students make is failing to appropriately counter a point of view that is opposite to their own. Including an opposing argument is a good technique to use, as long as you argue against it well. Otherwise, including it will weaken your own argument.

Activity 4

Rephrase each of the views below in a paragraph which argues the opposite. The first is done for you as an example.

1. Languages are taught in school, so there is no point in starting language learning before that, as you will only get bored repeating work you've already done.

> It is true to say that languages are taught at school, but why wait until then? Very young children can have lots of fun learning simple things like numbers, colours and animal names in another language. They get a lot of satisfaction being able to proudly assert their knowledge in games and songs while they're young and when they're in a foreign language class in school they'll be the expert in the class. Far from getting bored because they know it already, they'll have the foundations of learning the foreign vocabulary sorted and will be able to quickly move on to the more complicated lessons about construction and grammar.

2. There is no point in learning a foreign language; that's what Google Translate is for.

3. Learning a language is really hard. Why would you bother when people speak English to you when you go on holiday anyway?

Activity 5

Compare your responses to Activity 4 in a small group. Make a list of the most effective strategies you have used to counter the argument. For example, the techniques in the example above are:

- question ('why wait?')

- evidence that supports the opposing view using positive terms ('fun', 'proudly', 'expert')

- asserting a view that is completely opposite to the one proposed 'far from…'.

List useful phrases from your own writing which you will be able to learn and use whenever you counter an argument. You might be able to produce a class resource if each group offers their best strategies and phrases.

Progress check

Look at the techniques listed in the table below.
Assess how you feel about each of them by considering:

- which you think you could confidently spot
- which you feel you could then explain the impact of
- which you could use in your own arguments.

Make a copy of the table and fill it in using the numbers 1 to 3:

1 = you feel confident

2 = you know how to do it but need practice

3 = you are really unsure.

Technique	Ability to spot in what I read	Ability to explain the impact of the technique	Ability to use technique in my writing
Scientific research			
Varied language choices			
Commands			
Direct address			
Simile			
Analogy			
Pairing of opposites			
Examples to support your argument			
Counter-argument			

For any technique where you wrote '3', look back over the pages in this
chapter where that skill is addressed and set yourself a target to help you improve.

Assessment

Reading

Learning objective

- To assess progress made against reading skills taught in this chapter

Introduction

Throughout this chapter you have been learning how to follow a writer's argument and compare points of view, to comment on and compare the techniques used to make an argument persuasive, and to structure an engaging and persuasive written argument. The extracts in this assessment pose both sides of a debate about whether it is worth learning a foreign language. The first is from a *Daily Mail* newspaper article; the second is adapted from a blog on a website from a company providing foreign-language courses. The reading and writing activities in this assessment will give you chance to consider how successfully you can comment on and compare points of view, in addition to how well you can construct your own argument.

Extract 1

Why do the English need to speak a foreign language when foreigners all speak English?

By David Thomas

My roots read like a World Cup draw. My half-Welsh father was born and spent his boyhood in Argentina and thus speaks Spanish almost as naturally as English. My mother's family are Norwegian.

Because Dad was a diplomat, I spent the first five years of my life in Moscow and Lisbon, so my baby-talk was Russian (in which I later got an O-Level) and I then spoke kindergarten Portuguese. [...]

Given this absurdly multi-lingual background, you might think I'd be distraught at hearing that 380,000 teenagers in England did not take a single language at GCSE last year. Department for Education figures show that fewer and fewer of us are learning a foreign language, while more and more foreigners are becoming multi-lingual. This, say distraught commentators, will condemn us pathetic Little Englanders to a life of dismal isolation while our educated, sophisticated, Euro-competitors chat away to foreign customers and steal all our business as a result.

In fact, I think those pupils who don't learn other languages are making an entirely sensible decision. Learning foreign languages is a pleasant form of intellectual self-improvement: a genteel indulgence like learning to embroider or play the violin. [...]

Consider the maths. There are roughly 6,900 living languages in the world. Europe alone has 234 languages spoken on a daily basis. So even if I was fluent in all the languages I've ever even begun to tackle, I'd only be able to speak to a minority of my fellow-Europeans in their mother tongues. And that's before I'd so much as set foot in the Middle East, Africa and Asia. [...]

There is, however, one language that does perform the magic trick of uniting the entire globe. [...]

This is the language of science, commerce, global politics, aviation, popular music and, above all, the Internet. It's the language that 85 per

Global reach: English is the second language of 85 per cent of Europeans, and the default tongue of the European Union

cent of all Europeans learn as their second language; the language that has become the default tongue of the EU. [...]

This magical language is English. It unites the whole world in the way no other language can. It's arguably the major reason why our little island has such a disproportionately massive influence on global culture: from Shakespeare to Harry Potter, from James Bond to the Beatles.

All those foreigners who are so admirably learning another language are learning the one we already know. So our school pupils don't need to learn any foreign tongues. They might, of course, do well to become much, much better at speaking, writing, spelling and generally using English correctly. But that's another argument altogether.

Extract 2

◄ ► ⟳ ⊠ + [　　　　　　　　　　　　　　　　　　] ▾ Q▾

Reasons You Should Speak More Than One Language

may 20 by Mandy Menaker

Ok, we know there is an iPhone app for everything these days (apparently your phone can do everything except make phone calls). But seriously, it is time to stop looking up every word in a translator or asking Siri. [...] Need some convincing? Check out these reasons:

1) Expose Yourself to Culture
It's time to branch out and explore other musical artists. Spice up your playlist [...] with more foreign language artists. Instead of a new Angelina Jolie movie, consider netflixing *Pan's Labyrinth*, *The Class* or another fantastic foreign-language flick that will make you look way cooler in front of your mates.

Career Opportunities
Employers want people who speak more than one language. If you are looking for the fastest way to make yourself more marketable, [...] tack on Spanish, French or Chinese to your resumé. Fluency in foreign languages can also be the token to getting your boss to let you take an international business trip. If you are looking for a great way to get 15% off classes, check out our Corporate Membership Club and get your co-workers to sign up for a language class with you!

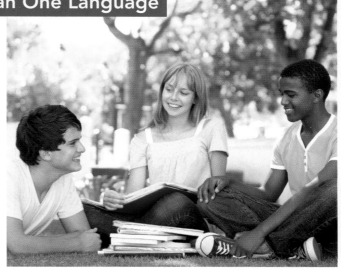

3) Brain Power
Keep your mind active. People who learn a new language as an adult and push themselves to do more cognitive thinking are less likely to have brain-related health problems later in life including Alzheimer's. [...]

So, survey says? Learning a new language is an absolute must. Consider a fun, casual group class at Fluent City where you can pick from French, Spanish, Italian, Portuguese, German, Arabic or Chinese. We promise, it will help you in more ways than one.

Activity 1

Read Extract 1 carefully and answer the questions below.

1. Look carefully at the headline. In what ways does it signal the possible viewpoint of the article? **[1]**

2. Focus on the first two paragraphs. Identify four things you learn about Thomas's own language experiences. **[4]**

3. What phrase in the next paragraph, beginning 'Given this absurdly multi-lingual background', signals that his argument will follow his headline and take the view that there is little reason for English people to learn a foreign language? **[1]**

4. In paragraphs 5–8, how does Thomas support his argument that 'those pupils who don't learn other languages are making an entirely sensible decision'? **[2]**

5. Re-read paragraphs 7–9 ('This is the language of science…' to the end of the article). How does Thomas persuade you that English is the most important language to know? Focus on:
   - factual information and opinions
   - lists
   - descriptive or emotive vocabulary choices
   - connections with the reader.

   Explain how these techniques persuade and why you think they are effective at supporting his argument. **[5]**

Activity 2

Now read Extract 2 carefully and answer the following questions.

1. List five reasons that Menaker gives to support her argument that 'learning a new language is an absolute must'. **[5]**

2. The reader of this blog is likely to be someone considering enrolling on a language course. The techniques below are used in paragraphs 1 and 5. Explain how Menaker uses each one to make the tone appealing to the reader. You must quote one specific example for each of the following techniques:

    *   questions
    *   use of the pronoun 'we'
    *   positive language. **[3]**

3. Look at paragraphs 2–4 only. What language strategies does Menaker use to try to persuade someone to enrol on a foreign language course? Choose three examples and explain how they are effective. **[4]**

Activity 3

Now you are going to consider both extracts together.

1. Write three sentences to compare and contrast what the article and the blog say about reasons for learning a language. You need to make it clear which text you get your ideas from and use comparative vocabulary in your answer. **[4]**

2. Identify the genre, audience and purpose of each text. **[6]**

3. Explain how the language has been shaped by the differing genre, audience or purpose of the texts. Select one example from each extract. Include quotations from the texts in your explanation. **[2]**

Assessment

Writing

Learning objective

- To assess progress made against writing skills taught in this chapter

Introduction

Plan the following writing task carefully, using whatever means you think will be most effective. You might take your ideas and techniques from the texts on pages 162–163.

Your school is about to make a decision about whether taking a language at GCSE should be compulsory. Write a letter to your head teacher, giving your view.

Before you start writing, think carefully about:

- which side of the argument you will support
- what ideas and examples you will select to appeal to your audience
- what counter-arguments you might need to knock down
- other techniques explored in this chapter that might persuade your reader.

As you write, check:

- the accuracy of your spelling, punctuation and grammar
- the structure of your writing and paragraphing
- the tone for your audience and your choice of persuasive techniques
- that you are maintaining and supporting your line of argument.

 Writing Tip Keep the tone of your writing fairly formal. Start your letter with the head teacher's name 'Dear Mr/Mrs...' and end it 'Yours sincerely...' with your full name.

5 PEOPLE

In this chapter you will develop your ability to evaluate. We are constantly making assessments, judgements or evaluations. We evaluate our own behaviour and actions as well as making judgements about those of other people. We constantly evaluate and assess the world around us as it affects us, from the programmes we watch on TV and the books we read to the appearance of objects, people and places. In this chapter you will encounter a range of activities (reading, writing, and speaking and listening) which build on what you already know. This will help you to become more effective when using your evaluation skills.

The focus of this chapter is 'People'. The extracts you read will spotlight different types of people from both the past and the present. While you are reading and analysing the extracts, try to evaluate the appearance, behaviour and actions of the people within them and consider how you feel about them as a reader.

'The key to good decision-making is evaluating the available information…'
Emily Oster

'You never really understand a person until you consider things from his point of view – until you climb into his skin and walk around in it.'
Harper Lee, To Kill a Mockingbird

'True genius resides in the capacity for evaluation of uncertain, hazardous, and conflicting information.'
Winston Churchill

Fiction and non-fiction

This chapter focuses on a range of the text types you have already covered in previous chapters. People feature heavily in almost every type of written text. From some of the earliest religious texts to newspapers, magazines, journals and contemporary books, almost every text will include or be influenced by people.

This chapter includes extracts from both fiction and non-fiction. You may like to consider how the presentation of people is different in each form of writing. The skill of the fiction writer is to create believable characters that we can identify with, admire or even despise. The characters in non-fiction writing are, of course, real people. Does that mean they are always presented in an accurate way? Which do you prefer: people in fictional writing or people in non-fiction?

Reading texts

In this chapter you will cover a wide range of fiction and non-fiction texts. From reviews and newspaper articles to transcripts and posters, the texts will give you an opportunity to read widely while making evaluative judgements on what you have read.

Writing

This chapter will focus on some narrative writing techniques that you will find useful when producing your own narrative accounts. You will also have the opportunity to produce some lively and humorous transactional writing, particularly when writing to review.

Exam link

Exam relevance

In the exams you will be asked to read from a range of texts. The Component 1 exam will include questions about a fictional text and require you to complete some creative writing of your own. The Component 2 exam will include questions on two non-fiction texts: one from the 21st century and one from the 19th century. It will also require you to complete transactional/persuasive writing tasks of your own. The skills you use when evaluating the texts in the exams will depend on the task you are given and the content of the text. In this chapter you will:

- read and evaluate a range of different texts

- develop skills for the writing section of the exam

- consider how you can use evaluation skills in speaking and listening activities.

Exploring people

Learning objectives

- To explore the overall theme of evaluation
- To reflect on your own experiences of people

Key terms

Evaluate: to form an idea of the state or value of something

Impression: effect produced on the mind, ideas

Introduction

The theme of this chapter is 'People'. Most of us will encounter hundreds of people each day, though we will only interact or communicate with a small number of them. Some people can be hugely influential in our lives, persuading us to dress or act in a certain way. Some people will become lifelong friends, while others may only feature in our lives for a short period of time. Throughout this chapter you will be reflecting on and evaluating people and their actions. By reflecting on the people you meet every day, you will broaden your evaluation skills without even thinking about it.

If you checked the dictionary for a definition of 'people', it would tell you they are:

1. human beings in general
2. men, women and children belonging to a place or forming a group or social class.

This certainly gives us a starting point, but it doesn't tell us much about the complexities of people, their amazing and terrible capabilities or the emotional reactions they can evoke in others. These are some of the things that writers explore in their work.

Activity 1

1. Make a list of the first ten people who come into your mind.
2. Think about each of these people – write down any words or phrases (both positive and negative) that you would use to describe each one.
3. Choose three of the people on your list. Discuss with a partner what you think or feel about each of them.

Activity 2

Think about the word '**evaluate**'.

1. Make a list of other subjects where you might be asked to evaluate something.
2. What do you need to think about when you are evaluating something?
3. Write down your own definition of this word, then share your definition with a partner. Are your definitions similar? Adjust your definition as you like.

Activity 3

Look at the three images on the right. Have you seen any of these people before? Can you describe what each of them looks like? Write down any words or phrases you would use to describe the people pictured in them.

Image A

Image B

Image C

The language or words you chose to describe each person in the pictures will have been based on your first (or visual) **impression** of that person. When you approach a new text you may have an initial impression of the person or events described in that text. Once you have read the information you will have a closer understanding of the person or events and will have added to, or changed your first impressions. When you are writing about a text for your exam, it is important that you record a range of ideas in your answer and support them with evidence from the text.

Activity 4

Think about any recent TV programmes, films or news reports you have watched or any books you have read. All of these probably featured people in various different situations and scenarios. What was the first thing you noticed about the main person or character? Can you remember what they were wearing? What did they look like? How did they behave?

Design and complete a table like the one below to show your recent experiences of people, recording specifically your first impressions of each person. Think carefully about the words and phrases you choose to describe the people.

Source	Person encountered
BBC News	Female news presenter. Smartly dressed, eloquent, tried to give a balanced view of the events (does not give an opinion). Professional but relaxed.

People from the past

1 What does an evaluation involve?

Learning objectives

- To understand the meaning of the term 'evaluation'
- To consider why we evaluate

Introduction

This unit focuses on one of literature's most famous detectives. Sir Arthur Conan Doyle's fascinating stories about the world-famous detective Sherlock Holmes were written between 1891 and 1927, and remain hugely popular. Books, films and TV programmes are constantly being made about this super sleuth and his assistant Dr Watson. In this unit you will develop your evaluation skills using a wide range of texts, all focusing on Sherlock Holmes.

Essentially, an evaluation is a judgement of something or someone. If you are asked to evaluate something, you are being asked to engage with a text or topic and think carefully about what is happening and how that might make you feel.

Activity

The first Sherlock Holmes short stories were published as a series in a magazine called *The Strand*.

1. Spend ten seconds looking at the original *Strand* illustration of Sherlock Holmes and Dr Watson on this page. Write down your first impressions of Sherlock Holmes (the character on the right) based on this image.

2. Now look more closely at the picture and answer the following questions.

   a. How is he sitting? What does his posture suggest?

   b. What is he doing with his hands? Why is he doing this?

   c. Describe his face. Why does he look so intense/direct?

   d. Write down your impression of his clothing. Why is he dressed differently from Dr Watson?

Activity 2

In recent years many different actors have played Sherlock Holmes. The pictures below show three of them.

Image A

Image B

Image C

1. Compared to the original illustration of Sherlock Holmes on page 170, which image do you prefer, and why?

2. Choose one of the pictures. Write down as many adjectives and descriptive phrases that you can think of to describe the actor.

Throughout Activities 1 and 2 you have been asked to give your impressions and feelings about the images and you have been using a range of evaluation skills without even thinking, such as considering:

- what you like and dislike
- how the images compare to others
- your overall impressions.

Activity 3

Support

We use evaluation skills most of the time but rarely write down what we are thinking. Complete the following activity to help you evaluate a lesson at school.

Think about a really good lesson you have enjoyed at school. What made the lesson enjoyable? What did you learn? How was the lesson different from other lessons? What could you add to the lesson to make it even better?

Exam link

Straightforward evaluations will:
- give personal opinions
- show some understanding of the text
- give straightforward supporting evidence.

Confident evaluations will:
- give an overview of the text as a whole
- see patterns within the text
- probe and explore the text in detail
- include convincing and persuasive supporting evidence.

2 Evaluating thoughts and feelings

Learning objectives

- To explore your reactions to a piece of text
- To evaluate your reactions to a character within a text

Tip If you are asked to evaluate your thoughts and feelings, you can use the first person to help you frame your answer (*I think…, I feel…*). If you are asked to evaluate the character or writer's thoughts and feelings, you can use the third person to help you frame your answer (*He thinks…, She feels…*).

When evaluating a text you may be asked to give a personal response. You should track through a text and consider your thoughts and feelings at various points to enable you to give a balanced personal evaluation. You might be asked to consider how a character is thinking or feeling in an extract – you need to track through the extract, collecting evidence and considering what the character might be feeling at specific points.

Read the following extract from a Sherlock Holmes short story.

Extract from 'A Scandal in Bohemia' by Sir Arthur Conan Doyle

His rooms were brilliantly lit, and, even as I looked up, I saw his tall, spare figure pass twice in a dark silhouette[1] against the blind. He was pacing the room swiftly, eagerly, with his head sunk upon his chest and his hands clasped behind him. To me, who knew his every mood and habit, his attitude and manner told their own story. He was at work again. He had risen out of his drug-created dreams and was hot upon the scent of some new problem. I rang the bell and was shown up to the chamber which had formerly been in part my own.

His manner was not effusive[2]. It seldom[3] was; but he was glad, I think, to see me. With hardly a word spoken, but with a kindly eye, he waved me to an armchair, threw across his case of cigars, and indicated a spirit case and a gasogene[4] in the corner. Then he stood before the fire and looked me over in his singular introspective[5] fashion.

'Wedlock suits you,' he remarked. 'I think, Watson, that you have put on seven and a half pounds since I saw you.'

'Seven!' I answered.

'Indeed, I should have thought a little more. Just a trifle more, I fancy, Watson. And in practice again[6], I observe. You did not tell me that you intended to go into harness[7].'

[1] silhouette – a dark shadow seen against a light background
[2] effusive – making a great show of affection or enthusiasm
[3] seldom – rarely, not often
[4] gasogene – a device for creating fizzy water
[5] introspective – concentrating on your own thoughts and feelings
[6] in practice again – Holmes means Dr Watson is working as a doctor again
[7] harness – routine, everyday work

Activity 1

1. In the extract, Dr Watson has decided to visit Sherlock Holmes. To help you develop your ability to produce an **overview**, write down, in not more than 30 words, a summary of what happens in the extract.

2. With a partner, discuss your initial reactions to Sherlock Holmes. What type of person is he?

Key term

Overview: a general summary, explanation or outline of a situation

Activity 2

This activity will help you to build up your own thoughts about what type of person Sherlock Holmes is. Follow the steps below:

1. Go through the passage and highlight any phrases that you think give information about Sherlock Holmes. The first two have been done for you.

2. Write down the phrases you have selected in a table like the one below.

Evidence	What does this suggest?
'He was pacing the room'	He seems preoccupied or restless.
'head sunk upon his chest'	He seems dejected, troubled or deep in thought.

Activity 3

Use the table you completed in Activity 2 to help you answer the following question:

What are your thoughts and feelings about Sherlock Holmes?

To answer a question like this, you need to work through the extract in order (tracking the text), picking out any words and phrases that give you clues about his character. Cover the whole extract and do not repeat any ideas. Constantly ask yourself what you think and feel about him.

Support

The first few sentences have been done for you. Complete the answer using your own ideas and evidence.

> I think that Sherlock Holmes is a preoccupied or restless individual. 'He was pacing the room' suggests he could be trying to collect his thoughts or solve a problem. Sherlock Holmes' head is 'sunk upon his chest' and I feel that this suggests he is deep in thought or reflection.

Activity 4

Look at your answer and use three highlighter pens to indicate the following:

- evidence
- your explanation
- the words 'think' or 'feel'.

You should see a balance of these three bullet points in your answer to ensure your response is focused and clear. If it is not balanced, go back and adjust your writing.

3 Review writing

Learning objectives

- To explore the features of a review
- To plan a review

After watching a film or TV programme, reading a book or listening to a CD, you will have opinions about it. To capture these opinions, you can write a review. The purpose of a review is not only to write down our views and opinions in an evaluation, but to share them with other people who may wish to read about them.

A review is an evaluation. Reviews can consider books, articles, films, cars, buildings, art, fashion, restaurants, performances and many other products or services. It is important that a review is a commentary, not just a summary. You may like or dislike the thing you are reviewing, but you should always:

- state your opinions clearly
- give some supporting paragraphs
- come to a conclusion.

Activity 1

Below are the main features of a review. Read them carefully and put them in the correct order.

A

Give a short summary of the piece. This includes a description and an idea of the purpose.

B

In addition to analysing, a review often suggests whether or not the reader will appreciate it.

C

Write down the title or name of the thing you wish to review.

D

Offer a critical assessment (your evaluation). This should include your reactions, whether or not the piece was effective or persuasive, and your personal opinions.

Activity 2

When producing professional reviews for newspapers, magazines or online forums, writers think carefully about the language they select. To maximize the impact of their review or evaluation, a writer will try to use a range of different persuasive techniques (you have already studied many of these in this book). Match each technique in the list below to its definition.

Humour

Puns

Assertive point of view

Compare or contrast

Direct appeal

A 'You' is often used to encourage the reader to watch or read it

B To be clear and direct in your opinions

C Comparisons with other films or books are used to make it sound better or worse

D Something amusing or comical

E Humorous use of words or a play on words

Activity 3

Read the film review below and answer the following questions.

1. The reviewer refers to him as 'Swashbuckling Sherlock'. What does this imply about the character?

2. Highlight any persuasive techniques you can find in the review. Why do you think the writer chose to use persuasive techniques?

3. Look at the comparison used for the two Sherlock characters (you may wish to use a dictionary to work out what these words mean): Conan Doyle – 'complex cerebral sleuth' and Guy Ritchie – 'bare-knuckle fighter'.

   a. What is the effect of the comparison?

   b. What does it suggest about Ritchie's Holmes compared to Conan Doyle's original?

4. Can you find any other comparisons? What effect do they have?

5. The writer tells us that the Holmes in the film is 'more indebted to comic strips'. What does this mean?

6. Why does the writer tell us that the adventure is 'enjoyably silly'?

7. What does the writer mean by the comment 'The story is of little importance'?

LATESTRELEASES

Swashbuckling Sherlock: Robert Downey Jr returns as a gun-toting, fist-fighting Sherlock Holmes and he's terrific fun

Sherlock Holmes: A Game of Shadows (12A)

Admirers of Sir Arthur Conan Doyle's complex, cerebral[1] sleuth[2] should stay away from Guy Ritchie's second film about a bare-knuckle fighter of the same name, played by Robert Downey Jr as a smart-alec spoiling for a fight.

The film's villain, Moriarty, and his climactic[3] fight with Holmes are all that remain of Conan Doyle's short story, 'The Final Problem'.

Downey's version of the detective is essentially Sherlock Hams, a swashbuckling eccentric[4], none-too-distantly related to Johnny Depp's Captain Jack Sparrow from the *Pirates Of The Caribbean* films.

But though he is more indebted[5] to comic strips than Conan Doyle, his new adventure is an enjoyably silly romp[6]. The story is of little importance…

Verdict: Action and fun

[1] cerebral – intellectual or linked to the brain
[2] sleuth – detective
[3] climactic – forming an exciting resolution or climax
[4] eccentric – slightly strange or unconventional
[5] indebted – owing gratitude to someone
[6] romp – rough and lively play

Look at the way the writer blends facts about the film with their views about the actors and the storyline. This is an effective technique to use when producing a review because readers of reviews like to read a balance of fact and opinion.

Follow these steps to plan your own review.

1. Write down the title of a story you have read or a film you have watched.

2. Briefly describe the main action. A flowchart might help you recall the order of events.

3. Start to evaluate the characters, storyline, special effects and ending (or anything that was important to you). Spider diagrams can be helpful when you are noting down detail about a lot of different elements.

4. Consider the audience. Who will enjoy it (or not)?

5. Note down your general conclusions.

Support

1. Look at step 3. Make a list of any words you would like to use to help you state your opinions about the book or film.

2. Write a paragraph that uses these words and gives an evaluation of what you have watched or read.

Stretch

Look at step 3. Think carefully about the characters, storyline, costumes, soundtrack and anything else notable about the book or film. Write two paragraphs, giving a clear evaluation of what you have watched or read.

Tip Remember: it is perfectly acceptable to write a review about something you absolutely detest. Make sure you give direct and honest opinions about it, but back these up with reasons. You must explain why a film is awful if that's what you believe.

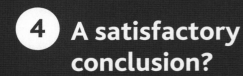

4 A satisfactory conclusion?

Learning objectives

- To explore reactions to a text
- To evaluate the effect of a concluding passage

When you reach the end of a book or a film, you may choose to spend a few minutes thinking about what you have just read or watched. Good readers should be able to reflect on what they have read and evaluate it. Sometimes you might be asked to read a section of text or the concluding paragraph, and evaluate how effective you found it.

Activity 1

Think about the books you have read or the films you have watched; you will have experienced a range of different endings, some of which you might use as ideas for your own writing.

1. What is your favourite book or film? How does it end? With a partner, discuss the ending in detail and try to explain why you enjoyed it.

2. With a partner, look at the following list of possible endings. Write down a brief definition for each of them.

   a. Cliffhanger

   b. Resolution

   c. Circular or 'tie back' ending

   d. Fairy-tale ending

   e. The sermon

Sir Arthur Conan Doyle invented a deadly enemy, Moriarty, to kill off Holmes. Doyle felt that the success and popularity of Holmes was distracting the world from his other achievements. In 'The Final Problem', Moriarty made his most significant appearance, falling with Sherlock Holmes to a watery grave at Switzerland's Reichenbach Falls. The extract below describes Dr Watson exploring the area of his friend's death.

Extract from 'The Final Problem' by Sir Arthur Conan Doyle

I stood for a minute or two to collect myself, for I was dazed with the horror of the thing. Then I began to think of Holmes's own methods and to try to practise them in reading this tragedy. It was, alas, only too easy to do. During our conversation we had not gone to the end of the path, and the Alpine-stock marked the place where we had stood. The blackish soil is kept forever soft by the incessant drift of spray, and a bird would leave its tread upon it. Two lines of footmarks were clearly marked along the farther end of the path, both leading away from me. There were none returning. A few yards from the end the soil was all ploughed up into a patch of mud, and the branches and ferns which fringed the chasm were torn and bedraggled. I lay upon my face and peered over with the spray spouting up all around me. It had darkened since I left, and now I could only see here and there the glistening of moisture upon the black walls, and far away down at the end of the shaft the gleam of the broken water. I shouted; but only the same half-human cry of the fall was borne back to my ears. [...]

An examination by experts leaves little doubt that a personal contest between the two men ended, as it could hardly fail to end in such a situation, in their reeling over, locked in each other's arms. Any attempt at recovering the bodies was absolutely hopeless, and there, deep down in that dreadful caldron of swirling water and seething foam, will lie for all time the most dangerous criminal and the foremost champion of the law of their generation.

Activity 2

Read this sample exam question:

> **What do you think and feel about these lines as an ending to the passage?**

You may be asked to evaluate the ending of an extract or a story in an exam. You need to go through the indicated section and think carefully about the following:

- What happens?
- Why does it happen?
- How do you feel about it?
- What does the writer do to manipulate your feelings?
- How successful is the ending? (If appropriate, reflect back on the rest of the story.)

With a partner, discuss the questions above and apply them to the extract from 'The Final Problem'. Write down two or three of your initial responses to each of these questions.

Support

Look at the highlighted sections in the extract. They are evidence that something dramatic has taken place in the story. Choose four of these from across the extract and write them down. Next to each piece of evidence, write down briefly:

- what you think has happened
- what the evidence adds to the ending and why (e.g. 'It adds tension because…').

Stretch

The highlighted sections in the extract are evidence that something dramatic has taken place. Write down each piece of evidence and then evaluate its effect, considering how the evidence contributes to the ending. For example:

'I was dazed with the horror of the thing': this word 'dazed' implies that Watson is truly shocked by what has happened and the 'horror' confirms that something dreadful has happened. Readers share Watson's fears as they realize that this could be the end of Sherlock Holmes.

Tip Refer back to the question to keep your answer focused.

5 Speculation and fact

Learning objectives

- To develop your skills of speculation
- To explore a character and their behaviour
- To develop speaking and listening skills

Some texts focus almost solely on one character. If you are given a text like this you will need to carry out a detailed character evaluation. In addition to stating the obvious things about the character, you will need to probe the text so you can make some informed judgements about their actions and appearance.

Activity 1

Look at the picture of the actor below who is playing a teenage Sherlock Holmes. Use the questions around the picture to help you make some speculations.

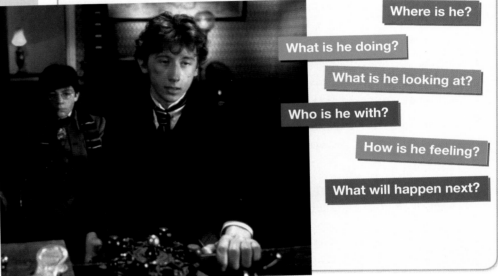

Where is he?

What is he doing?

What is he looking at?

Who is he with?

How is he feeling?

What will happen next?

Mycroft is Sherlock Holmes' older brother. In this extract, Mycroft has just taken the young Sherlock to their uncle's house for the summer.

Extract from 'Death Cloud' by Andy Lane

He turned towards Sherlock, and there was a look in his eyes that was part sympathy, part brotherly love and part warning. 'Take care, Sherlock,' he said. 'I will certainly be back to return you to school at the end of the holidays, and if I can I will visit in the meantime. Be good, and take the opportunity to explore the local area. I believe that Uncle Sherrinford has an exceptional library. Ask him if you can take advantage of the accumulated wisdom it contains. I will leave my contact details with Mrs Eglantine – if you need me, send me a telegram or write a letter.' He reached out and put a comforting hand on Sherlock's shoulder. 'These are good people,' he said, quietly enough that Mrs Eglantine couldn't hear him, 'but, like everyone in the Holmes family, they have their eccentricities. Be aware, and take care not to upset them. Write to me when you get a moment. And remember – this is not the rest of your life. This is just for a couple of months. Be brave.' He squeezed Sherlock's shoulder.

Sherlock felt a bubble of anger and frustration forcing its way up his throat and choked it back. He didn't want Mycroft to see him react, and he didn't want to start his time at Holmes Manor badly. Whatever he did over the next few minutes would set the tone for the rest of his stay.

He stuck out his hand. Mycroft moved his own hand off Sherlock's shoulder and took it, smiling warmly. 'Goodbye,' Sherlock said in as level a tone as he could manage. 'Give my love to Mother, and to Charlotte. And if you hear anything of Father, let me know.'

Activity 2

1. In the extract, Mycroft behaves carefully and deliberately as though he is warning Sherlock. Highlight any words or phrases that suggest Mycroft has concerns about leaving his younger brother.

2. Highlight any words or phrases that suggest how Sherlock is feeling about being left.

3. What does Mycroft mean when he says, 'they have their eccentricities'?

Activity 3

Work with a partner. Imagine you are being taken to visit a distant relative you have never met before. On the journey there, your older brother tells you that you will be staying for the whole summer.

1. Decide with your partner who is the older brother and who is younger. Spend five minutes on your own, jotting down some ideas. Think about:
   - how the conversation will start
   - the tone you will use and how this might vary
   - what you will say to one another
   - the body language/body position you will adopt when you are speaking
   - how you will react to each other
   - the types of questions you will ask
   - how the conversation will end.

   Thinking about these things will help you to act and answer questions in character.

2. Now have the conversation. Try not to refer to your notes too much as this will interrupt the flow of the conversation. Listen to what your partner says and try to respond spontaneously but in character, using your preparation to shape your answers and questions.

Progress check

You are going to carry out some peer-assessment on Activity 3. With your partner, judge your performance based on the following criteria:

- If things went well, write down particular examples of what worked.
- If you found this a challenging activity, try to note down what happened; it will help you to understand how you could do it differently next time. For example, it can be difficult to respond 'on your feet' to what the other character said. Next time, you could try predicting what the other character might say and preparing some responses.

What did we do?	Very good – we did well at this.	OK – we were happy but need more practice.	We struggled with the activity.
Managed to sustain the conversation			
Listened closely to each other and responded thoughtfully			
Challenged each other in a variety of ways			
Each referred to things the other said throughout the conversation			

People today

6 How writing presents achievement

Learning objectives

- To consider what achievement is
- To evaluate the characteristics of achievers

Introduction

In this unit you will look at people from across society and consider how their achievements are presented, and how they can be evaluated. You will continue to evaluate the impact of texts and the people in them while developing your skills in reading, writing, and speaking and listening.

What is **achievement**? We can't always remember our first taste of achievement – our first steps as babies or learning to feed ourselves. For some babies, simply leaving hospital after being born prematurely is an achievement. As we move through life, achievements can be small (making it to school on time) or large (academic success, developing sporting skills, or such things as overcoming emotional and physical barriers).

What do you think are achievements? Not everyone agrees on the same things. As you get older, your perception of what this is will also change. This will often depend on what an individual has done or achieved either for themselves or for the good of society.

Activity 1

1. What is achievement? Can any kind of success be an achievement?
2. The basketball player and coach, John Wooden, said, 'Never mistake activity for achievement'. Do you agree with him? Make a list of the kinds of thing you feel are achievements.
3. List three people who you feel have achieved something important.
4. What have these people done or achieved? Why do you admire them?

You thought about what makes someone a hero or heroine in Chapter 3. Often, achievements display an element of heroism. You don't have to be a hero to achieve something, but can you be a hero without achievement?

Activity 2

In small groups, discuss this question:

Can you be a hero without achievement?

Listen carefully to the arguments each person in your group makes; you need to evaluate each one and decide whether you agree with it, and if not, express why you don't agree.

Activity 3

1. Look at Image A. What does this picture suggest about the firefighters?

2. Think about the way they are sitting. What does their posture suggest?

3. Look closely at their faces. What do you learn by the way they look?

4. Look at Image B. Why do you think the suit is empty?

5. Look at the writing at the top of the advert. Why does the writer use the phrase 'new suit'? What do you normally associate with a 'new suit'? Why is this effective?

Image B

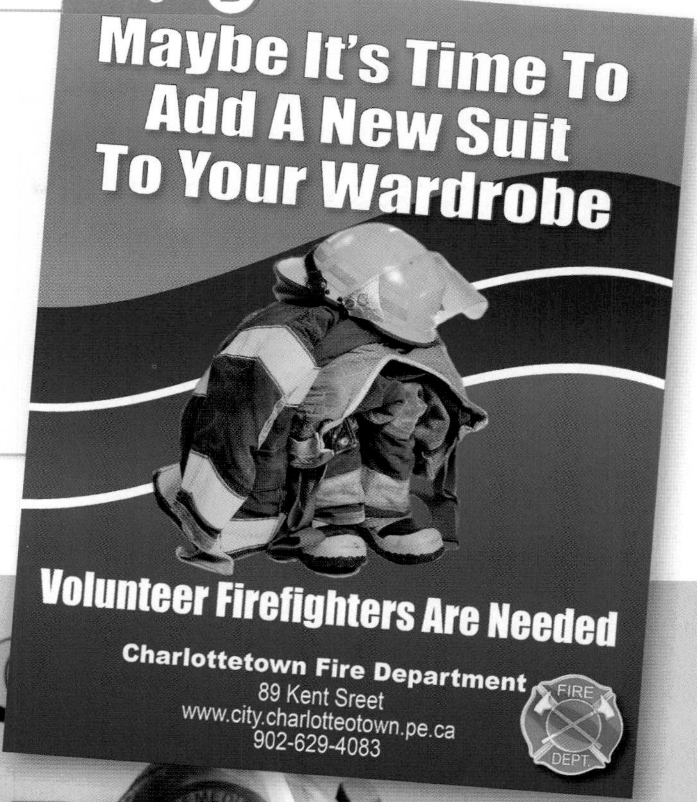

Maybe It's Time To Add A New Suit To Your Wardrobe

Volunteer Firefighters Are Needed

Charlottetown Fire Department
89 Kent Sreet
www.city.charlotteotown.pe.ca
902-629-4083

Image A

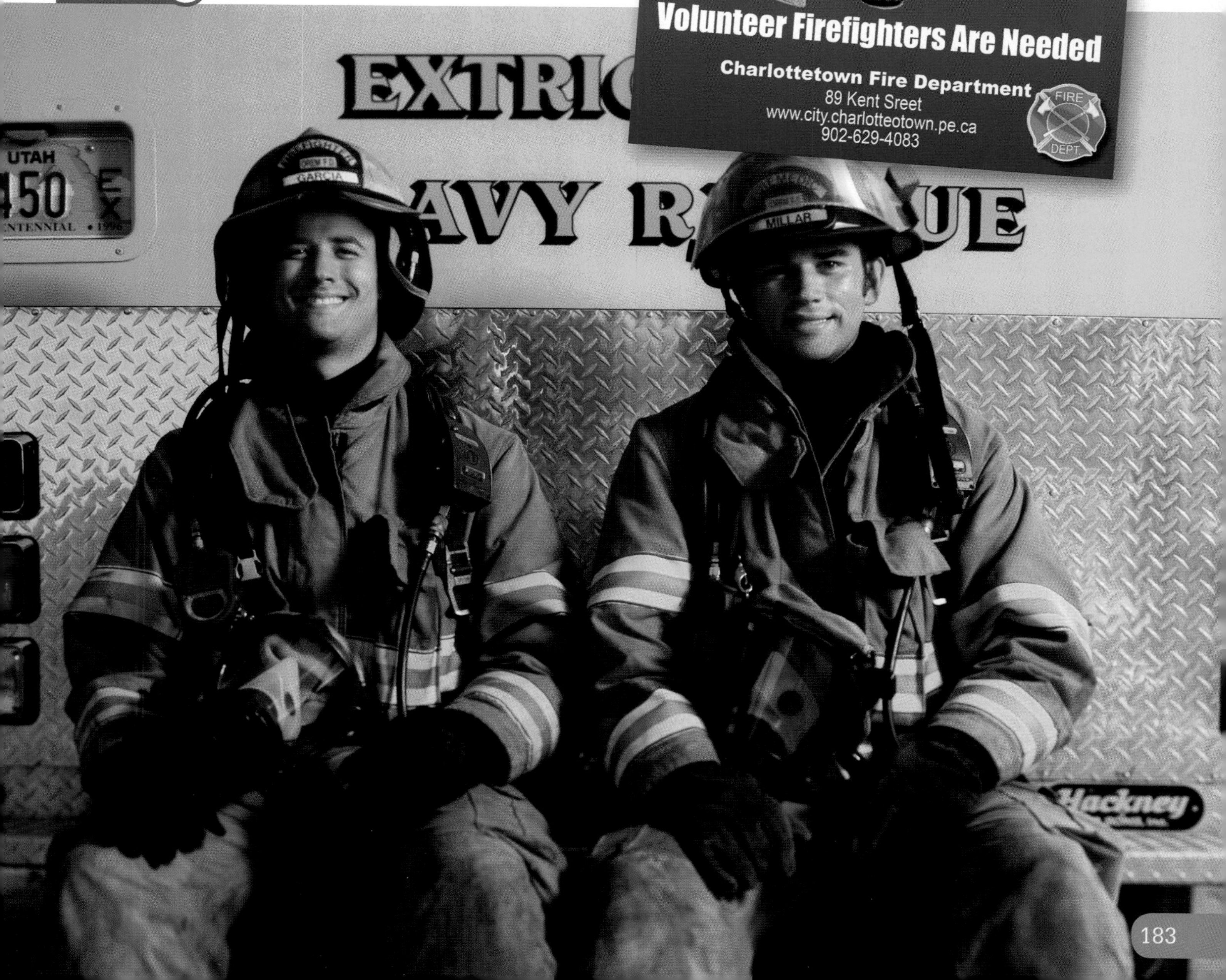

Read the following article about Rosie Chisnell, a nurse. As you read, keep in mind the ideas about achievement you discussed in Activity 1.

'Other nurses clock on and off – she is a constant': Meet Rosie, the unsung hero of a nurse who fights for sick children's lives as if she was their mother

There was never any question over what Claire Rumble would call her daughter when she was born last month. It was always going to be Rosie, the name of the specialist nurse who looked after her big brother Louis during his three-and-a-half year battle with leukaemia. [...]

The family, who live in Hemel Hempstead, in Hertfordshire, first met Rosie in September 2009, after a terrifying five days when Louis became suddenly and desperately ill.

'One day he was fine, playing with his twin sister Grace, then suddenly he stopped eating, was pale, exhausted and crying through the night for no apparent reason,' recalls Claire. 'When angry purple bruises appeared all over his body we rushed him to hospital.'

Just 12 hours after a barrage of tests at Watford General Hospital doctors revealed the shocking diagnosis: the 19-month-old had leukaemia. 'You can't imagine what being told your son has cancer feels like,' says Claire. 'The world just stops.'

As the hospital's paediatric oncology nurse, Rosie, 56, was there at the diagnosis. 'For the next two hours Rosie sat with us explaining everything in great depth, fielding our questions and laying everything out clearly and honestly.' [...]

From day one the Rumble family had her mobile number. 'Children aren't ill nine to five, Monday to Friday,' explains Rosie. 'I would hate to think something might happen and a family couldn't get hold of me.'

Claire and James, a 37-year-old aircraft engineer, frequently had to call Rosie late at night when Louis developed croup – a fierce barking cough – because of his weak immune system. [...]

Once Louis accidentally pulled out his nasogastric tube – a tube inserted via the nose into the stomach to administer medication. Unfortunately, it was on a weekend when Rosie wasn't working, but she knew putting it back would be a traumatic experience for a child, so dropped everything and drove the 40 minutes from home to the hospital to do the procedure herself. [...]

The next day Rosie called to say not to take Louis to hospital as she was coming to their house with the equipment to teach Claire how to administer the intravenous antibiotics at home.

'I couldn't believe anyone could be so kind. She arrived with a great crate of equipment and stayed until almost midnight, showing me exactly how it all worked; the pump, the syringes, everything.

'Louis's face lights up when he sees her and when he was in hospital if he heard her heels click-clacking down the corridor he would sit up in bed. [...]

'For a parent, you can't underestimate the impact of having someone like Rosie around. I'd have spent days stewing over Louis's health, endlessly worrying, but Rosie being just a phone call away

meant I was less anxious and felt more in control. She helped me and James to focus on the practicalities of his treatment and be better parents.'

So what drives this kind of dedication? 'It's the children,' Rosie explains. 'They're a model to us all. They just get on with it, the good and the bad. If I can improve their lives, or their families', even a bit, I'm happy.

'I know in this job I can make a difference. I've always loved children and got on with them easily and even as a little girl knew I wanted to be a nurse.' [...]

Rosie is adamant that she wouldn't be able to provide such high standards of care without the help of her colleagues. 'I couldn't be nearly so flexible without a strong team behind me.'

One member of that team is Vasanta Nanduri, a consultant paediatric oncologist who has worked with Rosie for the last 18 years. She says: 'She's my right hand, a great friend with far too much energy and someone I trust implicitly.

'But it's her knowledge and dedication to the children which is so impressive. She works out of hours, late into the night. She rarely takes a holiday, even though we try to make her. If she does, she writes 50-page handover notes. She's a real inspiration. Everyone on the ward looks up to her.'

Sentiments echoed by Claire. 'It will be a sad day when Rosie retires and I feel sorry for the families who won't get to meet her. We felt lucky every day that she was around and now we'll always be reminded of her kindness by baby Rosie.'

Heroic: Nurse Rosie Chisnell (right) has been nominated for a Health Hero Award by Claire Rumble (left)

Activity

In this activity you are going to use your reading skills to write an evaluation of Rosie Chisnell. Follow the checklist to help you write an answer to the question:

What has Rosie Chisnell achieved?

1. Read through the text, highlighting any words and phrases that show the following:

    a. what she has achieved for herself

    b. what she has achieved for other people

    c. how other people feel about her.

2. Look at the words and phrases. Think about these and explain why you think something has been achieved. You might like to annotate the text so you don't forget your ideas.

3. Write up your answer, one word/phrase at a time. Make sure you refer to the question so you are continually focused on what has been achieved. Try to keep each explanation focused, brief and clear.

> ### Support
>
> On pages 182–185 you have focused on firefighters and a nurse as people who have achieved. Can you think of any other groups of people whose achievements help to save the lives of others? Make a list of the qualities that these people need to help them with their work.

> ### Stretch
>
> You have been asked to help a design team to plan a poster encouraging people at school or college to take up a career as a doctor, nurse or carer. You will need to consider the following:
>
> *   how you could persuade young people to take up a career as a nurse, doctor or carer
> *   the qualities these people need to offer
> *   the type of picture/graphics you would use in the appeal
> *   the persuasive techniques you would use to appeal to your target audience.
>
> Draw a rough plan of your poster. You do not need to draw any pictures – a description of the picture will suffice. Plan carefully the words you would include to persuade people to take an interest in your poster.

7 Presentation skills

Learning objectives

- To explore the verbal and non-verbal techniques used during a presentation
- To plan a presentation and consider how to deliver it

Giving a presentation to an audience, large or small, can be a terrifying experience. Presenters worry about many things including how people will respond to them, whether they will be heard, what questions will be asked, how they will manage to remember everything and so on. To ensure a presentation goes well, you need to think about two main things:

- What am I going to say?
- How can I present myself effectively?

Activity 1

Imagine you have been asked to give a presentation about the achievements of your school or college. Follow the steps below to help you plan what you will say.

What do you want to include? Before you start, it is a good idea to note down all the things you would like to talk about.

1. Complete a mind map or other planning tool with a partner to show the areas you would like to cover in your presentation.

Prioritizing your information. Once you have decided on your main areas, you need to work out how you will sequence them. Think about which points are your key ideas, as you might like to place them at strategic points in your presentation.

2. Take the items from your plan and bullet point them in the order you would like to talk about them.

What are your key messages? Some students like to highlight their key messages under each of their bullet points to prompt them when they are talking. Some students like to make a list of key words to use when they are talking.

3. Under each bullet point add your key words and phrases. Try to avoid writing down complete sentences or you may end up just reading them from the sheet and losing fluency and effective non-verbal techniques.

Techniques to engage your audience. Once you have a rough plan for your speech you can go back through and give some consideration to the techniques you would like to include to engage your audience.

4. Look at your rough plan to see where you can improve your language and add persuasive techniques. Rhetorical questions and repetition are particularly effective when delivering a speech (if used sparingly) but remind yourself of other persuasive techniques on pages 156–157.

Final version. Now that you have your plan you need to produce a neater version. If your plan is very untidy you will struggle to use it effectively during your presentation.

5. Write up your plan either on cue cards or your tablet, paper or computer – whichever is best for you.

Rehearsal. Now you need to rehearse your speech!

Here is the start of a student's plan for this activity. You can use it to help you get started.

1. What does achievement mean in my school? What have students achieved?

2. Which are most important?
   • Sport because we're a specialist school and students come here because of that
   • Academic
   • Charity

3. Most important points for achievement in each area:
   • Sport: specialist school; unbeaten record inter-school football; students come here because of sports department
   • Academic: good GCSE results; improved A-Level results; new science equipment to promote achievement
   • Charity: link to local community; sharing and caring; voluntary work; personal skills
   REMEMBER: make sure audience aware of my key messages. Use headings to make them stand out?

4. Which techniques will engage the audience?
   • Address audience directly, make them feel they want to come to our school
   • Use positive vocabulary
   • Build feeling of positivity from the start – with rhetorical Q 'Is there anything West Stanton Academy doesn't know about achievement?'

> **Tip** It is a good idea to rehearse your presentation before presenting to an audience. Always speak out loud when rehearsing so you can practise when you will pause and which words you will emphasize.

Non-verbal features are all the non-talking things that accompany your presentation. They include the way you stand, the gestures you might make and the expressions on your face. Think about the presentations you have seen at school or interviews on the TV and what the speakers do to engage their audience.

Activity 2

1. Watch a TV or online news broadcast. Study the news reporter and take notes on what they do while they are talking. Record your findings in a table like the one below.

Facial expressions	Body movement	Hand movement	Props used

2. Think carefully about the news reporter. How did they emphasize a point using non-verbal features?
3. Did you find it easy to concentrate on what they were saying? Why?
4. How effective was the news reporter in engaging an audience?

Activity 3

Look at the transcript of an award speech below. In it, Declan Donnelly gives an acceptance speech for a surprise award marking his and Anthony McPartlin's 25 years of achievement in TV.

National Television Landmark Award 2013 Transcript

Declan Donnelly: This is kind of crazy and a bit bizarre but em, it's just the weirdest, weirdest thing ever.

There's so many people that we should thank for helping us in the past 25 years since we started when we were er eleven years old, um, when we got our first jobs, mine on *Byker Grove* and Ant's on *Why Don't You* as part of the Newcastle gang. There's hundreds of people that we've worked with and they've helped us and have taught us, er, everything we know and, we couldn't go into thanking every single person but every single person has put us on that journey and has put us here today. [...]

Erm, but it's just amazing. Thank you to, um, ITV, to James Grant, to everybody, um, that we've worked with from *Byker Grove* to our early days, erm, our first prime time job on the BBC, on *Friends Like These*. Thank you for that, erm, and for everybody we've ever worked with who has taught us, who has informed us, who contributed to who we are now, erm, but, but and everybody who featured there. But most importantly I think, you know, neither of us would be here if it wasn't for each other. So, ah.

Thank you so much, so, so much. Thank you everybody. Good night.

Award speeches are often unscripted. The speakers are often very emotional and have to give a speech in front of a large audience with no notes.

Activity 4

1. Look at the speech above. Do you think the speech is effective?

2. What do you notice about the speaker's use of language and grammar?

3. What would you change if you had to improve this speech? Use the steps in the plan on page 186 to make sure you consider every element.

8 Evaluating a newspaper article

Learning objective

- To evaluate a newspaper article and consider the effect it has on a reader

When you evaluate a text that has been written about a person, it is important that you understand exactly why the article was written about them. The text below was written about Laura Trott before she became an Olympic champion. Laura was interviewed by *The Guardian* newspaper and, as the title of the article suggests, she was determined to win a gold medal.

Laura Trott sick to the stomach in pursuit of 2012 glory

The Great Britain cyclist tells Donald McRae of the lengths she will go to in her bid for two gold medals

'I love the pain,' Laura Trott says, opening her eyes wide as she imagines the hurt that will accompany her pursuit of at least one gold medal at the Olympic velodrome this summer. 'Everyone goes on about the lactic burn and all that. They talk about the weird feeling you get in your mouth when the pain is bad – it tastes like blood – but I love that feeling. That's just me.'

Trott emits one of many infectious laughs, and then hammers home her point. 'Coping with that pain is the difference between winning and losing,' the teenage cyclist says as she prepares for a World Cup event in London later this month. 'You know it's going to [...] get you at some point in a race. But you can't exactly stop, can you? The important thing is to ride through the pain. I come out the other side and I'm going a heck of a lot better then.'

She is at her most interesting when detailing the physical trials she has survived in her short life. Born with a collapsed lung, which threatened her life, Trott then overcame asthma while continuing to struggle with an ailment that means she vomits after almost every race and serious training session. [...]

Trott [...] describes what happens to her on the track. 'They've given me some tablets to calm it down because I have such a high acid lining in my stomach. Whenever I tense, dead hard, it pushes all the acid up and makes me throw up. I've been throwing up since I was 10. As soon as I stop I can't control it for long. The worst was at the [2010] Commonwealth Games. It was on telly, wasn't it? Me being sick in a bucket.' She covers her face in mock embarrassment. 'But the tablets are working. I did a sprint the other day and didn't throw up afterwards for the first time in years.' [...]

The Olympics might see Trott emerge as one of the most distinctive faces in British sport – and it's easy to imagine the country going crazy about her with a couple of medals around her neck. 'I do think about how different life will be afterwards,' she says before a small smile breaks into another riotous laugh. 'But, right now, I'd better focus on winning the [...] thing!'

Activity 1

1. Why do you think *The Guardian* chose to write an article about Laura Trott?

2. To be able to analyse and evaluate a text, you need to understand what it is about. Write down no more than five words to summarize each paragraph. For example:

    1. enjoys the pain of competition

3. List the problems Laura has faced in her life.

4. What do you think drives her to win?

5. Trott seems light-hearted and fun during the interview. Make a list of any words that suggest this.

Exam link

Remember to analyse each reading question very carefully in the exam before you begin your answer. Ask yourself what you will need to do in order to answer the question. How will you structure your answer and what will you include? Remember to consider the number of marks available in the time allocated when working out how long to spend on each answer.

Activity 2

Using the article for reference, answer the question:

What are your thoughts and feelings about Laura Trott and her achievements?

Support

Use the table below to help you to plan an answer to the question. Think carefully about the answers you gave in response to Activity 1 as these will help you to cover a wide range of different areas in your answer. Try to cover the whole text. Give yourself ten minutes to complete your plan.

10 mins

What are your thoughts and feelings?	Evidence
She enjoys pushing her body to the limit…	'I love the pain'

Stretch

1. Use the skills you have developed throughout this book to answer the exam-style question above. Remember to support your answer with evidence from the text. You should spend no longer than 15 minutes writing up your answer.

15 mins

2. When you have written your answer, spend 5 minutes checking it against the following assessment criteria. If you have missed anything, annotate your answer in a different colour:

    *   I have taken evidence from across the text.

    *   I have supported each piece of evidence with an explanation as to how it makes me feel.

    *   I have covered a range of different aspects of Laura Trott's personality, background and achievements.

    *   I have tried to vary the vocabulary I have used in my answer.

9 Commonly confused words

Learning objectives

- To check your use of homophones
- To produce a personalized list of spellings to revise

Tip Dialect can cause errors that come across in writing. Some students may use *are* instead of *our*, while others use *a* instead of *I*. Although these errors might seem very minor they will affect the mark you are awarded in your exam.

When you are producing a piece of writing it is important that you try to make your work as accurate and as clear as possible. Remember, 20% of your whole GCSE grade will come from the vocabulary you choose, the way you structure sentences and the accuracy of your spelling and punctuation. Many GCSE students make careless errors with the selection and spelling of simple words, especially homophones. In this section, you will have the opportunity to check your knowledge of some of these commonly confused words and put them right.

Activity 1

Below are some homophones that are most commonly confused. Go through the list and write a sentence with each one in. If you do not know the difference, look them up in a dictionary or ask your teacher.

- affect/effect
- their/there/they're
- where/were
- of/off
- to/too/two
- practise/practice

Activity 2

Look at the passage below. The writer has used many incorrect words. See if you can spot all the errors and correct them.

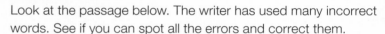

Jake and I had bin an item for months now. I was in every top set at school, he was struggling to get bye. I tried to help him as much as I could – staying in two revise and sharing my notes but it wasn't doing him any good.

One night while we where having a brake from are studies, he came up with a plan. 'Nobody collects in mobile devises in the exam and their are hardly any invigilators checking up on us,' he said. 'How about I use my phone to text you for advise?' Of coarse it was a huge risk but I wanted to help.

On the morning of the exam I felt sick. Mum tried to make me feel better. 'You have a flare for these things. You're dad and I are so proud.' I forced a smile. How could I except her compliment in this situation?

Halfway threw the exam I felt my pocket vibrate. I past my hand over my pocket but couldn't do it. Again and again I felt my pocket shake, it was having a dreadful affect on me. I was shaking and sweating and could bearly hold my pen. Five minutes to go. I couldn't bare it any longer. No one was watching. I slowly put my hand into my pocket. My fingers touched the cold metal screen but before I could take it out a hand clenched my shoulder. 'Can you please stand up Miss Jones?'

Activity 3

There are a number of common spelling errors that can be found in students' work. Look at the passage below and see how many spelling errors you can detect. Copy out the text, correcting all of the errors.

SPAG

Tip Over the coming months, make a list of the spelling errors that you make. You might like to display it somewhere where you will constantly see it to help you remember the correct spellings.

When using a computer you also need to take care, especially when using a spell-checker. If you are not careful you might select the wrong correction and completely change the meaning of what you write.

The que was enormous, like a huge snake it rapped itself around the building and dissappeared into the distance. There were allready alot of exited people standing with their family and freinds. It was quiet embarasing on this ocassion to be standing on my own. Choas broke out to my write where two women were having a viscious arguement about who would sucseed in the race to get to the shoe isle.

A couple at the back of the queue were stretching their muscles as though warming up for excercise. Standing seperately from his partner, the man clearly felt it nessessary to prepare for the exertions a head. His partner was having grate difficultie keeping her face strait as she copied his moves.

Suddenly the enviroment became more hostile. One woman began to remove her jewelry as she readied herself for the compitition. As I looked across at the other competitors, I sincerley began to wish I had stayed in bed. This was truely aweful. With a deep breathe, I turned and walked away.

People like you

10 Humour in evaluation

Learning objectives

- To explore the different types of humour
- To plan a piece of amusing evaluative writing

Introduction

This final unit in the chapter will give you the opportunity to reflect on and evaluate yourself, after considering how other writers write about themselves. You will also consider the role of humour for effect.

You will now explore different types of humour. Humour can make us laugh out loud, but depending on the type of humour it can also make us slightly uncomfortable. It can make us reflect on our own behaviour or it can lift our spirits.

Activity 1

Make a list of the things that make you laugh. Are there any specific people who you find amusing? Do any specific situations amuse you?

Activity 2

There are many different types of humour. Can you match the definition to the type of humour?

Anecdote	**A** A remark that seems to be praising someone or something but is really taunting or cutting – it can be used to hurt or offend, or for comic effect
Parody	
Sarcasm	
Irony	**B** The use of words where the meaning is the opposite of their usual meaning or what is expected to happen
Farce	
	C A short entertaining story
	D An imitation of something – particularly literature or a film – that is meant to make fun of it
	E Something that is intended to be seen as ridiculous, particularly a comedy based on an unlikely situation

Writers use a range of techniques to make anecdotes about relatively mundane events and these often sound very comical. People often **exaggerate** to make the incident seem even more humorous.

Activity 3

Think about an event, book or story that has made you laugh.

- What happened in the moments leading up to the amusing incident?
- Who was there?

- What happened before the incident?
- What happened during the incident?
- What were people's reactions?

In the following extract, comic writer Stuart Maconie writes about a childhood trip to Blackpool. Look at the annotations to see how he gives some specific details.

The writer *casually* suggests he was in danger.

The writer uses unusual vocabulary to describe usual people.

This means bizarre and is blunt.

Again, a blunt description.

Seems an extreme treatment.

Extract from *Pies and Prejudice* by Stuart Maconie

Blackpool is one of my earliest memories. [...] Working-class Lancastrians go or at least went to Blackpool so often and so regularly – for day trips, holidays, stag dos – that it's impossible to date accurately when my first trip was. The mid-sixties I imagine. Probably in a romper suit and on reins, always being likely to stray under a passing tram to Cleveleys.

I remember my first proper holiday there in an abstract way, anyway. We were with my Auntie Mollie and Uncle Cliff and Cousin Steven. The boarding house was full of Scottish people. They were the first Scots I'd ever met and seemed tremendously exotic creatures to me, with their milky skins, freckles, outlandish accents, incendiary ginger hair and a massive capacity for sticky orange fizzy pop that tasted like metal. One of them was a fat boy of about twelve who got so sunburned that he spent the rest of the week in bandages and cotton wool. Sotto voce, people were sympathetic but they did say it was his own fault. What with his skin and everything.

The writer gives unusual extra details, e.g. clothing.

The writer uses proper nouns to give clear details.

This means flammable and is not a description we expect.

Funny description for a well-known drink – Irn Bru.

Activity 4

Think of a place that you know well. You are going to write a lively and humorous guide to the area, featuring yourself. To help you write your guide, use the spider diagram on the right.

Think about the language you could use and the specific details you could include to make your writing lively. Plan five or six topic sentences, one to help you write each paragraph.

Where are you writing about?

What are the main features of the place?

Are there any amusing aspects/people/incidents that have happened there?

Planning a humorous guide

How will you feature — as an observer or as part of something that happens?

What do you like/dislike about the place?

11 Self-evaluation

Learning objectives

- To think about the value of self-evaluations
- To complete a self-evaluation of how you feel you are doing in English

During your time at school or college you will have been asked to complete a range of evaluations. These evaluations are often used to give you an opportunity to reflect on your achievements and areas that you feel you need to develop further. It is important that you are honest otherwise there's no real point in completing one.

Activity 1

Students complete self-evaluations so they can understand how well they are doing and what they need to develop in order to improve.

Think about your time at school or college. Make a list of the things that you enjoy and the things you don't like. Write next to each of these why you feel you like or dislike them.

You English course is separated into three areas:

- Reading
- Writing
- Speaking and Listening.

Each area has a number of assessment objectives (AOs) which you must demonstrate in your English language work. They are listed in the table here, designed to help you self-evaluate how you feel you are progressing in English.

Activity 2

Copy and complete the self-evaluation table.

Support

Using your answers, list the top three areas that you feel you need to develop in order to improve your English skills. Spend two or three minutes writing down:

- what you find difficult about each objective
- what you can do to improve
- what you need to get some extra support or help with.

Stretch

When completing a self-assessment or evaluation, it is a good idea to try to list your skills in terms of strengths and weaknesses. Look at the skills listed in the table and see if you can write a brief overview paragraph about your strengths and weaknesses in English Language.

	I feel confident about this; it is something I am good at.	I feel OK about this; it is something that I need to continue to develop.	I do not feel confident about this and need some extra help.
Reading			
AO1 – Reading texts and finding key information			
AO1 – Understanding or interpreting information			
AO1 – Selecting and synthesizing relevant evidence from different texts			

AO2 – Explaining why and how writers use specific language			
AO2 – Explaining why a writer chooses a specific structure and its effect			
AO2 – Using technical terminology to explain the effect of a text			
AO3 – Comparing writers' ideas across two or more texts			
AO3 – Comparing writers' perspectives on a topic			
AO4 – Giving a personal opinion about a text			
AO4 – Evaluating texts with supporting evidence			
Writing			
AO5 – Writing clearly			
AO5 – Writing imaginatively and effectively			
AO5 – Adapting writing for specific forms, purposes and audiences			
AO5 – Understanding the purpose of a piece of writing and adapting to suit this			
AO5 – Controlling the tone and style of writing to engage readers			
AO6 – Using paragraphs and structure to organize writing			
AO6 – Writing with accurate spelling and punctuation			
AO6 – Writing using a range of appropriate sentence structures and vocabulary			
Speaking and Listening			
AO7 – Giving a presentation in a formal setting			
AO8 – Listening carefully to other presentations			
AO8 – Responding appropriately to questions			
AO8 – Responding appropriately to feedback			
AO9 – Using Standard English effectively in speeches and presentations			

Assessment

Reading and understanding

Learning objectives

- To practise evaluative reading skills
- To practise wider reading skills
- To revise reading objectives

Introduction

During this chapter you have focused on the skills you need to be able to evaluate texts and characters. The extract below and the following questions will test your understanding of these skills and your ability to use them. Make sure you read the extract carefully and approach the text and your answers **chronologically**.

In this extract, Sara Maitland describes a period of heavy snow in County Durham.

Extract from *A Book of Silence* by Sara Maitland

Part of me became increasingly scared [...] What would happen if the weather did not improve? Was my family all right? But more of it was emotional – despite the fact that I was supposedly longing for quiet. I increasingly felt invaded. The silence was hollowing me out and leaving me empty and naked.

The cold intensified that sense of being exposed, and sometimes when the weather was particularly wild just getting the coal in from the coal shed was exhausting and even frightening. When the weather was calmer, however, I realised that snow produces a peculiar acoustic effect: it mutes nearby noises (presumably because the softer ground surface absorbs them) but causes distant sounds to carry further and with startling clarity. In addition the snow itself flattened everything visually. These effects disorientated me and made me increasingly nervy and jumpy. One day walking to my gate, the collar of my jacket blew up against the back of my head and I screamed aloud, viscerally[1] convinced I had been attacked from behind.

One afternoon I needed to break out and I took a walk up the undriveable road, despite the fact that there were flurries of 'snail' (a mixture of snow and hail) which, driven by the harsh wind, cut into my face. Then about half a mile from the house, I started to hear the most agonised wailing noises – the wailing, it seemed to me then, of the damned. I was completely terrified. I would be on this hill in this wind forever howling and desolate. I would never see another human being again. I would freeze in hell. It turned out that this strange and deeply disturbing noise was in fact no manifestation[2] of my inner torment, but caused by a strange and fascinating phenomenon. The unfenced roads in that part of the north-east have snow poles – tall posts marked in black and white foot-wide strips that show you both where the road is and how deep the snow is. Older snow poles are made of iron and have holes drilled in them for the wind to pass through. Essentially they were Aeolian harps[3] or organ pipes and they were responding to the wind with these extraordinary sounds. But I know I was lucky that I identified the source of the noise fairly quickly, because otherwise it would have driven me insane. I can only too easily understand how this sort of silence can drive anyone beyond panic and into true madness.

[1] viscerally – in a way that comes from deep inward feelings
[2] manifestation – an outward display
[3] Aeolian harp – a stringed instrument that makes sounds when the wind blows through it

Key term

Chronologically: in the order in which things occurred

Activity 1

1. Why is Sara scared in the first paragraph? **[3]**

2. What does the writer mean when she says, 'The silence was hollowing me out and leaving me empty and naked'? **[2]**

3. Look at paragraph 2. What are Sara's thoughts and feelings about the snow and the cold weather? You must refer to the text to support your answer. **[5]**

4. How does Sara suggest that she is terrified in paragraph 3? You must refer to the text to support your answer. **[10]**

5. We realize that noise is a major concern for Sara. Look back across the whole text. What does Sara think and feel about the noises she hears in this extract? You must refer to the text to support your answer, for example: **[10]**

> Sara comments that 'The silence was hollowing me out and leaving me empty and naked,' which makes me think that she feels very uncomfortable about silence. The 'hollowing' suggests that the absence of noise makes her feel empty as though it is weakening her. On top of this, 'naked' sounds as though the silence is making her feel particularly vulnerable.

Tip When you are asked to refer to the text to support your answer, you are being advised to include evidence from the text (or quotations) to support each of the points that you make in your answer. Some students find it helpful to highlight sections of the text that they intend to use in their answer to ensure that their response remains chronological.

Try to vary the vocabulary you use in your explanations. For example, when exploring the evidence don't continually use the word 'terrified' to show that she is frightened. Instead you could use: *afraid, petrified, apprehensive, anxious* or *uneasy*. You can also be creative in your vocabulary when explaining an effect: *'this shows that...', 'this suggests...', 'from this we can infer...', 'her choice makes it obvious that...'.*

How you make your point is as important as the point itself, and demonstrating a variety of vocabulary shows you have a mastery of language, which is something the examiners are looking for.

Assessment

Writing

Learning objectives

- To plan and write a review to suit your audience
- To structure your writing and ideas purposefully

Introduction

In this assessment you will have the opportunity to plan and write a review. Think carefully about the skills you have developed throughout this chapter and make sure you incorporate them into your writing.

You read the following review in a movie blog:

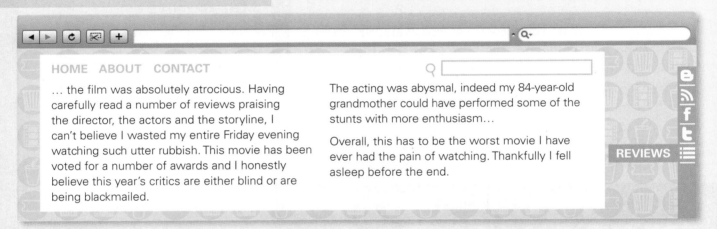

HOME ABOUT CONTACT

… the film was absolutely atrocious. Having carefully read a number of reviews praising the director, the actors and the storyline, I can't believe I wasted my entire Friday evening watching such utter rubbish. This movie has been voted for a number of awards and I honestly believe this year's critics are either blind or are being blackmailed.

The acting was abysmal, indeed my 84-year-old grandmother could have performed some of the stunts with more enthusiasm…

Overall, this has to be the worst movie I have ever had the pain of watching. Thankfully I fell asleep before the end.

REVIEWS

Activity 1

Imagine that the review you have just read was written about your favourite film. Write a review of your favourite film.

Planning

You should spend five minutes planning your work. Think carefully about how you are going to evaluate the film – making your opinions clear for the reader. Think carefully about the structure of your review. Make sure you cover a wide range of different angles about the film.

You may find it helpful to revise the structure of a review on page 175.

Points to consider before you start:

- Who is your audience?
- What will your opening sentence be?
- Why not plan four or five topic sentences that will begin each paragraph in your writing?
- Will your review be serious or will you include some humour?
- Do you want to make a brief reference to the negative review you have just read?

Peer-assessment

Share your plan with a partner. Make notes on each other's plans if you can think of any ideas or points that could be included in their work.

Activity 2

Now spend 30 minutes writing your review.

Self-assessment

Now that you have completed your work, spend two or three minutes reading through it to make sure it makes sense.

Tips for proofreading:

- Check your work one sentence at a time and make sure each sentence makes complete sense.
- Check your work for any homophone errors or errors that you commonly make.
- Swap your work with a partner and ask them to annotate your work (in pencil) with suggestions or corrections.

Features of good/competent writing

- Varied sentence structure and mostly secure sentence control and a range of punctuation
- Most spelling and tenses are secure, with developing vocabulary
- Clear understanding of task, purpose, format and audience
- Content is developed with appropriate reasons
- Writing organized into paragraphs with an overall fluency

Features of excellent/sophisticated writing

- All sentences are effective and accurate
- A range of punctuation is used effectively
- Wide range of ambitious vocabulary, with accurate spelling
- Sophisticated understanding of task, purpose, format and audience
- Ambitious content, convincingly developed

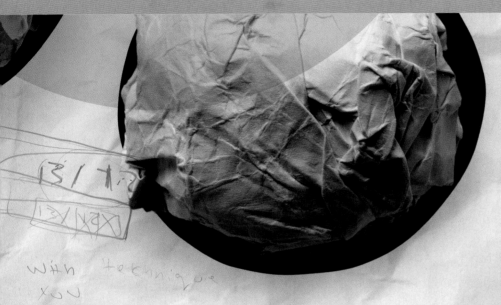

With technique
you
technique

In this chapter you will focus on your ability to look back on what you have learned and to apply that knowledge. In the five previous chapters you had the opportunity to learn many skills, and by engaging with some of the activities you will have developed both as a reader and a writer. Many of the skills you have learned are transferable, not just to different areas of English, but to other areas of your life and studies. Sometimes you will need to connect and combine the skills you have learned in order to achieve your aims. The ability to evaluate, for instance, which you practised and developed in Chapter 5, is a skill that you will use in many other school subjects and in your daily life.

Here, you will revisit some of the skills you have learned in order to make connections between them. If this sounds like revision, that's because it is! The revision unit of this chapter contains activities that will use some of the things you have learned and potentially make connections between them.

In the exam unit you will find a breakdown of what happens for GCSE English Language assessment and two practice exam papers with some guidance on how to approach them.

Revision

Revision can be defined as 'the process of revisiting work in preparation for an exam', and the ability to revise and remember skills you have learned is just as important in the study of English as in other subjects. English revision can take a number of forms, but it will essentially be based on practising the skills you have acquired and applying them in as many different situations as you can. While memorizing key information (such as features of persuasive writing or literary techniques) can be useful and help you to feel confident,

'You can't connect the dots looking forward; you can only connect them looking backwards. So you have to trust that the dots will somehow connect in your future.' *Steve Jobs*

'The test of a first-rate intelligence is the ability to hold two opposed ideas in the mind at the same time, and still retain the ability to function.' *F. Scott Fitzgerald*

'Creativity is the power to connect the seemingly unconnected.' *William Plomer*

it is most important that you expose yourself to a wide range of reading and writing experiences. Applying your skills in response to different texts will give you the confidence to be unfazed by whatever is presented in an exam.

Read as much as you can – and not just what is suggested in English lessons. Read fiction, non-fiction, things you know you like and new genres you have never tried. Keep in mind what you are learning in the classroom and ask those same questions about what you are reading at home. Making connections and using your English skills will help to make the exams less scary. Reading widely will also allow you to experience different writing styles, and give you ideas about how to structure and punctuate your work and develop your vocabulary.

Revision

 Recap on text and context

Learning objectives

- To distinguish between types of text
- To make connections between text and **context**
- To recap on the features of different texts

Introduction

It would be impossible to revise everything that is important in this book in just a couple of pages. Instead, this unit will show you how to pick out and apply some of the skills you have learned, so you can go on to do this with other skills on your own. Some connections between what you have learned will be made in order to demonstrate what can be done. It is then up to you to apply it elsewhere and to make further connections between your learning. In short, what you cover with your revision is up to you.

You have already learned some important skills for revising and recapping important information. Think back to Chapter 1, where you studied different reading techniques. The techniques of **skimming** and **scanning** are crucial when recapping details that you have learned: they will help you to locate information and key points quickly. You will be able to use these skills to access quickly what you have read and written during this course and isolate the details that you need.

Activity

You will take two exams in English Language. In order to fully understand how these exams work, it is essential that you understand the difference between fiction and non-fiction. This distinction was dealt with separately in Chapters 1 and 2.

1. Using your skills in skimming and scanning, glance through Chapters 1 and 2, and jot down in note form what we mean by fictional and non-fictional texts.

2. List three different examples of fictional texts and three of non-fictional texts.

3. Now connect these details to help you write a clear explanation of the differences between fictional and non-fictional writing.

Activity 2

Look at the texts below and on pages 206–207. Identify whether they are examples of fictional or non-fictional texts. Copy the table below and quickly complete the 'Fiction or non-fiction?' column.

	Fiction or non-fiction?	Text type	Features of text type	Context
Text 1				
Text 2				
Text 3				
Text 4				
Text 5				
Text 6				
Text 7				
Text 8				

Activity 3

Now look more closely at each of the eight texts.

a. Complete the 'Text type' column of the table, which identifies what kind of text each one is.

b. Note down in the 'Features of text type' column any details that helped you to work out what kind of text you were looking at.

Text 2

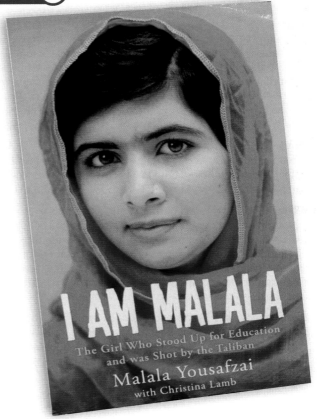

I AM MALALA
The Girl Who Stood Up for Education and was Shot by the Taliban
Malala Yousafzai
with Christina Lamb

Text 1

for the new
Who won the volleyball
tition Teams from high schools
entered the competition.
com·pet·i·tive /kəmˈpetɪtɪv/
situation is one in which people or
hard to be more successful than ot
petitive market | **highly / fiercely**
tive Advertising is an intense
products or prices that are
but still of good
servic

Text ③

Anna stands up and walks slowly round the gallery, coming to a stop in front of an old man, his white beard and turban set off against a wall of golden brick hung with pages of white, inscribed paper. Before him, on the floor, robed in vivid reds and blues, sit the children he teaches. A sun-striped cat reclines on a green cushion watching a pair of doves pecking at the spangled mat. In the half-open doorway, the smallest of the children hesitates.

In the street, Anna starts to hurry. It is four o'clock and the light is fading fast.

Text ④

GLOBE TROTTER

HOME   ALL ABOUT ME   TRAVEL BLOG   TRAVEL TIPS   CONTACT

Rediscovering America

By Sanjit | Published August 25th

Hello world! This month I will be rambling around the grand old United States of America, exploring the vast prairies, bustling cities and Grand Canyons of this star-spangled country.

First stop: New York – the city that never sleeps. No matter how many times I have visited NYC, I never tire of it. There is an indescribable buzz and energy to the city. Walking through the luminous Times Square, it almost feels like home. I can't wait to share my experiences with you!

Text ⑤

The Fault In Our Stars
Dying Young (Adult)

Plot
At a support group, teenaged cancer sufferer Hazel (Woodley) meets and falls for chirpy amputee Gus (Elgort). After introducing Gus to her favourite novel, Hazel is excited when he befriends the author by email. Will the pair meet their hero? The story eventually finds Gus using a Make-A-Wish-style arrangement to fly Hazel and himself to Amsterdam, where they meet the alcoholic, scornful author. Along the way, Gus and Hazel grow closer than ever, even as their disease continues to impact their lives.

Review
A teen cancer drama is like a rite of passage for a former child actress these days: Dakota Fanning did it in *Now Is Good*; now Shailene Woodley stars as a cancer patient with a similar desire to live life to the full while she can. [...]

While 16-year-old Hazel narrates, this also takes a look at the effect her condition has on her family. Laura Dern puts in a sensitive performance as the kindly, smiling mother fighting back the tears, torn between indulging her daughter and protecting her. Like the (bestselling) source novel by John Green, *The Fault In Our Stars* explores characters as much by what they don't say as what they do. Hazel's parents' strained faces speak volumes; as do Gus' cavalier jokes that help him avoid the truth.

Performances are likable and the casting's on the money: Elgort (Woodley's brother in *Divergent*) has a flirtatious sparkle while not an obvious hunk, while Woodley maintains the fresh-faced girl-next-door look that should win over the young target market. It's also quite brave for a mass-market film to feature a heroine wearing a breathing tube throughout.

Verdict
Despite a few missteps this is a spirited, touching romance and Shailene Woodley's best performance yet. *Divergent* fans after a weepie need look no further.

★★★★☆

 6   4   0

Text 6

Dear Editor,

I am a 17-year-old student. Despite what I read in the papers, I am fairly certain I am not a mindless idiot getting drunk in the park and trolling celebrities on Twitter.

It may surprise some of your readers, but I do try to think about other people. Two of these people are my nan and granddad who I regularly visit and enjoy spending time with. They are not rich, but they do not complain about what they have. However I think it's time someone stood up and complained for them.

Their council tax goes up, their fuel bills go up, but the service they receive goes down. Their home help rarely arrives on time, sometimes leaving my disabled nan stuck in bed for hours with my granddad fretting that he's not able to lift her himself. Now they're being told they may need to pay to go to their day centre and meet their friends. This is an appalling way to repay their years of hard work and commitment to this country.

Instead of patting themselves on the back and awarding themselves fat pay rises, why don't our politicians open their eyes and think about how other people have to live?

Yours faithfully,

Sean O'Grady

Text 7

Old Marley was as dead as a door-nail.

Mind! I don't mean to say that I know, of my own knowledge, what there is particularly dead about a door-nail. I might have been inclined, myself, to regard a coffin-nail as the deadest piece of ironmongery in the trade. But the wisdom of our ancestors is in the simile; and my unhallowed hands shall not disturb it, or the Country's done for. You will therefore permit me to repeat, emphatically, that Marley was as dead as a door-nail.

Scrooge knew he was dead? Of course he did. How could it be otherwise? Scrooge and he were partners for I don't know how many years. Scrooge was his sole executor, his sole administrator, his sole assign, his sole residuary legatee, his sole friend, and sole mourner. And even Scrooge was not so dreadfully cut up by the sad event, but that he was an excellent man of business on the very day of the funeral, and solemnised it with an undoubted bargain.

Text 8

Activity 4

In Chapter 4 you learned that the context of a piece of writing refers to the circumstances or background in which it was created, and the influences that made its author write it in the way they did. Sometimes it is possible to make an informed judgement about the context of a piece of writing from clues in the text.

Have another look at texts 1–8 and note down in the 'Context' column of the table on page 205 anything you can work out about their background from the information given.

Stretch

Think carefully about when fiction and non-fiction might overlap. Why do you think this might happen? Write down as many reasons as you can, with examples of when it might happen.

2 Reading skills

Learning objectives

- To identify the skills you have developed in earlier chapters
- To think about how those skills can be used

Skills can be defined as something we have the ability to do well. How then do we gain skills? Some people seem naturally able to do certain things, whereas others have to work much harder. However talented someone is, they can always improve by developing their skills. For example, footballers must take care of their bodies, practise and train, and musicians must spend hours refining their technique.

You have learned many skills in English, but you should not assume that you can now use those skills to the best of your ability. You will only be able to fully realize your ability by practising what you have learned, applying your skills to different situations and thinking about how you can take them further.

You need to know what you have learned in order to practise it. It might seem like hard work to think back over activities and lessons you have completed over the last year, but by actively doing this you will be forced to focus on your own learning and skills.

Activity 1

You are going to make a checklist of the skills you have gained while using this book that you might need to demonstrate in an exam. Use the table below as a starting point. A few of the boxes have been filled in with examples. Try to find at least 12 different skills – you may have practised these in more than one chapter and in more than one way. Make sure you make this clear in your table.

Chapter	Skills learned	Example/explanation	Why is this important?
	Recognizing different reading techniques	I know the difference between skimming, scanning and close reading.	I know how and when to use these skills to get to the meaning of a text.
1	Knowledge of how to track through a text in an exam answer		
1	Understanding of the importance of word choice		
2	Awareness of explicit and implicit information	I can identify explicit information and know how to draw conclusions from implicit information. I have also practised descriptive writing that featured implicit and explicit information.	
4		I can compare the different ways in which different writers present an idea.	
3	Using the context of a sentence to work out the meaning of an unfamiliar word		
5	How to evaluate my reactions to a character		

Activity ②

Read the extract below. Using some of the skills you identified in Activity 1, try to write ten questions about this extract that would provide a varied test of skills for a future Year 10 student.

HOME   NEWS   **ARTICLES**   DOWNLOADS

SEARCH

Experience: my microwave nearly killed me

It was the week of my 32nd birthday last September. I had been at a friend's house on Saturday night for some cake and cava. I came home to my flat in Pimlico and went more or less straight to bed. I didn't wake up until the Sunday, when I found myself in intensive care.

I have no memory of it, but I'm told that just after 11pm, about half an hour after I'd gone to bed, my microwave had exploded. It was empty, plugged in and switched on at the mains, as usual. The washing machine, which was beneath it, caught fire from the explosion. The fire spread. The firefighters found me in the hallway – I must have tried to escape. I had passed out because of the carbon monoxide. [...]

They took me to intensive care, where I was in and out of a coma for three days. It was like lying in a black room, just waiting. I remember feeling shocked because I felt weightless, but also feeling very peaceful. It was like being underwater. A policeman was sent to my parents' house in Swansea to inform them what had happened. They were told that I was probably going to die, and rushed straight to London where the hospital staff told them I would live but that I would have brain damage and need 24-hour nursing care.

Thankfully, they were wrong. On the Friday I woke up for a few seconds.
I remember feeling outraged that I was naked with all these people around me. [...]

After nine days in hospital, I moved back to Swansea with my parents for two weeks. That was tough. I am very independent, so I found it hard letting them do basic things. I was so tired I couldn't climb stairs. Lifting a fork to my mouth was an effort. By the second week, I was getting my strength back slowly, and I was then well enough to move in with a friend in London.

I went back to work as a mental health nurse after a month. My family said it was too soon, but I thought I was fine. I didn't like telling people what had happened in case they thought I was being a drama queen. But on the second day my manager asked me how I was and I just burst into tears. I wasn't ready.

Six weeks after the fire, I went back to my flat for the first time. It was a shell. Everything smelled terrible. I salvaged a few books. The insurance organized the rebuilding, and it took seven months to do all the repairs. I moved back in at the end of April last year. That was an awful time. It wasn't losing all my stuff, but coming to terms with nearly dying. I felt as if I was at risk all the time, as if the sky might fall on my head. I kept my door unlocked and I got rid of all my electrical goods. I couldn't see the point of life, because I realized that I could lose it all in just one moment.

I was diagnosed with post-traumatic stress disorder and I had counselling for four months, which really helped. Gradually, I learned to change the way I approached things. I began to think that, in case I died in the next five minutes, I should make the next four minutes and 59 seconds count. I made my flat my home again and even started to be able to laugh about it. I eventually realized how impractical life was without a fridge and a washing machine, so I started using them again, but I do switch off all electrical goods at the mains every night. I will never get another microwave, though. People tell me they're unhealthy anyway.

Activity ③

In Chapter 5 you completed a self-evaluation which asked you to consider your progress in English in relation to the assessment objectives (AOs). Look back at the AOs for reading and remind yourself of what they are asking you to do. For each of the questions you set for Activity 2, try to work out which AO you will be testing.

Stretch

Look again at the AOs that you have covered. With the exception of AO3, which doesn't fit here because there is no comparative piece, have you missed any AOs out of your questions? What questions could you set to address any missing AOs?

3 Recap on writing

Learning objectives

- To identify some of the writing skills you have learned
- To think about what you can do to develop your skills

Although these two pages deal specifically with writing skills, you should keep in mind that your writing ability will naturally be influenced by what you have read. The more you read, the better your writing will become. In developing your reading skills, you are becoming more aware of what a writer does to produce an engaging, informative or entertaining piece of writing. You can then use these skills yourself. Reading and writing are linked, and what you learn in one is relevant to both.

Activity

You have learned about and practised many different kinds of writing during your time in school. This book has included some of them and you will have come across others in previous lessons in English or other subjects. Match the writing activities and definitions below, and write them out in the correct order.

A Story/Narrative	**1** A complete piece of writing that discusses a specific topic
B Letter	**2** Writing on a given topic that is intended to form a talk to a given audience
C Review	**3** A printed sheet of information on a given topic
D Article	**4** A written message that is sent from one person to another
E Description	**5** Writing an account of an incident – either true or invented
F Speech	**6** Writing that shows what something is like (for example, a person or a place)
G Leaflet	**7** An assessment or evaluation of the merits of something

Activity

Are there any other types of writing that you have encountered or that you can think of? Add these to your list and write a brief explanation of what that type of writing involves.

The definitions above are quite general and can be improved on. In order to do this it is important that we consider some key concepts or ideas. These ideas will be familiar to you, but you should still consider them carefully. Understanding each of these concepts is an important part of your achievement in English and should not be underestimated.

Key writing concepts

Audience: the person or people a piece of writing is intended for. In non-fiction writing this can be quite specific, for example, a letter could be written to a friend/relative or as a complaint to a specific company. There are many potential audiences for a piece of non-fiction writing and recognizing who your audience is will enable you to make important decisions about how to write.

Purpose: the reason for a piece of writing. Does it intend to persuade or inform the reader? Is it being written to entertain or to enable the reader to imagine something? There are many reasons for writing and being clear on what those reasons are will enable you to respond to a task with clarity and focus.

Format: how you set out your piece of writing. In some writing you will not need to think beyond the structure of your writing and whether it is paragraphed with clarity and for effect. Other pieces will require more emphasis on headings and titles. In some areas of writing (for example, letter writing) there are specific rules. Are you certain what those are?

Formal/informal: Formal writing is writing that is addressed to an audience you don't know or whose purpose needs to be taken seriously, for example, a letter to a newspaper or a report on the facilities in your school. Informal writing can be more personal or lively, perhaps because you are more familiar with your audience or you are writing in a more relaxed way. Formality affects your choice of language, tone and literary techniques.

Exam link

The more you know about what is expected from different pieces of writing (and some of the different routes a type of writing can take) the better equipped you will be in an exam. Knowledge of the key writing concepts will enable you to work out quickly what a question is asking of you and the factors that you must keep in mind when planning your response.

Activity 3

Look back at the explanations you gave for each writing type in Activities 1 and 2. Think about how you can develop these explanations by including the key writing concepts described on page 211.

Now write a paragraph to explain each of the writing types from Activities 1 and 2, making sure you include references to the key writing concepts on page 211.

Keep in mind that for some writing types it may not be possible to specify all details, but you may have to consider others in more than one way. For example, in a fictional piece you might not be able to identify a particular audience unless you have elected to write in a specific genre (for example, science fiction), but some non-fiction pieces may be aimed at a variety of different audiences.

Support

Here is an example of how you might begin:

An article is a complete piece of writing that discusses a specific topic. The audience that an article is aimed at can vary from something very broad like the general public (for example, a newspaper article) to something much more specific like a particular age group or fans of a specific sport or hobby (for example, a formula-one racing magazine). Similarly, it is not possible to define the purpose of an article in only one way: it may aim to inform its audience or...

In addition to the importance of understanding what is expected of you and careful planning of a piece of written work, it is essential that you pay attention to the technical accuracy of your writing. During the course of this book you have undertaken activities in proofreading, improving the accuracy of your vocabulary choices and spelling, and improving your use of sentences and key punctuation. It is very important to improve and practise your skills in this area: 20% of your marks rely on your ability to communicate clearly and accurately.

Activity 4

SPAG

It is often quite easy to mark and correct someone else's work, but less easy to improve something you have produced yourself. Using a whole piece of writing you have produced in the last three months, do the following:

1. Circle any spelling errors and write the correct spelling in the margin.

2. Underline any errors in punctuation/grammar (for example, missing full stops, comma splicing, inaccurately punctuated speech, inaccurate tenses or agreement, inconsistent tenses).

3. Highlight any areas where you think you could improve your use of punctuation or grammar. For example, could you make your meaning sharper or offer more emphasis through the way you structure your writing?

4. Put a 'v' next to any words that you think would benefit from more specific or appropriate vocabulary.

5. Put a * next to any areas where you don't think you have made your meaning as clear or developed as you could have done.

Activity 5

SPAG

Rewrite three paragraphs from your piece of work, using the corrections and suggestions you have made above. They can be consecutive paragraphs or paragraphs taken from different parts of your assignment.

The exams

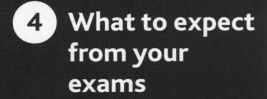

What to expect from your exams

Learning objectives

- To familiarize yourself with the ways you will be assessed
- To understand the structure of your assessment

Introduction

Your exams will seem much less scary if you know exactly what to expect from them. The chapters in this book were written to provide instruction, advice and practice to help you to become a rounded and competent student of English language. Everything you have studied is relevant to what you need to know for a GCSE English Language exam. As you approach the end of this book, this is a good time to consider what form that assessment will take.

Summary of Assessment

Component 1

What is tested?	20th-century literature reading and creative prose writing
How is it tested?	Written examination, 1 hour and 45 minutes
What is it worth?	40% of qualification
How is it broken down?	Section A – Reading (40 marks) This section will use structured questions to test the reading of an unseen extract from one 20th-century literary prose text (about 60–100 lines). This section assesses AO1, AO2 and AO4.
	Section B – Prose Writing (40 marks) This section will test creative prose writing through one 40-mark task. You will choose ONE title from a choice of four. These titles will give opportunities for writing to describe and narrate, and for imaginative and creative use of language. This response should be a narrative/recount. Candidates who write purely descriptively or use a different form (like poetry or drama) will NOT be able to access the full range of marks. This section assesses AO5 and AO6.

Reading of fiction that was written between 1900 and 1999

Writing your own fiction or fictional narrative, e.g. a story or an account of something that has happened to you

This is worth 40% of the qualification.

You will read 60–100 lines of fiction and answer questions on what you have read.

You will have a choice of four Writing questions. You should only choose one.

You should not write anything other than a story or recount, as these are the only types of writing which can allow you to gain the highest marks in the exam.

Component 2

What is tested?   19th- and 21st-century non-fiction reading study and transactional, persuasive and/or discursive writing

How is it tested?   Written examination, 2 hours

What is it worth?   60% of qualification

How is it broken down?   Section A – Reading (40 marks)
This section will use structured questions to test the reading of two high-quality unseen non-fiction texts. One of the texts will have been written in the 19th century, the other in the 21st century. Non-fiction texts may include, but will not be limited to: letters, extracts from autobiographies or biographies, diaries, reports, articles and digital and multi-modal texts of various kinds from newspapers, magazines and the Internet.

This section assesses AO1, AO2, AO3 and AO4.

Section B – Writing (40 marks)
This section will test transactional, persuasive and/or discursive writing through TWO equally weighted compulsory tasks (20 marks each). Across the tasks candidates will be offered opportunities to write for a range of audiences and purposes, adapting style to form and to real-life contexts in, for example, letters, articles, reviews, speeches, etc.

This section assesses AO5 and AO6.

Reading of non-fiction that was written between 1800 and 1899, and 2000 to the present day

Writing non-fiction for a given audience/purpose

Although both exams are out of 80 marks, this one is worth 60% of the qualification.

You will need to read two different non-fiction texts.

One will definitely be from 1800–1899 and one will definitely be from 2000–present.

You will need to produce two pieces of non-fiction writing. You must complete both tasks set.

Component 3

What is tested?   Spoken Language

How is it tested?   Through your work in class

What is it worth?   Work on Spoken Language does not form part of your final mark/grade in English Language. Achievement in Spoken Language will be reported as part of the qualification on your exam certificate alongside the overall grade you achieve for English Language.

How is it broken down?   You need to complete one formal presentation or speech.

You will also be assessed on your responses to questions and feedback following the presentation or speech.

Standard English should be a feature of all parts of your work for this component.

This component assesses AO7, AO8 and AO9.

You need to speak in Standard English, not slang or abbreviated language.

5 How to approach Component 1

Learning objective

● To develop awareness of what to expect in the Component 1 exam

You are about to see what the Component 1 exam paper will look like. Exposure to different exam papers and practice at timing yourself will be helpful in preparing you for what is to come at the end of your GCSE. For now, it is important that you take on board some essential information that will help you tackle your first practice paper.

Important information

On the front cover of your Component 1 exam paper you will be told the following:

● You have 1 hour and 45 minutes to complete the Component 1 exam paper.

● You should answer **all** of the questions in Section A (the Reading section).

● You should select only **one** title to use in Section B (the Writing section).

● You should time your approach carefully. You are advised to spend your time as follows:

    Section A   – about 10 minutes reading
                  – about 50 minutes answering the questions.
    Section B   – about 10 minutes planning
                  – about 35 minutes writing your narrative/account.

● The number of marks each question is worth will be written in brackets at the end of the question.

 How to start the Component 1 exam successfully

Don't panic and don't rush to answer without taking some simple steps at the start. Before you begin, make sure you have thought about the following:

Section A

1. Know roughly how long you will need to spend on each question before you start and keep an eye on the time. Check how many marks a question is worth – you will probably need to spend more time on a question that is worth 10 marks than on one that is worth 5 marks.

2. Read the question carefully – make sure you know what you are being asked to do.

3. Make sure you know exactly which lines you have been asked to look at.

4. Use a pencil or highlighter when reading the text to highlight key evidence that will help you answer the question.

5. Re-read the question – be absolutely sure that you know what you are being asked to do.

6. Track carefully through the relevant lines when answering the question.

Section B

1. Read each of the options. Think carefully about which one appeals to you. Keep in mind that you need to present a clear narrative with a beginning, middle and end that will appeal to a reader.

2. Choose your title.

3. Spend a few minutes planning your work. Think about key characters, settings and events.

4. Write your narrative and try to leave enough time to finish properly rather than just stopping because you've run out of time.

5. Don't write for the sake of it because you've got a few minutes spare. Keeping your reader interested is all important.

6. Use any remaining time to proofread your work. Writing at speed means you are likely to have made errors.

6 How to approach Component 2

Learning objective

- To develop awareness of what to expect in the Component 2 exam

You are also about to see what the Component 2 exam paper will look like. As with Component 1, it is important to take the opportunity to look at different exam papers and practise timing yourself when answering questions. Below is some essential information that will help you tackle the practice paper.

Important information

On the front cover of your Component 2 exam paper you will be told the following:

- You have 2 hours to complete the exam.
- This exam will contain extra Resource Material for use in Section A.
- You should answer **all** of the questions in Section A (the Reading section).
- You should answer **all** of the questions in Section B (the Writing section).
- You should time your approach carefully. You are advised to spend your time as follows:

  Section A   – about 10 minutes reading
                          – about 50 minutes answering the questions.

  Section B   – spend 30 minutes on each question
                          – about 5 minutes planning for each one
                          – about 25 minutes writing for each one.

- The number of marks each question is worth will be written in brackets at the end of the question.

 Exam Tip **How to start the Component 2 exam successfully**

Don't panic and don't rush to answer without taking some simple steps at the start. Before you begin, make sure you have thought about the following:

Section A

1. Check how many marks a question is worth. You will probably need to spend more time on a question that is worth 10 marks than one that is worth 5 or 2 marks.
2. Read the question carefully. Make sure you know what you are being asked to do.
3. Use a pencil or highlighter when reading the text to highlight key evidence that will help you answer the question.
4. Re-read the question. Be absolutely sure that you know what you are being asked to do.
5. When you are asked to look at two texts together in the same question, make sure you identify which one you are referring to when answering.

Section B

1. Read the question carefully.
2. Make sure you are clear on the purpose and audience of your piece of writing.
3. Spend a few minutes planning your work. Have an idea of the points you want to make and in what order.
4. Keep an eye on timings. Try to leave enough time to conclude properly.
5. Remember you have two writing questions to complete.
6. Use any remaining time to proofread your work. Writing at speed means you are likely to have made errors.

Assessment

Sample Component 1 exam paper

Section A: 40 marks

Read the passage below carefully. Then answer all the questions which follow it.

This story is told by a character named Joan. She is looking back to an event which happened in her childhood.

I was not [thin], and this is one of the many things for which my mother never quite forgave me. At first I was merely plump. In the earliest photos in my mother's album I was a healthy baby, not much heftier than most, and the only peculiar thing is that I was never looking at the camera; instead I was trying to get something into my mouth: a toy, a hand, a bottle. [...] Though I didn't exactly become rounder, I failed to lose what is
5 usually referred to as baby fat.

When I reached the age of six the pictures stopped abruptly. This must have been when my mother gave up on me, for it was she who used to take them; perhaps she no longer wanted my growth recorded [...].

My mother [...] enrolled me in a dancing school, where a woman called Miss Flegg, who was almost as slender and disapproving as my mother, taught tap dancing and ballet. [...] My mother took this step partly
10 because it was fashionable to enroll seven-year-old girls in dancing schools [...] and partly because she hoped it would make me less chubby. She didn't say this to me, my mother said it to Miss Flegg; she was not yet calling me fat.

I loved dancing school. I was even quite good at the actual dancing, although Miss Flegg sometimes rapped her classroom pointer sharply on the floor and said, 'Joan dear, I wish you would stop thumping.' Like most
15 girls of that time I idealized ballet dancers. [...] I used to press my short piggy nose up against the jewellery store windows and goggle at the china music-box figurines of shiny ladies in brittle pink skirts, with roses on their hard ceramic heads, and imagine myself leaping through the air, lifted by a thin man in black tights. [...] I worked hard at the classes, I concentrated, and I even used to practise at home, wrapping myself in a discarded lace bathroom curtain. [...] I longed for a pair of satin toe shoes, but we were too young, Miss
20 Flegg explained, the bones in our feet had not hardened. So I had to settle for black slippers. [...]

Miss Flegg was an inventive woman; I suppose these days she would be called creative. She didn't have much scope for her inventiveness in the teaching of elementary steps to young children, [...] but she let herself go on the annual spring recital. The recital was mostly to impress the parents, but it was also to impress the little girls themselves so they would ask to be allowed to take lessons the next year.

25 Miss Flegg choreographed the entire program. She also constructed the sets and props, and she designed the costumes and handed out patterns and instructions to the mothers, who were supposed to sew them. [...]

Miss Flegg organized the recital into age groups, which corresponded to her dancing classes. There were five of them: Teenies, Tallers, Tensies, Tweeners and Teeners. Underneath her spiny exterior, the long bony hands, the hair wrenched into a bun, and the spidery eyebrows, done, I realized later, with a pencil, she had a layer of
30   sentimentality, which set the tone for her inventions.

I was a Teenie [...]. 'The Butterfly Frolic' [...] was my favourite, and it had my favourite costume too. This featured a gauzy skirt, short, like a real ballerina's, a tight bodice with shoulder straps, a headpiece with spangled insect antennae, and a pair of colored cellophane wings [...]. The wings were what I really longed for but we weren't allowed to put them on until the day itself, for fear of breakage.

35   But it was this costume that was bothering my mother. [...] The problem was fairly simple: in the short pink skirt, with my waist, arms and legs exposed, I was grotesque. [...] With my jiggly thighs, [...] plump upper arms and floppy waist, I must have looked obscene. [...] I was the kind of child, they would have thought back in the early months of 1949, who should not be seen in public with so little clothing on.

My mother struggled with the costume, lengthening it, adding another layer of gauze to conceal the outlines,
40   padding the bodice; but it was no use. Even I was a little taken aback when she finally allowed me to inspect myself in the [...] mirror [...]. Although I was too young to be much bothered by my size, it wasn't quite the effect I wanted. I did not look like a butterfly. But I knew the addition of the wings would make all the difference. I was hoping for magic transformations, even then.

The dress rehearsal was in the afternoon [...]. As I was putting on my butterfly costume [...] Miss Flegg looked
45   over at me; then she walked over, followed by my mother. She stood gazing down at me, her lips pressed together. [...] She was seeing [...] her 'Butterfly Frolic' being reduced to something laughable and unseemly by the presence of a fat little girl who was more like a giant caterpillar than a butterfly, more like a white grub if you were really going to be accurate.

Miss Flegg could not have stood this. For her, the final effect was everything. She wished to be complimented
50   on it, and wholeheartedly, not with pity or suppressed smiles. [...]

She knelt down and gazed with her forceful black eyes into mine. [...]

'Joan, dear,' she said, 'how would you like to be something special?'

I smiled at her uncertainly. [...]

'I've decided to change the dance a little,' she said. 'I've decided to add a new part to it; and because you're the
55   brightest girl in the class, I've chosen you to be the special, new person. Do you think you can do that, dear?'

I had seen enough of her to know that this kindness was suspect, but I fell for it anyway. I nodded emphatically, thrilled to have been selected. [...] Maybe I would get bigger, more important wings. I was eager. [...]

'What am I going to be?' I asked as she led me away.

'A mothball, dear,' she answered serenely, as if this were the most natural thing in the world. [...]

60   I was wounded, desolated in fact, when it turned out Miss Flegg wanted me to remove my cloudy skirt and spangles and put on one of the white teddy-bear numbers the Tensies were using for their number, 'Teddy Bears' Picnic'. She also wanted me to hang around my neck a large sign that said MOTHBALL. [...] Her idea was that once the butterflies had finished their cavorting, I would lumber in among them in the white suit and the sign and the butterflies would [...] scatter.

(from *Lady Oracle* by Margaret Atwood)

Read lines 1–5

A1   List five things you learn about Joan.   **[5]**

Read lines 6–12

A2   How does the writer show what the relationship between Joan and her mother was like?   **[5]**

You must refer to the language used in the text to support your answer.

Read lines 13–20

A3   What does Joan think and feel about dancing?   **[10]**

You must refer to the language used in the text to support your answer.

Look at lines 21–30

A4   What impressions do you get of Miss Flegg in this section? How does the writer create these impressions?   **[10]**

Look at lines 31–64

A5   'Towards the end of this passage, the writer encourages the reader to feel sympathy for Joan.'

To what extent do you agree with this view?   **[10]**

You should write about:
* your own impressions of Joan and her situation as she is presented here and in the passage as a whole
* how the writer has created these impressions.

You must refer to the text to support your answer.

Section B: 40 marks

In this section you will be assessed for the quality of your creative prose writing skills.

24 marks are awarded for communication and organization; 16 marks are awarded for vocabulary, sentence structure, spelling and punctuation.

You should aim to write about 450–600 words.

You should write about:

Choose **one** of the following titles for your writing: **[40]**

Either,   (a)   Write about an occasion when you felt disappointed

Or,   (b)   The Gift

Or,   (c)   Write a story which begins:

Everything changed after that day.

Or,   (d)   Write about a time when you had to look after someone

Sample Component 2 exam paper

Section A: 40 marks

*Answer **all** of the following questions.*

The Resource Material for use with Section A is:

A newspaper article, 'Quiet, please!' by John Humphrys (page 222).

AND

A letter written by Charles Dickens to support a proposal that the government introduce laws to stop street performers creating a public nuisance (page 223). This was published in 1864.

Read the newspaper article by John Humphrys.

A1 (a) What are two ways that the British Medical Journal claims that children exposed to constant noise can suffer? **[2]**

(b) What problems does the article say were caused for children living near a railway line when compared to children who lived somewhere quieter? **[1]**

A2 Humphrys is trying to persuade us that noise is a serious problem. How does he try to do this? **[10]**

You should comment on:
- what he says to influence readers
- his use of language and tone
- the way he presents his argument.

To answer the following questions you will need to read the letter by Charles Dickens.

A3 (a) What instruments does the writer suggest the 'brazen performers' use? **[2]**

(b) What does the writer mean by the phrase 'seeking to be bought off' in line 12? **[1]**

A4 What do you think and feel about Charles Dickens's views about the street entertainers? **[10]**

You should comment on:
- what is said
- how it is said.

You must refer to the text to support your comments.

To answer the following questions you will need to use both texts.

A5 According to these two writers, what steps have people taken to get away from noise? **[4]**

A6 Both of these texts are about the effects of noise. Compare the following:
- the writers' attitudes to the effects of noise
- how they get across their arguments. **[10]**

You must use the text to support your comments and make it clear which text you are referring to.

John Humphrys is a well-known radio presenter. He presents the Today
programme on BBC Radio 4, from 6 to 9 in the morning.

'Quiet, please!' says news presenter John Humphrys

The world is getting louder, and the noise is damaging our health. It's time we all turned down the volume.

5 It is inevitable that if you present the *Today* programme, you will become obsessed with noise. The first question strangers ask is always: "What time do you get up?" (Answer: the middle of the night.) The second is: "What time do you go to
10 bed?" (Answer: absurdly early – long before the average 10-year-old.) And the third is: "How do you manage to sleep?"

Which is where noise comes in. Because it depends. If it is quiet, I sleep like a contented baby.
15 If it is noisy, I sleep like a fractious baby with a particularly nasty teething problem. The difference is that if I am kept awake, I do not scream for attention but lie still, cursing all those selfish souls who think it acceptable to walk past my house at
20 nine in the evening without lowering their voices to a whisper. Yes, I know this is seriously weird, but I would contend that there is no sentient being who is indifferent to noise.

I happen to be on the extreme end of the spectrum
25 for obvious reasons, but you, dear reader, are on it, too. Do you not dread the approach of Christmas with the certain knowledge that every shop you enter will welcome you with canned Christmas carols? Or the fellow passenger who pulls out their
30 mobile to make a phone call, forcing the entire carriage to listen in? Or the hotels who believe you cannot make it through a meal without music in the background? Even at breakfast, for God's sake!

Do you not want to take a large hammer to the
35 small jet engine your neighbour insists on using to blow away the tiny handful of leaves that have settled in his front garden, smash it into even tinier pieces and hand him a broom that would do the job in a fraction of the time (and quietly)?
40 Do you not nod in (silent) agreement at the result of the survey last week that asked office workers what most annoyed them about the behaviour of their colleagues and found that they put eating noisily at the top of the list by a large majority? Do
45 you not applaud the hotel chain that has installed noise meters in its corridors that flash a warning light if people are talking too loudly and offer a refund to guests who failed to get a good night's sleep because of noise? We can even – just – forgive

the company for calling them "ssshhh-o-meters".
50 The man who cancelled his long-standing membership at his gym when they started playing loud music (and successfully encouraged other members to join him) asked the obvious, if rhetorical, question: "Who wants a raving disco
55 at 7am?" The music, said the gym owners, was "motivational".

If you are old enough to have children, you may by now be starting to feel a little uneasy. You may fear that you are settling into a stereotype – the
60 selfish old grump who wants to stop others having fun/expressing themselves in their own way/ indulging your own old fogeyism. You should resist that temptation. You should instead feel virtuous. It's for their own good.

There have been many studies proving the
65 damaging effect of noise at work. Hearing loss is the most obvious problem, but more recent research also suggests that another effect is raised blood pressure.
70 Even more worryingly, perhaps, is the effect of noise on children. The British Medical Journal has reported research that shows the ways in which children exposed to constant noise can suffer. One study looked at children of primary school age
75 living in 32-floor blocks of flats near a main road. The children on the lower floors were affected much more severely than those living higher up. Not only was their hearing damaged, but it was shown that they did less well at school. They had greater
80 difficulty processing information, had poorer memories and more difficulty concentrating.

Another study that compared children living near a railway line with pupils at the same school who lived in a quieter area found significant differences
85 in reading ability; the mean reading age of the railway children was three to four months behind the others. The solution to this is obvious, if not achievable, given the difficulty of rehousing half the
90 population of any big, noisy city.

But noise exists on a different level, too, and it's much trickier to see how we deal with that. Modern society demands that if we have something to say, we must make a great deal of noise about it or it
95 will not be heard. The days of the quiet thinkers who were listened to because of what they thought rather than how they said it have long gone.

CONTENTS

WJEC EDUQAS GCSE **BOOK 1**

English Language

Developing the skills for
Component 1 and Component 2

Michelle Doran
Natalie Simpson
Julie Swain

Consultant:
Barry Childs

Endorsed by

educ
Part of WJEC

OXFORD
UNIVERSITY PRESS

Home in the Rain

BOB GRAHAM

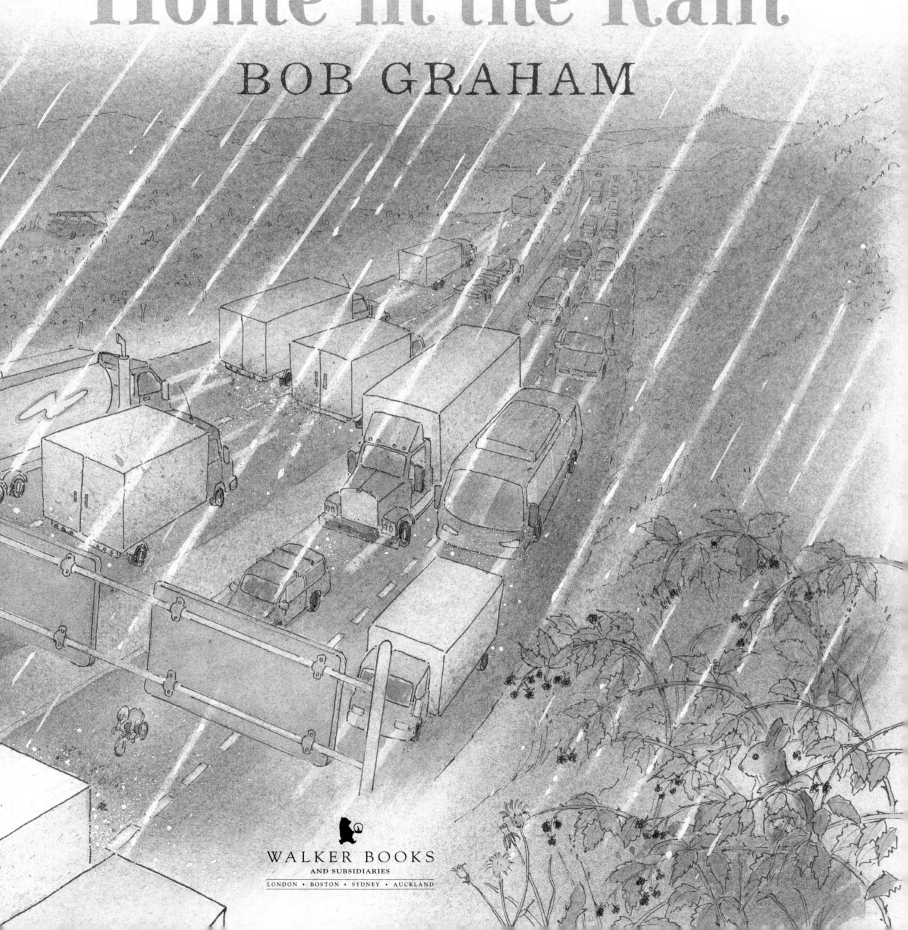

WALKER BOOKS
AND SUBSIDIARIES
LONDON · BOSTON · SYDNEY · AUCKLAND

Didn't it rain!

It hit the highway, bucketing down on Francie and her mum and her baby sister on their way home from Grandma's.

It rained on endless lines of cars and buses, oil-tankers and trucks – the windscreen wipers in despair. *Shoo-shoo-shoo!*

But the rain was going nowhere.
Except down.
Francie, Mum and Baby Sister,
a long way from home.

A big rig passed on a long-haul trip,
headed for Heaven knows where!
It rocked them in road spray and
washed them up into the picnic area.

Above the highway it rained on the hill
and a baby rabbit dived for cover.

It rained on a field mouse wet and confused
in the blackberries – and lucky too ...

because three hundred
feet up, a kestrel had lost
sight of its prey!

It rained on the canal –
turning the water white –
and it rained on the fishermen,
wet as the fish below.

Young Marcus, water
running down his neck,
his fingers smelling of bait,
wished he were
somewhere else ...

while the water ran off the
backs of ducks.

The rain soaked two men on the Western Highway interchange.
They argued while steam rose from their hot engines.

And not looking where it was going, the countryside ran straight into the edge of the highway, bringing with it the faint smell of farmyards.

Francie, Mum and Baby Sister,
such a long way from home.

Inside Francie's car the fog
moved in. She wrote her name
in her breath on the side window.

She wrote her mum's name
with her finger squeaking on the glass.

And then her dad's name.
Her dad working far out to sea,
gone three weeks now.
She wrote it clear across
the front window.

"My little sister.
 What will her name be, Mummy?"
"Well, she's not quite with us yet," said Mum.
"But when will she have a name, Mummy?" said Francie.
"Soon," said Mum. "Sometime soon."

Francie saw a whole back window
just waiting for a name ...

a window just waiting for Francie's wet finger.

"Could it be Alice, maybe? Or Isabel ... Emma ... or, um, Zoe?"

"Well, they're nice, Francie," said Mum, "but there's a name somewhere out there that will fit her just right."

They ate the picnic Grandma had packed.
Plum jam sandwiches and hard-boiled eggs
with a little sprinkle of salt.
They shared the two stale toffees found
under old parking tickets in the door.

"When is Daddy coming home?" said Francie.
"Soon," replied Mum. "Sometime soon."
"Like the new baby, then," said Francie,
  and felt a small movement against her ear.
"Well ... yes," said Mum, brushing crumbs
  from her knees. "Like the new baby."

Then the radio played.
"This is 3LFM – your spot on the radio.
It's wet on the road. So you take care, folks."

Francie and her mum
and her baby sister pulled
back out into the traffic.

Far off down the road they found a service station.
Hail hit the roof, and oil on the puddles made rainbows
around Francie's toes.

What was about
to happen would
not be noticed
by anyone.

Not by Sam Miller
feeding his dog fried
chicken legs.

Nor by Kate Calder losing her Sour Fruity Fizzes
from a hole in her pocket.

Not even by a seagull
who was eating them.

Perhaps it was something unremarkable,
not to be seen by strangers passing in the rain.
For it was just a mum lost in thought
and a small girl dancing.

"Francie, come here,"
said Mum.

"**Grace!** Your new sister ...
we'll call her Grace!"
And Mum hugged Francie as best
as she could with Francie's sister
Grace in between.

The three of them.

They staggered and toppled
a bit; did a slow and awkward
little dance of their own.
Until Francie's feet found
the ground again.

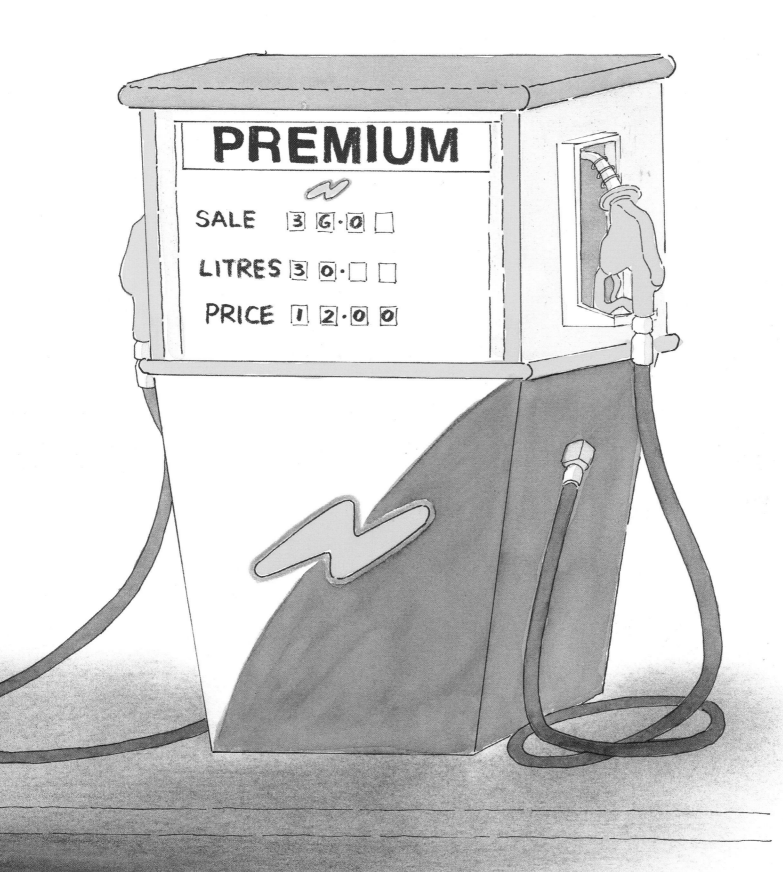

Francie had a feeling.

Francie knew that right here, with the smell of petrol,

her feet all wet on this driveway in the rain ...

that she would remember the moment for ever!

"Wait until Daddy hears," said Francie.

"Daddy will love that," replied Mum.

And way back down the highway Francie's grandma sipped tea, rabbits and field mice were deep in their burrows, young Marcus headed home for a hot bath, and somewhere, kestrel chicks went without dinner.

Then the sun covered the countryside – far off and away
from Grandma's place to home, and out across the sea.
Their little car, now full of courage, bumped off down the
road, the windows rolled down and wind rushing through.

One window was still fogged up.
It had Francie's fading breath
and *GRACE* still faintly showing.

First published 2016 by Walker Books Ltd, 87 Vauxhall Walk, London SE11 5HJ ∗ This edition published 2019 ∗ © 2016 Blackbird Design Pty Ltd
The right of Bob Graham to be identified as the author and illustrator of this work has been asserted by him in accordance
with the Copyright, Designs and Patents Act 1988 ∗ This book has been typeset in Garamond Ludlow ∗ Printed in China
∗ British Library Cataloguing in Publication Data: a catalogue record for this book is available from the British Library
ISBN 978-1-4063-7978-5 ∗ www.walker.co.uk ∗ 10 9 8 7 6 5 4 3 2 1

Extract from "A Soft Spring Night in Shillington" taken from *Self-Consciousness: Memoirs* by John Updike (Penguin Books, London. Alfred A. Knopf, New York 1990)
Copyright © John Updike, 1989, and included here with kind permission of Penguin Books Ltd.

For Cormac and Dervla

Rain is grace; rain is the sky condescending to the earth; without rain, there would be no life.
John Updike

"Goodbye, Grandma."

"Goodbye, Francie," said Grandma. "You both take care.
It's wet out there and such a long way home."

"We will ... won't we, Mummy?" replied Francie.

"Of course we will," said Mum.

Their little red car seemed to muster all of its courage
as it waited outside, ready for the road.